∞

All for Jesus

Frederick William Faber

All for Jesus

The Easy Ways of Divine Love

SOPHIA INSTITUTE PRESS®
Manchester, New Hampshire

This 2000 edition of *All for Jesus* by Sophia Institute Press is an abridgment of the fourth edition, published in 1854. It includes the author's revisions for that edition, as well as subheadings and minor editorial revisions to the 1854 text.

Printed in the United States of America

Jacket design by Lorraine Bilodeau

The jacket artwork is Raphael's *Madonna of the Chair*, Galleria Palatina. Palazzo Pitti, Florence, Italy (photo courtesy of Alinari / Art Resource, New York).

Sophia Institute Press®
Box 5284, Manchester, NH 03108
1-800-888-9344
www.sophiainstitute.com

"We approve highly of the republication of the work styled *All for Jesus*, by the Reverend F. W. Faber, which has been received so favorably by the Catholics of England."
Francis Patrick, Archbishop of Baltimore
January 20, 1864

Library of Congress Cataloging-in-Publication Data

Faber, Frederick William, 1814-1863.
All for Jesus : the easy ways of divine love / Frederick William Faber.
p. cm.
Abridged ed. of: All for Jesus, or, The easy ways of divine love. 4th ed. Westminster, Md. : Newman Press, [1854?]
Includes bibliographical references.
ISBN 1-928832-13-X (pbk. : alk. paper)
1. Spiritual life — Catholic Church. I. Title. Easy ways of divine love. II. Title.

BX2182.2.F33 2000
248.4'82 — dc21 00-040003

00 01 02 03 04 05 10 9 8 7 6 5 4 3 2 1

Contents

Preface vii

1. Further the interests of Jesus 3

2. Serve Jesus joyfully out of love 27

3. Be sorry for sin 41

4. Pray for others 69

5. Make use of the many riches God gives you 101

6. Learn to grow holier in every moment and instance . . . 131

7. Offer thanks to God 163

8. Praise God for His goodness 207

9. Assist the souls in Purgatory 261

Frederick William Faber 277

Editor's note: The biblical quotations in the following pages are based on the Douay-Rheims translation of the Old and New Testaments. Where applicable, quotations have been cross-referenced with the differing names and enumeration in the Revised Standard Version, using the following symbol: (RSV =).

Preface

In these pages, I am not putting forward what is perfect, but what is easy. I am not trying to guide souls in high spirituality; God forbid I should be so foolish or so vain! As a son of St. Philip,[1] I have especially to do with the world, and with people living in the world and trying to be good there and to sanctify themselves in ordinary vocations. It is to such I speak, and I am putting before them, not high things, but things which are at once attractive as devotions and also tend to raise their fervor, to quicken their love, and to increase their sensible sweetness in practical religion and its duties. I want to make piety bright and happy to those who need such helps, as I do myself. I have not ventured to aim higher. If it causes one heart to love our dearest Lord a trifle more warmly, God will have blessed both the work and its writer far above their deservings.

Frederick William Faber
St. Mary's, Sydenham Hill
St. Philip Neri's Day 1853

[1] St. Philip Neri (1515-1595), Italian priest who founded the Congregation of the Oratory.

All for Jesus

Chapter One

Further the interests of Jesus

Jesus belongs to us. He vouchsafes to put Himself at our disposal. He communicates to us everything of His which we are capable of receiving. He loves us with a love which no words can tell — nay, above all our thought and imagination — and He condescends to desire, with a longing which is equally indescribable, that we should love Him, with a fervent and entire love.

His merits may be called ours as well as His. His satisfactions are not so much His treasures as they are ours. His sacraments are but so many ways that His love has designed to communicate Him to our souls.

Wherever we turn in the church of God, there is Jesus. He is the beginning, middle, and end of everything to us. He is our help in penance, our consolation in grief, and our support in trial. There is nothing good, nothing holy, nothing beautiful, and nothing joyous which He is not to His servants. No one need be downcast, for Jesus is the joy of Heaven, and it is His joy to enter into sorrowful hearts.

We can exaggerate about many things, but we can never exaggerate our obligations to Jesus, or the compassionate abundance of the love of Jesus to us. All our lives long, we might talk of Jesus, and yet we would never come to an end of the sweet things that are to be said about Him. Eternity will not be long enough to learn all He is or to praise Him for all He has done; but then that matters not, for we shall be always with Him, and we desire nothing more.

He has kept nothing back from us. There is not a faculty of His human soul which has not had to do with our salvation. There is not one limb of His sacred body that has not suffered for us. There is not one pain, one shame, one indignity that He has not drained to its last dreg of bitterness on our behalf. There is not one drop of His most Precious Blood that He has not shed for us, nor is there one beating of His Sacred Heart that is not an act of love toward us.

We read wonderful things in the lives of the saints about their love of God, wonderful things that we dare not think of imitating. They practiced fearful austerities, or they spent years in unbroken silence, or they were ever in ecstasies and raptures, or they were passionately in love with contempt and suffering, or they pined and wasted away in holy impatience for death, or they courted death and expired in the long tortures of an excruciating martyrdom. Each one of these things separately fills us with wonder. Yet, put them all together, conceive all the love of Peter, Paul, and John, of Joseph and of Magdalene, of all the apostles and martyrs, the confessors and virgins of the Church in all ages, thrown into one heart made, by miracle, strong enough to hold such love; then add to it all the burning love that the nine choirs of multitudinous angels have for God, and crown it all with the amazing love of the Immaculate Heart of our dear Mother; and still it comes not near to — nay, it is but a poor imitation of — the love that Jesus has for each one of us, however lowly and unworthy and sinful we may be!

We know our own unworthiness. We hate ourselves for our own past sins. We are impatient with our own secret meanness, irritability, and wretchedness. We are tired with our own badness and littleness. Yet, for all that, He loves us with this unutterable love and is ready, if need be, as He revealed to one of His servants, to come down from Heaven to be crucified over again for each one of us.

The wonder is not merely that He should love us so much, but that He should love us at all. Considering who He is, and what we are, have we any one single claim to His love, except the excess and, without Him, hopelessness of our misery? We have no claims upon Him, but those which He Himself in His compassion has invented for us. What can be more unlovely than we are, or more ungenerous, or more ungrateful? And yet He loves us with this excess of love!

Oh, how is it that we can ever turn ourselves away from this one idea? How is it that we can take an interest in anything but this surpassing love of God for His fallen creatures? It is almost surprising how we can bear to go through our ordinary duties, or how it is that, like men in love with created loves, we do not forget to eat and drink and sleep, feeling ourselves every hour of the day and night the object of the most profuse tenderness and the most unutterable abundance of the love of God, the Almighty, the All-Wise, the All-Holy, the All-Beautiful, the Everlasting!

Oh, most incredible of startling wonders! Blessings are heaped upon us until we are almost out of breath with them. Graces are multiplied upon graces until they get beyond our power of reckoning. His compassions are new every morning. And then, after all, there is yet to come the recompense which eye has never seen, nor ear heard, nor heart conceived![2] This is His side of the question.

Alas, for our dearest Lord! Up to this day, what have we done for Him? And see what He has done for us, and the end of His

[2] Cf. 1 Cor. 2:9.

doing it all was to gain our love! We look upon a crucifix, and it hardly moves us. We hear of His bitter Passion, but our eyes are dry and our hearts indifferent. We kneel down to pray, but we can hardly keep our thoughts fixed upon Him for a quarter of an hour together. We go into His own most holy presence, and we hardly bend the knee before the tabernacle, lest it should spoil our clothes. We see others sin, and what matter is it to us that Jesus is offended, so long as it is not we who are risking our souls by offending Him?

Oh, these are strange signs of love! Surely Jesus cannot be much to us if this is the way we feel about Him. Yet so it is. We go our own way, and do our own will. The great thing is to please ourselves and to make things easy to us. Life must be taught to run smoothly. As to penance, it must be kept at arm's length. We must have bodily comforts and worldly conveniences, and our spiritual life must be nothing but a sufficiency of those inward consolations without which our souls give us pain, because they are not at rest. If we worship God, it is for self; if we do good to others, it is self we are seeking, even in our charity. "Poor Jesus Christ!" as St. Alphonsus[3] used to say, "poor Jesus Christ!" Who thinks of Him? Who weds His interests?

∞

Become familiar with the interests of Jesus

Now, let us try to get an idea of the interests of Jesus, so that we may be able to advance them.

You know what it is to have an interest. If you look over the world, you will see that everybody has some interest at heart and is

[3] St. Alphonsus Liguori (1696-1787), moral theologian and founder of the Redemptorists.

working hard for it. There are almost as many interests in the world as there are men. Everyone you meet in the streets is going after something. You see it in his face, his quick eye, and his rapid walk. Either it is political, or literary, or mercantile, or scientific, or fashionable, or simply ambitious, or dishonest. Still, whatever it is, every man has wedded the interest of his choice and is doing his duty to it. He works hard for it all day; he goes to bed with the thought of it, and he wakes with it in the morning. Even on Sunday, it is his hand that is resting, rather than his head or his heart: they are full of his interest. Look what men will do, singly or banded, to put down slavery, or to get free trade, or to compete for a large order, or to carry the mail, or to make new railroads. It is plain that men have interests enough in the world, that they love them dearly and work for them manfully. Oh, that it were all for God, the good, the merciful, the eternal God!

Beware the Devil's interests

The Devil also has his interests in the world. He has been allowed to set up a kingdom in opposition to God, and, like all sovereigns, he has a multitude of interests. Thus he has agents everywhere, active, diligent, unseen spirits, swarming in the streets of the cities, to push forward his interests. They canvass the laborers in the field. They see what they can do with the monk in his cloister and the hermit in his cell. Even in the churches, during Mass or Benediction, they are hard at work, plying their unholy trade.

Our fellowmen also, by thousands, let themselves out to him as agents — nay, numbers work in his interests for nothing. And, what is more shocking still, many do his work and almost fancy it is God's work they are doing, it looks so good and blameless in their eyes. How many Catholics oppose good things, or criticize good persons? Yet they would never consent to be the Devil's agents, if they really knew what they were about.

These interests of the Devil are various. To cause mortal sin; to persuade to venial sin; to hinder grace; to prevent contrition; to keep back from the sacraments; to promote lukewarmness; to bring holy people and bishops and religious orders into dispute, and to stand in the way of vocations; to spread gossip; to distract people at prayer; to make men fall in love with the frivolities and fashions of the world; to get men to spend money on comforts, furniture, jewels, knick knacks, parrots, old china, and fine dress, instead of on the poor of Jesus Christ; to induce Catholics to worship great people and put their trust in princes,[4] and fawn upon political parties in power; to make them full of criticism of each other and quick as children to take scandal; to diminish devotion to our Blessed Lady; and to make people fancy that divine love is an enthusiasm and an indiscretion: these are the chief interests of the Devil.

It is amazing with what energy he works at them, and with what consummate craft and dreadful ability he advances them in the world. It would be a thing to admire, if it did not make us afraid for our own souls, and if all things which are against God were not simply abominable and to be hated.

The dark enemy of the Creator is mysteriously allowed a marvelous share of success in that creation which the All-Holy once looked down upon and blessed in His unspeakable complacency. Men's interests put the interests of Jesus on one side, partly as troublesome, more often as insignificant. The Devil's interests are directly opposed to those of Jesus and, where they are successful, either debase them or kill them altogether.

[4] Cf. Ps. 145:2 (RSV = Ps. 146:3).

∞

See Jesus' interests throughout the Church

Now, let us look at the interests of Jesus. Let us take a view of the whole Church, which is His spouse. Look first into Heaven, the Church Triumphant.[5] It is the interest of Jesus that the glory of the most Holy Trinity should be increased in every possible manner, and at every hour of night and day. And this glory, which is called God's accidental glory, is increased by every good work, word, and thought, every correspondence to grace, every resistance to temptation, every act of worship, every sacrament rightly administered or humbly received, every act of homage and love to Mary, every invocation of the saints, every bead of the Rosary, every Sign of the Cross, every drop of holy water, every pain patiently endured, every harsh judgment meekly borne, every good wish — even if it ends only with the wishing and never sees fulfillment — provided there be a devout intention along with all these things, and they are done in union with the merits of our sweet Lord.

Every hour, at least so we trust, a new soul lands in Heaven from Purgatory or from earth and begins its eternity of rapture and of praise. Each soul that swells the throng of worshipers, each silent voice added to the angelic choirs, is an increase to the glory of God; and so it is the interest of Jesus to make these arrivals more frequent, and that they should bring more merits and higher degrees of love with them when they come.

Next, look at that vast kingdom of Purgatory. All those countless throngs of souls are the dear and faithful spouses of Jesus. Yet

[5] The members of the Church in Heaven are known collectively as the Church Triumphant. The members on earth and in Purgatory are known, respectively, as the Church Militant and the Church Suffering.

in what a strange abandonment of supernatural suffering has His love left them! He longs for their deliverance; He yearns for them to be transferred from that land, perpetually overclouded with pain, to the bright sunshine of their heavenly home. Yet He has tied His own hands, or nearly so. He gives them no more grace; He allows them no more time for penance; He prevents them from meriting. How, then, stands the case with the souls in the Church Suffering? Why, it is a thing to be meditated on when we have said it: they depend almost more on earth than they do on Heaven, almost more on us than on Him; so He has willed it on whom all depend and without whom there is no dependence.

It is clear that Jesus has His interests there. He wants His captives released. Those whom He has redeemed He now bids us redeem — us, whom, if there be life at all in us, He has already Himself redeemed. Every satisfaction offered up to God for these suffering souls, every oblation of the Precious Blood to the eternal Father, every Mass heard, every Communion received, every voluntary penance undergone, every indulgence gained, every jubilee whose conditions we have fulfilled, every *De Profundis*[6] whispered, every little alms doled out to the poor who are poorer than we — if they be offered for the intention of these dear prisoners, the interests of Jesus are hourly forwarded in the kingdom of Purgatory.

See how men work at the pumps on shipboard when they are fighting for their lives with an ugly leak. Oh, that we had the charity so to work, with the sweet instrumentality of indulgence, for the holy souls in Purgatory!

The infinite satisfactions of Jesus are at our command, as are Mary's sorrows, and the martyrs' pangs, and the confessors' weary

[6] The prayer that begins, "Out of the depths"; Ps. 129 (RSV = Ps. 130).

perseverance in well-doing. Jesus will not help Himself here, because He loves to see us helping Him, and because He thinks our love will rejoice that He still leaves us something we can do for Him.

There have been saints who have devoted their whole lives to this one work — mining in Purgatory — and to those who reflect in faith, it does not seem, after all, so strange. It is a foolish comparison, simply because it is so much below the mark, but on all principles of reckoning, it is much less work to have won the battle of Waterloo, or to have invented the steam engine, than to have helped free one soul from Purgatory.

Now look at the Church Militant on earth. The interests of Jesus are rich and plentiful enough here. There are things to be done, and things to be left undone; hearts to be persuaded and hearts to be dissuaded. There is so much to do; the puzzle is where to begin and what to do first. Men who do not love Jesus are to be made to love Him, and men who love Him, to love Him a great deal more.

∞

Pray for final perseverance for the dying

Each of us might take one department, and we would find more work to be done in it than we can get through in our best of times. There are so many people in their agony, and dying every minute, all over the world. Oh, in what danger the very dearest interests of Jesus are at their dying beds! Satan is hard at work, temptations thicker than flakes in a snowstorm; and whosoever wins this battle, Jesus or the Devil, is so far conqueror forever, for there is no fighting it over again.

There are Catholics who have not been near the sacraments for years, and there are saints whose half-century of merits and heroic love is positively in peril of being lost; they want only one thing, and let them suffer ever so much, they cannot merit it, and that is final perseverance.

There are heretics who never suspected they were in heresy, and heretics in bad faith, who have told falsehoods about the Church and have run down the Mother of God. There are men whom the unthawing snows whiten, and men whom the fierce heats of the south scorch, on the mountain tops, in the deep valleys, in the city and in the wilderness, on the land and on the sea, in the dungeon and in the palace — all dying, many a minute, in the most frightful unpreparedness that can be conceived.

And Jesus died for every one of them, as exclusively as if there had been nobody else to die for, and He is ready this moment to come down and die for each one again, if it were needed. Go all through His long Passion. Mark His steps, His tears, His drops of blood. Count the thorns, the blows, the spittings, and the falls. Fathom the interior depths of the shame and shrinking, the torture and the sickness of His Sacred Heart. And it was all for that poor person, dying far away this hour; and if he dies and is not saved, it will have been in vain.

This is but one department of the interests of Jesus: men in their last agony; and St. Camillus[7] was raised up to found an order expressly for them. What might I not say of souls in mortal sin, of heretics and infidels, of criminals in prison, of persons under calumny, of others in scruples or temptations? I would never finish if I described all the interests of Jesus upon earth.

As, however, I have mentioned the dying, and the dangers of the deathbed, as the object of a special devotion, it will not be out

[7] St. Camillus of Lellis (1550-1614), founder of the Ministers of the Sick.

of place to remind you that Pius VII[8] attached indulgences to the recital of three Our Fathers and three Hail Marys for the dying, in honor of the Agony of Jesus, which are found in the *Raccolta*.[9]

Many saints and holy persons have had this special devotion for souls in their agony. In the life of one of the first mothers of the Visitation, we read that, as she was watching before the Blessed Sacrament during the night of Holy Thursday 1644, she saw a vision of our Lord in His Agony, and with this vision there was given her a light and an efficacious grace to pray for the intentions of persons in their agony. "Alas!" she said. "The agonies of poor creatures are strange hours," and, in truth, that moment, decisive of eternity, is the only important affair we have to transact. From the hour she received this admirable grace, she often seemed to hear the sighs of dying persons; and the effect this had upon her was so great that ever afterward she said, night and morning, the prayers of the Church for those in their agony. She often meditated on the words that our Lord said of Himself a little before His death: "The prince of this world is come, and finds nothing in me,"[10] as if all life was to be so directed as to enable us to make these words in some measure our own when we come to die.

See Jesus' interests everywhere

There is not a public house or a gin palace, not a theater or a casino, not a ballroom or a concert, not a public meeting or a

[8] Pius VII (1740-1823), Pope from 1800.

[9] A book of prayers and pious exercises to which the popes have attached indulgences. An indulgence is a remission of the temporal punishment due to sin that has been forgiven, in virtue of the merits of Christ and the saints.

[10] Cf. John 14:30.

parliament, not a shop or a wharf, not a fair, a racecourse, or a market, not a carriage or a ship, not a school or a church where Jesus' interests are not in danger at all hours, and where He is not calling on us to help Him. This is the fighting part of the Church. No wonder there is so much to do, and so little time to do it in.

There is not a thing that has not two sides, and one side belongs to Jesus, and the other side is against Him. The Devil has other interests besides sheer sin. He can fight against Jesus with low views almost as successfully as with mortal sins. The slow poison of souls sometimes does his work better than the quick. See, then, the multiplicity, the ubiquity, and the urgency of the interests of Jesus.

Yet although it is impossible to go through all the interests of Jesus on earth with anything like minuteness, it is necessary to have somewhat more of a clear and definite view about them. If we study the Sacred Heart of Jesus, as He has revealed it to us in the Gospel, in the history of the Church, in the lives of His saints, and as we have found it ourselves in prayer, we shall see that the multitudinous and manifold interests of our most dear Lord may be gathered up into four classes: the glory of His Father; the fruit of His Passion; the honor of His Mother; and the esteem of grace.

Glorify the Father

When we study our blessed Lord as He is represented to us in the Gospels, nothing, if we may venture to use such an expression, seems so like a ruling passion in Him as His longing for His Father's glory. From the time when, at the age of twelve, He left Mary, and stayed behind in Jerusalem, to His very last word upon the Cross, this devotion to the glory of God comes up at every turn. As it is said of Him on one occasion that the zeal for God's house ate Him up,[11] so may we say that He was eaten up continually with hungering and thirsting after His Father's glory. It was as if God's glory had been lost upon the earth, and He was come to seek it and to find it, and how was His Sacred Heart straitened until He did find it! Thus was He our example! For this end does He give us grace, that we may glorify our Father who is in Heaven.

Now, who can look into the world and not see how God's glory is lost upon the earth? It is the interest of Jesus that we should seek and find it. Apart from clear acts of great and grievous sin, how is God forgotten, clean forgotten, by the greatest part of mankind! They live as if there were no God. It is not as if they openly rebel against Him. They pass Him over and ignore Him. He is an inconvenience in His own world, an impertinence in His own creation. So He has been quietly set to one side, as if He were an idol out of fashion and in the way. Men of science and politicians have agreed on this, and men of business and wealth think it altogether the most decent thing to be silent about God; for it is difficult to speak of Him, or have a view of Him, without allowing too much to Him.

Here is a desperate — if it were not for grace, we would say altogether desperate — obstacle to the interests of Jesus, this great, huge impenetrable mass of forgetfulness of God, of ignoring God.

Oh, how it turns our hearts sick, for what can we do in so hopeless an affair as this? Yet we must try. A string of beads and a blessed medal: there is no saying what they cannot do! And a single Mass: is its power far short of infinite?

Then, unfortunately, there are a great many religious people who by no means give God's glory its fitting place; many, called spiritual, who give Him but the second best of everything. They

[11] Ps. 68:10 (RSV = Ps. 69:9).

want light to know God's glory when they see it. They want discernment to detect the world and the Devil under the show of reason and moderation, whereby they would defraud Him of His glory. They want bravery to set the world's opinion at defiance, and consistency to make their lives all of a piece with their religion. Good souls! They are the very pestilence of the Church, and yet they never for one moment suspect it. And it is very much for the interest of Jesus that they should see themselves, and other things as well, in their true light. So here also we have some work to do: to pray that all good men, and men trying to be good, should be able to see what is for God's glory and what is not. Oh, what ground we lose every day for the want of this discernment!

Then, there are religious orders, set apart with the blessing of the Church, each in its own particular way, to work out this glory of God. There are bishops and priests, all supposed to be toiling with a single aim and an exclusive perfection for this one thing. There are guilds and confraternities without number, and is not this their end? Calamities have to be endured, dangers faced, scandals exposed; the Church has to yield to the world today and to rough-ride it tomorrow. And Jesus has interests in all these things, and it is our work to help Him. Half a dozen men, going about God's world, seeking nothing but God's glory — they would move mountains.[12] This was promised to faith; why should not we be the men to do it?

∞

Increase devotion to Christ's Passion

The second great interest of Jesus is the fruit of His Passion. Every sin we can prevent, no matter how venial, is a great thing for the interests of Jesus. We can see how great a thing it is if we

[12] Cf. Matt. 17:19.

remember that even if we could shut Hell forever, save all the souls that are in it, empty Purgatory, and make all the men and women on earth persevering saints, equal to St. Peter and St. Paul, by telling one little — and such a little — lie, we may not do so on any account; for God's glory would suffer more by that little lie, than it would gain by all the rest.

What a work, then, will it be for the interests of Jesus to prevent one mortal sin! Yet how easy!

If, every night, before we go to sleep, we begged our dear Lady to offer up to God the Precious Blood of her dear Son for grace to hinder one mortal sin somewhere in the world during that night, and then renewed the same offering in the morning for the hours of daylight, surely such an offering, and by such hands, could not fail to win the grace desired. And then each one of us might hinder 730 mortal sins every year. And if a thousand of us made these offerings, and persevered in them for twenty years, why, it would give none of us any trouble, to say nothing of the merit we should gain, and there would be more than fourteen million mortal sins prevented. Ah, at this rate, the interests of Jesus would prosper, and how happy, how immensely happy, would we be!

So, again, every time we get anyone to go to Confession who stands in need of it, even though it be only to confess venial sins, we increase the fruit of our beloved Redeemer's Passion. Every act of contrition we persuade men to make, or by prayer obtain for them the grace to make, increases the blessed fruit. Every additional strictness or trifling penance of which we are the promoters answers the same good end, and so do all our efforts to advance frequent Communion.

When we get people to join in devotions to our Lord's Passion, or to read about it, and meditate upon it, we are forwarding the interests of Jesus. Someone said — if my memory does not fail me, it was St. Albertus Magnus[13] — that one tear shed over the sufferings of our dear Lord was worth more than a year's fast on bread and water. What, then, if we get others to weep with us in our tenderness for the Passion of Jesus! What a great deal a little prayer will do!

Jesus, why are we so hard and cold? Oh, kindle in us the sweet fire which Thou camest to kindle on the earth![14]

∞

Honor Christ's Mother

The honor of His Mother is another chief interest of Jesus, and the whole history of the Church shows how near it lies to His Sacred Heart. She was the chosen one of the Most Holy and Undivided Trinity, the elected daughter of the Father, the predestinated Mother of the Son, and the chosen spouse of the Holy Spirit. The right doctrine of Jesus has in all ages been wrapped up with true devotion to Mary; and the Mother can be wounded only through the Son.

Thus, Mary is the heritage of humble, obedient Catholics. As devotion to her increases, so does holiness. The saints are molded on the love of her. Sin has no greater enemy than Mary, for the thought of her is a charm against it, and the devils tremble at her name. No one can love the Son without the love of the Mother growing in Him also; no one can love the Mother without his heart melting with tenderness toward the Son. Thus has Jesus put her in the front of His Church, so that she would be the token of all good, and the stumbling block of His enemies.

[13] St. Albertus Magnus (c. 1206-1280), medieval theologian, philosopher, and scientist.

[14] Luke 12:49.

What wonder, then, that His interests are deeply concerned with Mary's honor. Every heretical blasphemy against her dignity, for which you make reparation by an act of love, or an act of thanksgiving for her Immaculate Conception and her perpetual virginity, gives you an opportunity of advancing the interests of Jesus. Everything you can do to spread devotion to her, and especially to make Catholics feel more tenderly toward her, is a distinct work for Jesus, and one that He will most lovingly repay. To get people to go to Communion on her feasts, to be enrolled in her confraternities, to have a picture of her, to gain indulgences for the souls in Purgatory that in their lifetime were most devoted to her, to say the Rosary every day — everybody has an opportunity of doing one or another of these things, and they are all for the interests of Jesus.

Ah, there is one devotion I will mention! I wish we were all inspired with it. We would do well, then, for the interests of Jesus, and our dear Lord would get such abundance of new love the world over! It is to have more confidence in our Blessed Mother's prayers, more undoubting trust, more bold petition, more real faith in her. There would be more love for Mary if there were more faith in Mary.

Jesus, animate our confidence in Mary, not only so that we may work more for Thy sweet interests, but also so that we may work in the way Thou wouldst have us work, letting no creature be dearer to us than the one who was dearer to Thee than all other creatures put together!

∞

See the value of grace

Another of the chief interests of Jesus is the esteem of grace. The world would be quite a different place if men only valued grace at its proper value. What is there in the world worth anything except grace? Oh, how childishly we let ourselves be carried away by all manner of follies that have nothing to do with the interests of Jesus. How stupid it is of us! What time we waste! What harm we do! What good we leave undone! And how sweetly patient Jesus is with us all through it!

If people esteemed grace rightly, every one of the other interests of Jesus would go right. When they go wrong, it is just for the want of this esteem. Graces keep coming, merits keep multiplying, almost as fast as the blessed beatings of the Sacred Heart. Meanwhile, all the time that Heart is yearning over us with enraptured love, we are saying, "I am not obliged to do this. I need not forego this pleasure. I must keep down religious enthusiasm."

God help us! I wish we could get a peep of any enthusiasm there is to keep down! Poor Jesus Christ! And all this is for want of a true esteem of grace. Better to die than to forfeit one increase of grace. Do we all believe this? No, but we say we believe it.

To receive (this is what theologians tell us) all the natural gifts and ornaments of St. Michael — his power, strength, wisdom, beauty, and all the rest — would be nothing compared with one additional degree of grace, such as we get a score of if we resist an angry feeling for a quarter of an hour; for grace is a participation of the divine nature.

Oh, do we carry this out in our own lives, while we try to persuade others to carry it out? Fix upon any evil or calamity of the Church you please, and I am ready to show you that it would never have taken place if her children had had a true esteem of grace; and moreover, that it would be set right by tomorrow morning, if they all took up with a true esteem of grace. To gain the whole world will be of no profit to a man if he suffers detriment, any detriment, to his immortal soul.[15]

[15] Cf. Mark 8:36.

Go and persuade people of this; show them what store they should set by grace, and how one grace brings another along with it, and how all these things are merits, and how all merits turn to glories — glories that are eternal in the heavens. Ah, you will indeed forward our dear Lord's interests if you do this; you will forward them far more than you have any idea of. Only pray that men may have a truer esteem of grace, and you will be a secret apostle of Jesus. All graces are in Him; He is the fountain and the fullness of them all; He longs to pour them out over dear souls — souls that He died for — and they will not let Him, because they must esteem the graces they have in order to gain new ones.

Go and help Jesus. Why should a single soul, for which He died, be lost? I say, why should *one* be lost? It is a horrible thing to think of a lost soul — most horrible. And why should it be lost? There is Precious Blood to be had for the asking, and what it gives is grace. But men do not care about grace. St. Paul spent his whole life teaching people about grace, and praying for grace for them, and praying that they might use grace rightly when they got it. When the Fountain of all grace is springing up like a living well of joy in the heart after Communion, ask Jesus to open all men's eyes to the beauty of His grace, and so will you cause His grace to multiply and, with the multiplication of grace, His interests to prosper; for thus stands the case with our dear Lord, that the more He gives away, the richer He becomes.

Dear King of souls! How is it that we can think anything but Him? To think that we should be allowed to take His interests in hand: it is amazing! I wonder why it does not send us into an ecstasy. But we do not know our own privileges. And why not? Because we do not study our dearest Lord enough. Why not begin in time what we shall be delighted to do for all eternity — study Jesus? Heaven is Heaven only because Jesus is there; and I do not understand why earth has not become Heaven already, since Jesus is on earth also. Ah, alas, it is because we have the wretched power to offend Him. Take that away, and there is Heaven at once, or Purgatory, which is the porch of Heaven.

Will the day really come when we can sin no more, no more wound the Heart of Jesus? O blessed Lord, let the sun rise soon that is not to set until that dear privilege is ours.

Why fret and question whether it is to be Heaven at once or Purgatory first? What matter? The great thing is not to be able — for we would be sure to do it if we were able — ever to offend our dearest Lord and Love again.

∞

Be an apostle of prayer

These are the interests of Jesus, or rather, these are samples and specimens of those interests. It may seem strange that our blessed Lord should make use of such poor and vile instruments as we are for so great a work; but it is the same Lord who called simple fishermen from mending their nets to be His apostles and to convert the world. True it is that we have sins enough of our own to look after, that we have imperfections enough to turn away the Heart of our heavenly Spouse from us, and that there is no place in the whole world that we know of where the interests of Jesus are in so much danger as they are in our own souls. Yet even we must be apostles. Woe unto us if we are not apostles!

We must serve the souls of others, even while we have so much to do for our own. The Gospel is a law of love, and the Christian life is a life of prayer. As the apostle tells us, we must make intercession for all sorts of men.[16] Indeed, we shall never prosper with

[16] Cf. Eph. 6:18.

the work in our own souls if we do not strive to advance the interests of Jesus in the souls of others. Many persons complain that they make no headway in religion, and that they do not get on with the mortification of their evil passions, their sinful infirmities, and their tiresome self-love. They are just where they were a year ago, and that is disheartening. This often comes to pass because they are selfish, because they care only to stand by themselves. They do not think they have anything to do with the souls of others, or with the interests of Jesus, or with intercessory prayer; and so they keep on a low level, because they do nothing to merit higher graces.

But it is important to remember that the interests of Jesus do not follow the same rule as the interests of the world. If we were not to remember this, we would soon be disheartened at the little good we seem to be doing. The interests of Jesus are, for the most part, invisible interests. We must take the power of prayer on faith. We shall never know until the last day all the answers there have been to our prayers, nor how they have told upon the Church for hundreds and hundreds of years.

Look, for example, at St. Stephen's prayer when he was stoned to death.[17] It obtained the conversion of St. Paul, who was holding the clothes of Stephen's murderers. Then think of all St. Paul has done, and continues to do daily, and will go on doing until the end of the world. And all that he does St. Stephen does also, for it is all St. Stephen's prayer.

Suppose somebody asks for prayers so that obstacles to his vocation to the religious life or the ecclesiastical state may be removed, and it is granted. He becomes a priest; he saves hundreds of souls; these souls save others, some by becoming priests themselves,

[17] Acts 7:59 (RSV = Acts 7:59-60).

some by becoming nuns, some by becoming holy fathers and mothers in the world; and so the prayer goes on spreading and spreading, and may very likely be found actually at work in the dead of that night when all the earth will be awakened to see our Lord coming in the East.

Thus you must not look too much to visible fruits and to public results. What the world calls misfortunes often turn out to be the good fortune of Jesus. For instance, a man is suffering a great injustice because he happens to be a Catholic. You pray for him. The injustice goes on; his persecutors outwardly have the best of it and are as cruel and triumphant as ever. You fancy that your prayer has not been answered. There could not be a greater mistake. Jesus wants to make that man a saint. It is better for him to be the helpless victim of that injustice. Meanwhile, because of your prayers, Jesus has granted him additional grace, to which he has corresponded. So, actually, because of your Our Father and Hail Mary, he will be higher in Heaven for all eternity than he would otherwise have been. There will be a gem sparkling in his crown that would not else have been there; you will see it and admire it in Heaven, and you will know it was your Our Father and Hail Mary that put it there.

So it is with the Pope, and the Church, and religious orders, and in fact everything that has to do with Jesus. His interests do not follow the rules of the world, but the rules of grace. We must measure them by different measures and not use the measures of the world. Our measures, weights, and coinage must all be of the sanctuary. Jesus was never so triumphant as when He let Himself be nailed to the Cross, yet the silly world thought it had it all its own way then and had carried the day completely. It is of importance that you should bear this in mind. It is of faith that God always answers right prayers, and in a way and to a degree beyond our most enthusiastic expectation, but He does not yet let us see how. We must take it on faith. We are quite sure that in the long run, we shall not be disappointed.

We must still say a few words on the way in which it belongs to us to advance the interests of Jesus. There are many ways of doing this: good example, preaching, writing books, lending good books, arguing gently with people and persuading them, using your influence where you have any, and exercising your authority, as parent, teacher, or master. All these ways are good, and if we truly love Jesus, we shall never neglect any one of them, according as opportunity presents, and in keeping with the modest propriety of our condition and place in life.

People pray very little nowadays. Indeed it is sad to see how little faith men put in prayer. They think they are to do everything by their own cleverness, or by bustle, fidget, and activity. They think that the same things that made England a great proud country will suit the interests of Jesus and advance His kingdom upon earth.

Everything these days goes by sight, not by faith. If Catholics undertake anything and little seems to come of it, they are cast down, and think it has come to nought. If we cannot publish figures and show great results, if we cannot satisfy the world that we are doing a great work even in its discerning eyes, we all set to work to criticize each other, and we sin. We have public meetings, and we sin. We gossip, and we sin. We form angry committees, and we sin. We break up the work, and we sin. And then everybody writes a letter to the newspapers and, as likely as not, sins again. And after that we go on as before. We have tried to do a good work, and because we tried on natural principles, it has ended in a number of additional sins. All this is for want of prayer, and for want of faith in the power of prayer.

All for Jesus

We may be sure that, in an unbelieving age, simple-hearted prayer will have great power with God and a special reward. They who remembered Sion, when others were forgetting her, were wonderfully remembered by the Lord. So let us pray in a world that is forgetting prayer, and is trusting in itself, and leaning on an arm of flesh, and God will be with us as He has never been before, and the interests of Jesus will prosper on the earth. Oh, the interests of Jesus! Would to God they burned at our hearts the whole day long! Life is short, and we have much to do, but prayer is mighty, and love stronger than death, and so let us all set to work, with singing and with joy, angels and men, sinners and saints, for the interests, the dear interests, the sole interests, of Jesus!

Chapter Two

Serve Jesus joyfully out of love

When Jacob in his exile dwelt with Laban, he fell in love with Rachel, Laban's daughter, and he said to her father, "I will serve thee seven years for Rachel, thy younger daughter"; and the Holy Scripture adds, "So Jacob served seven years for Rachel, and they seemed but a few days, for the greatness of his love."[18]

Now, do we not often find life long, and our days to pass heavily? Is not perseverance a weary thing, and does not duty many a time turn out irksome and uninteresting? There is such a thing as wishing life over because of a holy impatience whereby we desire to be dissolved and to be with Christ.[19] Sin, the power of sinning, and the chance of sinning become intolerable to us, and we pine to be with God, as one pines for his absent love. But this is not what I mean.

Life, and especially our spiritual life, often drags on heavily for very different reasons. It is weary work to be always fighting with our evil passions and disheartening work to make so little way. Temptations tease us, and scruples worry us; and to be dead, buried, and safe in Purgatory seems the limit to our peevish ambition.

[18] Gen. 29:18, 20.

[19] Cf. Phil. 1:23.

And why is this? Because we do not serve Jesus for love. If we did, it would be with us as it was with Jacob. Years would seem but days, for the greatness of our love. Now let us see if it is, after all, so impossible for us to serve our dear Lord out of love.

It is possible to serve God, and so to do something for the interests of Jesus, in a stiff, dry, awkward way; just as we can do another a favor ungracefully, and as if it were an annoyance, but we cannot very well help ourselves. But it is not possible to serve God by prayer, or to advance the interests of Jesus by prayer, in this dry and unaffectionate way. Prayer with no heart in it is not prayer at all; it is either irreverence or distraction.

Oh, if only one of you could be persuaded to serve Jesus out of love, what joy would there be in Heaven, what delight to Mary, what consolation to the Sacred Heart of Jesus! One more soul in the world who is serving Him for love! It is worth a thousand years of penance to obtain for Him this consolation! The colored sunsets and the starry heavens, the beautiful mountains and the shining seas, the fragrant woods and the painted flowers are not half so beautiful as a soul who is serving Jesus out of love, in the wear and tear of common, unpoetic life.

If people could see this, everyone would wish to be a saint. This surely is true. They would wish to love God as much as the saints did. They would wish to have always that abounding and overflowing joy which the saints always had, and to go straight to Heaven without any delay in Purgatory, and to be high up in Heaven because of their exceeding love.

∞

Recognize what makes a saint

We may know that we are very far indeed from being saints, and we may fear there is very little chance of our ever becoming saints. We may have no heart for their great austerities and bodily mortifications, no courage for their valiant detachment from the world, no supernatural appetite for crosses and sufferings such as they had. Still, for all this, who would not wish to be a saint, if he could?

Now, I am not going to bring before you any very hard duties, much less any severe austerities. I do not want to drive you beyond your grace, but I wish you to observe this. Look at all the saints in all ages, no matter what their history may be, or their lot in life. You will find, when you compare them one with another, that it was not their austerities that made them saints. They differ very much from one another; yet after all they are very much alike. Some have worked miracles all their lives long, such as St. Joseph of Cupertino,[20] the Franciscan; and some hardly worked any at all, as was the case with St. Vincent de Paul;[21] and as to St. John the Baptist, of whom our Lord said such marvelous things, he never worked a single miracle. Some saints have practiced dreadful austerities, such as St. Rose of Lima;[22] others have contented themselves with taking God's will as it came their way, and mortified their wills; this was the case with St. Francis de Sales.[23]

But whether they did miracles or not, whether they practiced bodily penances in excess or not, still they have a distinctive character of their own. They have certain tastes and inclinations by which we could always know them if we met them. And the delightful thing is that their chief peculiarities as saints lie close to

[20] St. Joseph of Cupertino (1603-1663), mystic.

[21] St. Vincent de Paul (c. 1580-1660), founder of the Lazarist Fathers and the Sisters of Charity.

[22] St. Rose of Lima (1586-1617), third order Dominican and first canonized saint of the Americas.

[23] St. Francis de Sales (1567-1622), Bishop of Geneva.

our own doors; and we can make them our own without wonderful miracles or frightening penances.

I do not mean to say we can easily be equal to saints. No! But what I say is that the ways in which they loved God and served the interests of Jesus, and the tastes which made them so dear to the Sacred Heart, are quite easily in our power, if we choose to adopt them. In a word, while the saints differ in almost everything else, there are three things in which they all agree: eagerness for the glory of God; touchiness about the interests of Jesus; and anxiety for the salvation of souls. In these three things consists sympathy with Jesus, and sympathy is at once the fruit and food of love, and love is sanctity. And a saint is simply one who loves Jesus above the common run of pious men and has had unusual gifts given him in return.

Be eager for God's glory

Now, it is plain that if we love God, we shall be eager for His glory, and the more we love Him, the more eager we shall be. What we have set our hearts upon we are sure to follow out fervently and perseveringly.

When, then, a man comes to love God devoutly, he becomes what we call a man of one idea. He looks at everything from one point of view. He considers trades and professions as so many necessary evils, as distracting him from his one work. He is seeking everywhere and in everything the glory of God. It is his last thought at night, his first on waking. If he obtains any power, authority, or influence, his first impulse is, "How shall I use this for the glory of God?" If a calamity befalls him, this is the first question he asks of himself. If a sum of money is left him, this is the first idea it suggests to his mind.

For instance, a man of the world looks at the immense system of railways and steam navigation that now covers the earth as with a net. He calculates its probable effect on governments, popular rights, science, literature, commerce, and civilization. The problem fascinates him. The man of God looks on the same thing and thinks how it will forward missionary enterprise, how it will bring Catholics together, how it will facilitate communication with the Holy See, which is the freedom of the Church, and how in these and many like ways, God will have glory out of it all.

When a man's mind is engrossed in politics, whether in the government or in the opposition, everything that happens comes before him simply with reference to his one absorbing interest. The state of the crops, the chance of a bad harvest, our foreign relations, internal discontent, strikes of workmen, papal bulls — his view of them is, "How will they affect the political party with which I am acting?" So it is with the man who loves God. His one view of everything, however unlikely, has to do with the glory of God. I do not mean to say that he is always thinking of it with an actual and present intention. That would be almost impossible, almost beyond the condition of man. But I mean that it is his most frequent thought, and that he recurs to it ever and again, as a man does to something he loves affectionately and desires intensely.

Now, this is not very hard. There is no austerity in it. We can begin it quietly, take it easily at first, and then let it grow upon us, just as habits grow. We might make a little prayer to God every morning for love to seek His glory and for light to find it all day long. We might renew our intention twice a day to seek His glory. We might ask it in Communion, at the end of our Rosaries, and in our examinations of conscience. If we often forget it, never mind; it will come by use, and God Himself will begin to help us wonderfully, when we have persevered for a few months in the practice.

But not before, remember; for this is His way, to wait awhile and see whether we persevere, although He is really helping all the time, or else we never could persevere. But He will help us in another way later on. This not hard; yet it would bring us nearer the saints, and oh, what interests of Jesus would it not advance by the time a year was gone round!

∞

Be "touchy" about the interests of Jesus

In speaking of touchiness about the interests of Jesus, I use the word *touchiness* purposely, because it so exactly expresses my meaning, and I do not know any other word that expresses it so well. We know perfectly what is to be touchy about our own interests, or the interests of those who are near and dear to us. We fire up at the hint or suspicion of an attack. We are always on the lookout with a watchful jealousy, as if everybody we meet has a design upon us. We are quick to complain and quick to discern. Sometimes, if we do not take care, we judge others censoriously, or we lose our temper and speak rudely.

Now, apply all this to the interests of Jesus, and you will get a very fair idea of what it is to be a saint. Yet even good people do not understand it, and they condemn it as extravagance and indiscretion, simply because they do not know what it is to serve God with a service of love.

A man who is thus touchy about the interests of Jesus hears of some scandal, and it makes him perfectly miserable. He broods over it day and night; he talks querulously about it; it takes the sunshine out of his life for the time being. His friends cannot conceive why he should make so much of it, or take it so to heart. It is no affair of his, and there is no blame attached to him in the matter. They are ready to accuse him of affectation, but they do not see that all his love is for Jesus, and that it is positive pain to him that his dear Lord's interests should be injured. They could fret for a month over being vexatiously entangled in a spiteful and unjust lawsuit; but what is that to the least hindrance thrown in the way of the interests of Jesus? Surely a man who does not see this can hardly be a Christian.

Another way in which this touchiness about the interests of Jesus is shown is in the delicate perception and keen abomination of heresy and false doctrine. The purity of the true faith is one of the very dearest interests of Jesus; and, consequently, one who truly loves his Lord and Master is pained beyond the power of words by the expression of false doctrine, especially among Catholics. Opinions about our Lord's ignorance, or in depreciation of His grace, or in derogation of His Mother's honor, or lowering the sacraments, or dishonoring ever so little the prerogatives of His Vicar upon earth — these things, merely in passing conversation, sting him so that he feels even bodily suffering from them.

Unreflecting people are almost scandalized at this, yet if they heard the honor or chastity of their mother or sister called in question with coarse or wanton rudeness, there is hardly any violence short of bloodshed that would not be thought warrantable and creditable. Yet what is my mother's honor to the dignity of Jesus, or my sister's good name to the least tittle of our Blessed Lady's majesty? And is there not to me more of the mother's love, and of the sister's affection, in the See of Peter, than in all my flesh-and-blood relations put together? I am not bound to die, to seal with my blood my conviction of my mother's honor; but I would be a wretch if I shrank from dying for the lawful honor of the Holy See.

Thus you will not find a single saint who has cherished this pain of love in his heart of hearts, this inability to endure the sound of heresy or false doctrine; and where this is not, then, as sure as the sun is in the heavens, the love of Jesus is but poor and weak in the heart of man.

The same touchiness may be shown, as occasion requires, about all the interests of Jesus mentioned in the last chapter. One remark, however, must be made. It will often happen, when a man's love of our Lord is beyond the formed habits of virtue he may have at the moment, that he is indiscreet, or impatient, or rude, or bitter. He suspects where there is no ground for suspicion, and he does not bear with the slowness or coldness of others, as he would do if the habit of charity were more perfectly formed in him. This often brings discredit on devotion, for there are no persons judged with more unfeeling than those who make profession of a devout life. But they must have their faults and imperfections; they must have the less lovely stages of the spiritual life to pass through. And it must be their consolation that many a time when men blame them, Jesus does not, and the very imperfections of their young love are dear to Him, while the sage criticism and pompous moderation of their censors are hateful in His eyes.

Now, it would not be hard to cultivate this touchiness about the interests of Jesus, and yet it is one of the chief instincts of the saints. Is it not worthwhile trying? Can there be a pleasure in life so great as loving Jesus and serving Him for love? We may begin today. There is no hardship in it, no sudden or violent change that we need to make in our lives. We have only to think a little more about love, and to ask for more love, and then we will be fairly on the road.

∞

Desire and work for the salvation of souls

This is the third and last instinct of the saints that puts us in sympathy with Jesus. The world and the material interests of the world are all against us. They carry us away. What we see is so much more impressive than what we believe. Yet Jesus came into the world for the saving of souls. He died for them; He shed His Precious Blood for them. In proportion as souls are saved, His interests prosper; in proportion as they are lost, His interests as the Savior of souls are injured. The soul is the only thing worth caring for.

Only think what it is to be lost — lost eternally! Who can fathom the horror of it? Who can rightly picture to himself the utterness of the ruin, the breadth, the wretchedness, the unendurableness of the torture, or the helpless wildness of the despair? Yet St. Teresa[24] saw the souls of men flocking daily through doors of Hell, like the showers of dry leaves that the wind drives about in autumn. And Jesus hung for three hours upon the Cross for every one of those souls! And they might all have now been gleaming bright and beautiful in the courts of Heaven! And they loved us, perhaps, and we loved them, and there was much to love in them! Generous, kind, and unselfish they once were, but they loved the world and were ruled by their own passions, and, although they hardly thought of it, they crucified our Lord afresh. And now they are lost — lost eternally!

No wonder His servants should yearn for those over whom Jesus yearned Himself! Thus it is that they are always alert about missions, schools, religious orders, retreats, indulgences, and jubilees. They are full of plans, or, if not of plans, at least of prayers. They care for little else but souls. They sacrifice all for souls, no matter what rebuffs they meet with, what disappointments they find, or into what mistakes they fall at first. They are all for souls. They begin afresh every day to plan and plot for souls. They are

[24] Probably St. Teresa of Avila (1515-1582), Carmelite nun and mystic. — Ed.

not cast down when they do not see clearly that there will be money or men to go on with all the good works they plan; but their consolation is that all work for souls is complete work by itself, and for as long as it lasts, because all dispensing of grace and of the Precious Blood is a desirable and blessed thing in itself. While some talk and take views, and criticize, and despond, and weaken the hands and hearts of others, those who love Jesus work on in simplicity, not thinking of tomorrow.

Volumes might be written about this passion for souls. It must come where there is a true love of Jesus. It is not the rule for Peter only, but for all who love. "When thou art converted, confirm thy brethren."[25] "Lovest thou me more than these? Feed my sheep."[26] And have not we, each of us, many little ways by which we can help in the saving of souls? And in intercession, at least, is not the whole Church open to the genial and immense influence of our prayers, as much as it is to the Pope himself?

Cultivate the three characteristics of the saints

The saints, then, are made up chiefly of these three things: eagerness for the glory of God, touchiness about the interests of Jesus, and anxiety for the salvation of souls. These three things make a most beautiful and angelic character, and go further than anything else to assure us of our predestination. Yet we have seen how easy they are, if only we will learn to love Jesus, and to serve Him for love. There is neither sex, nor age, nor station which is not equally convenient for the practice of these three things. And

[25] Luke 22:32.

[26] Cf. John 21:15, 17.

what a difference it would make in the world if a few people would take them up seriously and carry them out quietly in daily life and in daily prayer.

I want to collect for you from the lives of the saints and the works of spiritual writers a number of easy and interesting practices that will help you to form these three things in your soul, so as to be advancing the interests of our dear Lord every hour of your life, and yet all the while, in the most pleasant manner possible, becoming something like the saints yourself.

You can take your choice of these practices. None of them is of any obligation. You are not even bound to choose, if you choose at all, the highest, best, and most perfect, for it is quite possible such would not be best for you. Take what is most to your taste; there is no need to turn your devotions into mortifications. This is one of the un-Catholic notions that converts should take pains to drive out of their heads. It sounds fine, but it works ill, and it ends in carelessness and lax ways. I want to beguile you into serving Jesus out of love, and so I want you to enjoy yourself and follow your bent in your devotions.

Serve Jesus happily

Now you see exactly what it is I want of you. You must serve Jesus in some way or other, or else you will not save your soul. You are absolutely dependent upon Him. You cannot do without His faith, His life, His death, His Blood, His Church, or His sacraments. You cannot take a step toward Heaven, but by Him. Nothing that you think or do or say is worth anything until His worth has touched it. Dependence cannot be conceived that is more utter and absolute, more incessant and indispensable, than is your dependence upon Him.

Thus, in some way or other, you must serve Jesus. The question is whether it is not best to serve Him out of love. But has your religion been a service of love hitherto? Or have you doled out your duties to Him as a poor man pays a debt to a rich creditor, looking him in the face between each shilling to see if he really intends to forget his poverty and take the full amount of his debt? Has not the problem been to find out the least that you must do to gain Heaven? Weighing commandments, clipping precepts, interpreting rules, begging dispensations — is not this the kind of thing you have called your religion, your worship of an incarnate God, beside Himself with love and hanging bleeding on a Cross?

Now, I maintain to serve Jesus out of love is so much easier than all this. Nothing is easy that we are not happy while doing. Have you been happy in your religion? Far from it! It has been a simple burden to you. If it had not been for Heaven and Hell, you would have made short work of it long since. But Heaven and Hell are facts; there they are, and there is no help for us.

As, then, we must be religious, I am for a happy religion. I see no use in an unhappy one, if God gives me my choice.

But He has done more than that. He wishes me to be happy in my religion. Nay, He wishes my religion to be the happiness and sunshine of my life. Now, a happy religion means a religion of love. Everything comes easy to love. Thus, I am dependent for my happiness on no one but Jesus; my religion makes me happy all the day long.

If serving Jesus out of love were some prodigiously difficult thing, such as the contemplation of the saints, or their austerities, then it would be another matter. But the fact is, it is nothing of the kind. To serve God because you are afraid of going to Hell, and wish to go to Heaven, is a great blessing and a supernatural work, but it is very difficult. Whereas, to serve God because you love

Him is so easy that it is hard to account for so many men in the world neglecting to do it. Stupid souls, so miraculously blind!

And what is a further blessing is that what makes you happy makes our dearest Lord happy also; and the thought of this again makes us so happy that we can hardly contain ourselves, and then that again makes Him happier still. And thus religion gets sweeter and sweeter. Life is one long joy, because the will of God is always being done in it, and the glory of God is always being gotten from it.

You become identified with the interests of Jesus; you wed them as if they were your own, as indeed they are. His spirit steals into you and sets up a little throne in your heart and crowns itself, and then most sweetly proclaims itself king. It gained the crown by a dear conspiracy; you never suspected what divine love was about all the while. But so it is. God's glory becomes dear to you. You get quite touchy about our Lord, for He has become the apple of your eye. You are drawn to save souls, because it is what He is always doing, and so you get an instinct and a taste for it yourself.

And so it all goes on; and so you live, yet not you, but Christ lives in you;[27] and so you die. You never suspect you are a saint, or anything approaching one. Your life is hidden with Christ in God,[28] and hidden from no one more than from yourself. You — a saint indeed! Your humility would either laugh or be frightened at the bare thought.

But oh, the depth of the mercies of Jesus! What will be your surprise at His judgment seat, to hear the sweet sentence, to see the bright crown! Why, you will almost argue against your own salvation! Our Lord makes the elect do so in the Gospel: "Lord, when did we see Thee hungry and feed Thee? When did we see

[27] Cf. Gal. 2:20.

[28] Cf. Col. 3:3.

Thee thirsty and give Thee drink?"[29] They cannot make it out. In all their love for Jesus, they never dreamed it was so great a thing as this.

Ah, only serve Jesus out of love! You cannot beat God in the strife of love! Only serve Jesus out of love, and what an unspeakable surprise will you have had at the judgment seat of your dearest Love, while the songs of Heaven are breaking on your ears, and the glory of God is dawning on your eyes, to fade away no more forever!

[29] Matt. 25:37.

Chapter Three

Be sorry for sin

It is said of one of the first fathers of the Oratory, the companion of St. Philip, that he used to prefer those writers on grace who made most of God's sovereignty and least of man's free will. He had developed a habit of taking God's side in everything and of always looking at things from God's point of view. And this is exactly what I am venturing to recommend to you.

A false doctrine is odious, because it is untrue; it is odious also because it gives scandal, or hinders devotion, or injures souls. On all these grounds, good men hate it. But those who love God with a very tender and delicate love do not think of it so much in these respects, as because God's honor is wounded by it. God's honor is their first thought. They range themselves at once on God's side. Suppose, again, that a good man is overwhelmed by an unjust persecution or a cruel calumny. Those who love God with such a delicate love are not without the most tender sympathy and the most generous self-sacrifice for the sufferer. But their first thought, their strongest thought, their abiding thought, is the wound inflicted on God's honor by the persecution of His servant, and of the sin almost necessarily committed by the persecutors. So in cases of spiritual destitution, or of great public sins, or of important political changes, or of local calamities, or of Catholic triumphs, or of getting souls out of Purgatory, these men, by an instantaneous instinct, feel and find where God's glory is touched. They are at once so absorbed in it that they often seem unaffectionate or ungenerous, or uncordial in sorrowing and rejoicing with others, although it is not really so in their hearts.

Now, this taking God's side on every occasion may easily be formed in us as a habit, by time, prayer, and quiet assiduity in devotion; and surely it is a considerable help to us in loving and serving God. It is a great thing gradually to grow in the conviction that there is no real sorrow in the world but sin, that we have no real enemy but sin, and that warfare with sin, in others as well as in ourselves, in prayer as well as in action, is the one work we have to do and is the one work that is worth doing. And it is this conviction which comes of our always taking God's side and which, when it has once come, causes us to persevere all the more steadfastly in taking that side. As creatures, we are in our proper place when we are taking the side of our Creator, defending His interests, protecting His majesty, and advancing His glory. There is happiness in the darkest lot, peace in the wildest trouble, when we are thus engaged.

∞

Love God as your Father

But God is not our Creator only; He is our Father also. Oh, that we all felt the importance of this! The man who serves God as his Creator is a very different character from the man who serves Him as his Father. We do not serve God out of love, because we do not have a loving idea of God. We are dry, cold, and grudging with Him, because we will persist in looking at Him only as our Lawgiver, Master, Sovereign, or Judge. Far more persons would try to go on to perfection, far more would persevere in it, and there would be a far narrower gulf between saints and common Catholics, if only we all agreed to serve God as our Father and to look upon Him as our Father.

It is astonishing what an amount of jealous and unkindly feeling there is even among good people toward God, His sovereignty, and His majesty. It is at the root of all the unhappiness and want of comfort in religious duties. It brings with it all sorts of temptations against the Faith and starts all manner of scruples in the mind, which hamper the tenderness of devotion and freeze the joyful spirit of loving mortification. Why, it is the very sunshine of life to believe and feel at every turn that God is our Father and is acting toward us out of a Father's love and in a Father's way!

See what pains God has been pleased to take to prevent this unkindly view of Him on the part of His children. He has committed all judgment to the Son. It is our dear Lord, as man, who is to judge us at the last. Our very last appeal is to His Sacred Human Heart. When God invites His rebellious people to return to Him, by the mouth of Jeremiah, He sums up all their sins, and then pleads so compassionately, rather for Himself than with them: "Therefore, at the least, from this time call to me: Thou art my Father."[30]

The apostle sums up the whole work of the Gospel in this very thing, that we have received the spirit of adoption, whereby we cry, "Abba, Father";[31] and when our Lord teaches us to pray, it is by the name of Father that He bids us call on God. He has provided one of the seven gifts of the Holy Spirit, that of piety, for the express purpose of enabling us to exercise, even in a heroic degree, a really filial tenderness toward God. This gift is defined to be a habitual

[30] Jer. 3:4.

[31] Rom. 8:15.

disposition that the Holy Spirit infuses into our soul to excite in us a filial affection toward God, and St. Thomas tells us that works done to God as our Father are more meritorious than works done to Him as our Creator, because the motive is more excellent.[32]

St. Paul, not content with the passage already cited from the letter to the Romans,[33] repeats almost the same words to the Galatians. He speaks as if, under the old dispensation, God had not, so to say, succeeded in persuading the Jews to look upon Him as their Father, and that, therefore, "when the fullness of time was come, God sent His Son, made of a woman, made under the law, that He might redeem them who were under the law, that we might receive the adoption of sons. And because you are sons, God hath sent the Spirit of His Son into your hearts, saying, 'Abba, Father.' Therefore, now you are not a servant, but a son."[34] Yet even in the Old Testament, who does not remember the pathetic language of Israel? "Thou art our Father, and Abraham has not known us, and Israel hath been ignorant of us; Thou, O Lord, art our Father, our Redeemer; from everlasting is Thy Name."[35]

Lancisius, in his *Treatise on the Presence of God*, gives a number of acts of love, addressing God as "my most holy Lord and dearest Father," and at the end, he puts into the mouth of an objector this question: "Why in these interior acts of love do you add the name of Father?" He replies that it is for four reasons. First, because it is desirable that such acts of love should be elicited from the soul, not merely by the affections of humility and religion implied in

[32] St. Thomas Aquinas (c. 1225-1274; Dominican philosopher and theologian), *Summa Theologica*, II-II, Q. 121, art. 1.

[33] Rom. 8:15.

[34] Cf. Gal. 4:4-7.

[35] Isa. 63:16.

the title of Lord, but by an affectionate filial feeling toward Him. Second, because of the greater merit thus acquired, according to the doctrine of St. Thomas: "It is more excellent to worship God as our Father than to worship Him as our Creator and Lord." And Leo says, "Great is the sacrament of this privilege, and this gift exceeds all gifts, that God should call man son, and that man should call God Father."[36] Third, because the remembrance that God is our Father excites confidence in us; and it is on this account, says Tertullian, St. Cyprian, and St. Chrysostom,[37] that the Lord's Prayer begins, "Our Father"; for, to quote St. Thomas again, "Confidence is chiefly excited in us by considering God's love toward us, whereby He wishes us good things, and on which account we call Him Father."[38] Fourth, "we call Him Father," says St. Augustine,[39] "that by the kind name of Father, we may win His favor and, by that appellation, move Him to grant what we are asking."

There is a very beautiful passage in the revelations of St. Gertrude, showing how acceptable with God are titles of reverent yet familiar endearment. Our Lord told her that as often as anyone says to God, "My Love," or "My Sweetest," or "My best Beloved," and the like, with a devout intention, he receives a pledge of his salvation, in virtue of which, if he perseveres, he shall receive in Heaven a special privilege of the same sort as the special grace that St. John the Evangelist, the beloved disciple, had on earth.[40]

[36] St. Leo the Great (d. 461; Pope from 440), *Sermo 6 de Nativ.*

[37] Tertullian (c. 160-c. 225), African Church Father; St. Cyprian (d. 258), Bishop of Carthage; St. John Chrysostom (c. 347-407), Bishop of Constantinople.

[38] *Summa Theologica*, II-II, Q. 83, art. 9.

[39] St. Augustine (354-430), Bishop of Hippo.

[40] *Revelations of St. Gertrude* (1256-c. 1302; German mystic), Bk. 3, ch. 9.

Now, if we fully feel that God is our Father, if our daily way of thinking of God, and of approaching Him, is as our dearest Father, it must soon come to pass that there will be nothing on earth half so dear to us as His majesty and honor. We should feel as if it belonged to us, and was really our own, and we should take up any offense against it as warmly as we would now take up an injustice toward ourselves. But it is sin that offends Him, and therefore it should be sin that we should feel to be our one enemy, our only care, our single misery on earth, whether in ourselves or in others. Yes, other men's sins would cease to be matters of indifference to us, because they are offenses against the majesty of God. We should fully enter into that constant cry of St. Philip: "Only let there be no sin!"

When we are full of this view of God, not a day goes by without our detecting something fatherly in Him that we never observed before. Prayer changes, and sacraments accomplish greater things than heretofore. Everything about us alters by degrees. Duties grow into privileges; penances brighten up into pleasures; pains soften the heart with a delicious humility; and sorrows are heavenly presences. Work becomes rest, and weariness of limb and brain almost touches on the sweet languor of contemplation. It is as if earth were making itself into Heaven; and at the commonest sights and sounds, something tingles in our hearts as if God were just on the point of speaking or appearing.

What another thing is life when we have discovered God to be our Father; if we work, it is beneath His eye, and if we play, it is in the light and encouragement of His smile. Earth's sunshine is Heaven's radiance, and the stars of night are as if the beginnings of the Beatific Vision. So soft, so sweet, so gentle, so reposeful, so almost infinite have things become, because we have found our Father in our God.

∞

Love God for His goodness

When we love God, we rejoice that He is God, that He is so good and perfect as He is. We call this feeling the love of complacency. We transfer His joy to ourselves; we rejoice in it as if it were our own simply because we love Him.

But this is not the only office of love. If it makes us happy because the Object of our love is happy, by transferring His happiness to our hearts, and so making His interests our own, the same love will equally make us sorrowful — because the Object of our love is wronged and oppressed — by transferring His injury to us, and placing His wrongs in our hearts, as if they were ours rather than His. What I mean is this: that to sorrow over the sins of others is no far-fetched devotion, or subtle refinement of religious feeling, but that it follows inevitably upon the love of God. Where there is no such sorrow for sin, either in ourselves or others, there is no love of God; and in proportion to the amount of love will the degree of sorrow be. What was it that made our Blessed Lady's dolors more intolerable than all the tortures of the martyrs, but that her love exceeded all the martyrs' love? Thus, if God is wronged and outraged, we take the wrong into our hearts, and it wounds us by means of the love we have for Him.

∞

Cultivate a compassionate love for our suffering Lord

As sympathy and compassion are feelings more easily excited in us than those of complacency, it seems as if God wished to cultivate what theologians call the love of condolence, even more than of complacency. This is one reason why devotion to the Passion is the great popular devotion of the whole Church. It may also be a reason why our Lord was pleased to suffer so much more than He need have done, and with so many unnecessary touching circumstances: so that to condole with Him in His Passion might be all the easier, and so He might have more of our poor love.

And it does not require any rare amount of love to feel this sacred compassion. The women of Jerusalem were no saints, yet they wept over Jesus in the way of the Cross. Job's friends were the meanest-hearted of men, yet compassion mastered even their pompous dryness and unamiable pedantry. What we want of all things is our heart's softening, and sorrow softens them sooner and more effectually than joy.

I have no hope that we shall get any further loves into our heart if we do not first domesticate this love of condolence there. We do not find such great fault with a man who does not joy in another's joy, as we do with him who grieves not with another's grief. Sympathy belongs to our position in the world, and there is hope for the most sinful heart, if it only keeps its quick and affectionate sympathies. Out of all evil comes good, and so from sin and the Passion our dear Lord, as from two perennial fountains, flows this blessed love of condolence in our hearts.

And see what this love can do! Mary's compassion is said, in a certain sense, to have cooperated with our blessed Lord's Passion in the saving of the world. How many instances we have on record of God showing mercy to sinners, just because they kept up some trifling tender memory of His loving Passion! We must grieve with Him now if we wish to rejoice with Him hereafter. I wish you would reflect on this. St. Francis de Sales says that the ardent desire of our Savior to enter our souls by this dolorous love is inexplicable.

Here, then, is a sweet way of loving Him, a sweet way of giving Him greater glory. You will not refuse Him when it is so easy. I am sure you love Him. I am sure you wish to love Him more. I will not believe that it is not so. Dear Lord! Who can help loving Him? Is there such a thing as a heart that does not love Him? But it is not our business now to go in search of such strange things, or to see whether such dreadful wonders exist upon the earth. We love Him; blessed be His grace for that! There was His old Passion two thousand years ago; there is His daily passion now, and His nightly agony, because sin abounds. Cruel sin! Cruel sinners! But He shall take refuge with us; only listen at your hearts, and hear what He says. Is it not clear? "Open to me, my sister, my love, my dove, my undefiled; for my head is full of dew, and my locks of the drops of the nights!"[41]

But you may say, "Sorrowing for other men's sins is all very well for saints; we know the saints have done so. But it is a thing rather to be admired than imitated. It is above us. It would be an injudicious practice in us. We do not have half enough sorrow for our own sins yet; we must not go so quickly; we must learn a little more of that first."

Alas, do not make such an objection as this. Let me take you on your own ground. You have not, you say, half enough sorrow for your own sins. There is nothing you regret so much as this, nothing that seems to you more uncomfortable and unpromising in your spiritual life. But why do you not have more sorrow? Because you look more at sin as it affects the interests of your own soul than as it affects the interests of God. I do not mean to say that you are not to look at it in that way — God forbid. You must do the one, but you must not leave the other undone.

Now, if you look at sin simply as it regards your own reward and punishment, it is clear that you will never get an adequate hatred of sin; for your punishment is far from being the chief evil of sin. Its

[41] Cant. 5:2 (RSV = Song of Sol. 5:2).

chief evil is its outrage of the majesty of God; and if you could see it in this light, you would have a much keener sorrow for your own sins than you have. But, then, in order to see it in this light, you must learn to look with an eye of sorrow on the sins of others, for there you have no interests of your own; there you are contemplating simply the injured glory of our heavenly Father. And thus, in order to sorrow more deeply and more effectually for your own sins, you must mourn for God's dear sake over the sins of others. And this is the practice that I wish now to recommend to you: sorrowing for the sins of others, and making reparation to God's injured glory for them.

∞

Be sorry for the sins of others

We sorrow for other men's sins, because God's glory is injured by them, because the fruit of our dear Lord's Passion is spoiled or wasted, and because souls are damaged and lost thereby. You see these same three things over and over again, and you must not be weary of my repeating them so often.

But, when I use the word *sorrow*, you must not misunderstand me. I am not putting before you anything melancholy or disagreeable — far from it. The sorrow I speak of is one of the greatest pleasures in life, enough to lighten a heavy heart, rather than to depress a light one.

Hear how the eternal Father vouchsafed to explain this to His beloved daughter St. Catherine of Siena. After speaking to her of the five kinds of tears men shed, He speaks of a state of the soul at once blessed and yet sorrowing. "It is blessed, indeed, from its sensible union with me, wherein it tastes the divine love. Its sorrow arises from its view of the offenses that are committed against me, who am the Eternal Goodness, whom it beholds and tastes in its knowledge of itself and of me. Neither does this hinder its state of union with me; for the tears that it sheds are of great sweetness, proceeding from its knowledge of itself in its love of its neighbor. For it finds the plaintiveness of love in my mercy, and the sorrow of love in the miseries of its neighbors. So it weeps with those who weep, and joys with those who joy; for the soul rejoices when my servants pay honor and glory to my name." And again, "This unafflicting pain, arising from my being offended, and from the misfortunes of its neighbors, is founded on a most real charity, and fattens the soul. Nay, a man rejoices and exults in this pain, because it is a most convincing proof that I am in his soul by a very special grace."[42]

Thus it has been that the saints who have received the most eminent gift of tears, have also been inundated above others with spiritual joy. The old biographer of St. John Climacus[43] tells us that words cannot express the ravishing effects that his gift of tears produced in his soul; and the saint himself, in the seventh step of his *Ladder of Perfection*, says, "They who have received the gift of tears spend every day of their lives as a spiritual feast." Truly there is no bitterness in the tears of those who love; and what can there be but peace and joy in tears that are a gift of Him who is the love and jubilee, as St. Augustine calls Him, of the Father and the Son?

But I shall make myself clearer by giving you instances, from the saints themselves, of this sorrow for all sins against the glory of God, and you will thus see how sweet and easy the practice is.

[42] St. Catherine of Siena (c. 1347-1380; Dominican tertiary), *Dialogue*, chs. 88, 89, 95.

[43] St. John Climacus (c. 570-c. 649), ascetic and writer on the spiritual life.

God made the following revelation to the same St. Catherine. "I am greatly pleased, my dearest daughter, with this desire of enduring every pain and toil, even until death, for the salvation of souls. For the more a man endures, the more he shows his love of me; and loving me, he knows more of my truth; and the more he knows of me, the more he feels the pain and intolerable grief of all sin against me. You asked to take punishment of other people's faults upon yourself, and you did not perceive that in asking that, you were all the while asking love, light, and knowledge of the truth; for, I have already said, the greater love is, the greater is the pain; so, as love grows, sorrow will also grow."[44]

St. Mary Magdalene de' Pazzi[45] said, "In this life, the exercise of sorrow pleases God more than the exercise of love, because the former is a sort of martyrdom, by which souls resemble Him hanging on the Cross, and their sorrow is compassion for His great pains and, as it were, tears of love for His Passion. And when this sorrow rises to the point of affliction, it cleanses the soul from its sins. Love is certainly more delectable, but, as we are in this world to be cleansed, it is rather the time for sorrowing and suffering for the love of our God; and so it is that God takes more complacency in sorrow than in love."

On another occasion, after Communion, our Lord told the same saint to mourn like a turtledove and to compassionate Him because He was so little known and loved by His creatures.

Still more remarkable is the proof of the power over the Sacred Heart of this practice of sorrowing for the sins of others, which we find in the life of St. Mary Magdalene de' Pazzi. It is full of the most encouraging sweetness and soothing consolation for us, for, in our

[44] *Dialogue*, ch. 5.

[45] St. Mary Magdalene de' Pazzi (1566-1607), Carmelite mystic.

measure and degree, how easy it is for us to follow her footsteps, although far behind, in this holy practice!

When she was a little girl, only eight years old, she heard one person abuse another in such a way as to commit a sin thereby. She was so shocked by this offense to God that she could not sleep all the night after, because of her weeping over the outrage committed against the majesty of God. Sixteen years elapsed, and the saint probably had forgotten all about it, when God, in a revelation, told her that in consequence of that act of sorrow for another's sin, there was prepared for her a special glory, which He represented to her under the figure of a glorious flame-colored garment.

He who does not forget the cup of cold water[46] can still less forget these interior acts of loving sorrow or of sorrowing love. What a treasure is here for us, if our love would only be wakeful and watch for the opportunities!

St. Bonaventure says of St. Francis that he filled the groves with his moanings and everywhere shed tears and beat his breast, as he murmured in his talk with God, or at times called out with clamorous cries, begging mercy for sin. "Nay," says the Seraphic Doctor, "when he saw souls, redeemed with the Precious Blood of Jesus Christ, polluted by any stain of sin, he wept over them with such tenderness of compassion, that it seemed as though, mother-like, he was every day bringing them to the birth in Christ."[47] The glory of God, the interests of Jesus, and the love of souls so run and blend into one in the blessed patriarch of Assisi that the three motives do duty for each other. He begins with one and ends with

[46] Cf. Matt. 10:42.

[47] St. Bonaventure (1221-1274; Franciscan theologian known as the Seraphic Doctor), *Life of St. Francis of Assisi* (c. 1182-1226; founder of the Franciscan Order), ch. 8.

another, for, in good truth, of them it may most reverently be said, "And these three are one."

St. Lawrence Justinian, the patriarch of Venice, says, "He cannot help sorrowing for other people's sins who sorrows truly for his own. A healthy limb on the body, which helps not the others when they are sick, occupies its place in vain. These members, likewise, of the Church, who see their brethren's sin and do not weep over it, or compassionate the ruin of their souls, are useless members. When our Redeemer wept over the city that was to perish, He considered it the more to be deplored as it knew not its own deplorable condition. "As many, therefore, as are set on fire by the torch of love weep over other men's sins if they were their own. Yet no one worthily deplores the sins of others who by voluntary falls neglects his own. We must at least cease to sin wilfully if we desire to mourn over the falls of others."[48]

Chrysostom[49] says that Moses was raised above the people because he habitually deplored the sins of others. "He," says the same holy Doctor, "who sorrows for other men's sins, has the tenderness of an apostle, and is an imitator of that blessed one who said, 'Who is weak, and I am not weak? Who is offended, and I burn not?' "[50]

"Who," says St. Augustine, "is not angry when he sees men renouncing the world, not in deeds but merely in words? Who is not angry when he sees the brethren plotting against each other and breaking faith with each other, faith that has been pledged in the sacraments of God?"[51]

[48] St. Lawrence Justinian (1381-1456; Bishop and first Patriarch of Venice), *Fascic. Amor.*, ch. 14.

[49] St. John Chrysostom (c. 347-407), Bishop of Constantinople.

[50] 2 Cor. 11:29.

[51] *On Psalm 30*.

In a similar strain, Lancisius quotes St. Chromatius of Aquileia:[52] "Do you wish to know what the pious grief of saints is like? Hear what is said of the prophet Samuel, who mourned for King Saul, even to the day of his death. Jeremiah, also, when he bewailed the sins of the people, said, 'My eyes have poured out floods of water over the contrition of my people.' And again, 'Who will give water to my head, and a fountain of tears to my eyes?' Daniel, also, was affected with sorrow and heaviness for the sins of the people, as he himself testifies, saying, 'In those days I, Daniel, mourned the days of three weeks. I ate no desirable bread, and neither flesh nor wine entered into my mouth, neither was I anointed with ointment.'

"The apostle mourned with a like sorrow over some of the Corinthians, saying, 'Lest when I come, God humble me among you, and I mourn many of them that have sinned before, and have not done penance.' This is the kind of grief which the Lord recompenses with the consolation of perpetual joy, as Isaiah says: 'He will appoint to the mourners of Sion a crown for ashes, the oil of joy for mourning, and a garment of praise for the spirit of grief.' "

Now, have we thought sufficiently of this? We live in a world where we see God offended every day and every hour. We see souls perishing for want of faith; we hear blasphemies on all sides; "truths are diminished among the children of men." Does all this grieve us? Have we felt it as personal calamity?

Or have we shut ourselves selfishly up in our own hearts, thanking God, with an unamiable gratitude, that we at least have the true faith and the living sacraments, and looking on all the rest as a doomed multitude, who are of no concern to us one way or another?

[52] St. Chromatius (d. 406 or 407), Bishop of Aquileia.

If you have no tie to the souls of all these, and indeed you have, for Christ shed His Precious Blood for them as well as for you, at least you have a tie to the glory of God; and can you feel that you really love God, in your own sense of the word *love*, if you do not feel His dishonor?

But it is not to upbraid you that I write. God forbid! It is rather to explain to you and urge upon you the practices that will cultivate more and more that sweet spirit of which we have been speaking.

Hear, then, what God said to St. Catherine of Siena: "It is with reason that you, my elect, are in bitter grief of heart because of the offenses I am continually receiving from men, and out of compassion for their culpable ignorance, by which they gravely sin against me, to the damage, nay, to the condemnation, of their own souls. This I gratefully accept from you, and it is my wish that you should act so."[53]

See also what was the experience of Bl. Angela of Foligno[54] in this matter. Before her death, she made a sort of devout will, in which she bequeathed certain admonitions to her spiritual children, and this is one: "I tell you that my soul has received more from God when I mourned for the sins of others than when I grieved for my own. The world makes light of what I say, that a man can deplore his neighbor's sins as much as his own — yea, more than his own, because it seems to be contrary to nature; but the charity which does so is not of this world."

When St. Ignatius[55] was living in the house of John Pascal, at Barcelona, and was spending the night in prayer, he was seen raised

[53] *Dialogue*, ch. 28.

[54] Bl. Angela of Foligno (1248-1309), Umbrian penitent and mystical writer.

[55] St. Ignatius of Loyola (1491-1556), founder of the Society of Jesus.

to some height above the ground, and the whole room was illuminated with the brightness that proceeded from his face, while he kept repeating over and over again these words: "O my Lord, my heart, my beloved! Oh, if men did but know Thee, they would never sin!" Thus it is said of Fr. Peter Faber,[56] the companion of St. Ignatius, that he had an abiding sadness of mind because he was touched to the quick by the sight of men sinning.

As St. Augustine says, "This is the persecution which all suffer who desire to live piously in Christ, according to the true and biting sentence of the apostle. For what persecutes the life of the good more sharply than the life of the wicked, not because it forces the good to imitate what displeases them, but because it compels them to grieve over the life they behold? For, in the sight of a pious man, an evildoer, although he does not oblige him to consent to his sin, yet tortures him with the sight and sorrow of it."[57]

Thus it is said of St. Clare of Montefalco,[58] in her life, that when she heard of anyone in mortal sin, she turned at once to the crucifix, and weeping inconsolably and sighing from the bottom of her heart, she said, "Ah, then, is all lost, so far as this soul is concerned, which my Lord suffered for it?" And then, unable to bear the thought, she prostrated herself upon the ground and prayed for the conversion of the sinner.

Oh, that there were such a heart in us that we would make these dispositions ours! Oh, that we would feel sin to be indeed the one solitary evil of the world! Oh, that the hunger and thirst for the glory of our most dear Lord were consuming us all the day long!

[56] Bl. Peter Faber (1506-1546).

[57] *Epist.* 141.

[58] St. Clare of Montefalco (c. 1268-1308), third order Franciscan who later embraced the rule of the third order of St. Augustine.

Yet how soon these feelings come, if only we set ourselves in earnest to seek them and to ask them of God. What does He want but to be loved — loved always, loved everywhere; and how, then, if we ask this love of Him, can He refuse it to us? Why not turn all our prayers into one, and pray early and late for more love of God?

But you may say, "In what ways are we to practice this sorrow for the sins of others?"

∞

Strive to see how God should be served and glorified

We should strive in our meditations to see how God ought to be served and glorified by His creatures. We should put before ourselves His infinite perfections and attributes, His beauty and loveliness in Himself. We should picture to ourselves the perfect obedience with which His will is done in Heaven, and try to unite ourselves with the interior dispositions of the Sacred Heart of Jesus, of the Immaculate Heart of Mary, and all the hierarchies and choirs of angels. We should count up the benefits and blessings that in His infinite love He has bestowed upon His creatures, and especially in the four great wonders of mercy: Creation, the Incarnation, the Holy Eucharist, and the Beatific Vision.

Then, when we have worked this well into our minds, we shall see what sin really is, how terrible it is to offend so great a majesty, and how base beyond words to wound so unutterable a love. We shall then hardly be able to leave the house and follow our worldly occupations without finding food for this sorrow over sin. At every step almost, we shall be called upon to make acts of reparation to the injured glory of God. The amount of the world's forgetfulness of God will strike us every day as more and more astonishing.

So far from getting used to it, the more the beauty and the tenderness of God's majesty grow in us, the more will the hatefulness of sin come upon us with startling force. The sort of common consent by which men ignore God, His rights, His claims, and His interests will seem to us almost more hideous than overt acts of sin. Life will become a burden, the world feel like a strange and unhomelike place, and a blessed weariness will come over us, which will find no repose except upon the sweet and satisfying thought of God.

∞

Sorrow over those who do not love Christ

Another method of practicing this sorrow for sin is the one suggested by St. Bernard to Pope Eugenius:[59] "Lift up the eyes of your reflection, and behold the nations. Are they not rather dry for the fire than white for the harvest? How much is there that looks like fruit, which yet, on nearer inspection, is but briers? Nay, not even briers, but old and knotted trees, bearing only such mast and acorns as the swine can eat."[60]

Take a map of the world; look first at Asia, where our Lord was born and suffered. How few Christians are to be found in the whole extent! Fearful systems of idolatry, Islam, and communities bearing the name of Christ yet in truth denying it in heresy and schism — these exercise an almost unlimited sway over those beautiful regions, and only here and there is there one to be found who calls on the saving name of Jesus and worships His Precious Blood. Yet there was man created, and Eden planted; there was the home of the chosen people; there the Son of God taught and suffered; there the Apostles preached, and Athanasius, Basil,

[59] Bl. Eugenius III (d. 1153), Cistercian and Pope from 1145.

[60] St. Bernard (1090-1153; Abbot of Clairvaux), *De Consideratione*, ii, 6.

Gregory,[61] and Chrysostom upheld the Faith and trampled upon heresy. As to Japan and China, their very soil is soaked with the blood of our dear Lord's martyrs. Yet how scanty is the harvest of His glory.

Look along the Mediterranean shores of Africa, where once more than four hundred bishops had their thrones! On how many leagues of country the sun shines where none call on Jesus or know of His blessed Cross! America is better, and so also is Australia, for thanks to the Spaniards and the Irish, there is the knowledge of the Gospel there. Yet how many people are still unconverted, and how many millions of heretics bear the Christian name in vain!

Look, too, how heresy has eaten into the fair fields of Europe! Nations are all more or less its prey, and multitudes are daily passing into perdition within the sound of the true Gospel and within reach of the holy sacraments! This was the picture that St. Lawrence Justinian looked upon when he wrote his *Treatise on the Complaint of Christian Perfection*. This was the picture God Himself beheld when He complained so bitterly to St. Catherine of Siena that priests and prelates cared not for His glory and, in their idleness and self-seeking, trod His dear interests underfoot.

Oh, what a field is there here for acts of love! Think of the day when the compassionate Creator looked over His own beautiful creation, virgin and undefiled, and blessed it because it was all so good. Think of the day when, to bring back that primal benediction — nay, to give it a new and better benediction — Jesus hung upon the Cross on Calvary. And this is the result! This is the sinner's recompense to God!

[61] St. Athanasius (c. 296-373), Bishop of Alexandria; St. Basil (c. 330-379), Cappadocian Church Father; possibly St. Gregory I (c. 540-604), Pope from 590. — Ed.

As our thoughts wander on, and our eyes rest on the provinces of heathens and heretics, do we not feel drawn to offer to God all the acts of adoration that the angels have made this day in Heaven, in reparation for the glory these poor outcasts have not given Him?

Let us also resort to the merits of Jesus Himself, to the heroic virtues of His ever-blessed Mother, to the apostles, martyrs, virgins, Doctors, and confessors, so that we may supply with loving intention the praise that should rise to the Divine Majesty from all these peoples and nations.

∞

Make spiritual visits to the world's tabernacles

Another practice is suggested by Fr. Balthazar Alvarez, St. Teresa's confessor. It is to journey over the world in spirit and visit the many churches and tabernacles where the Blessed Sacrament is reserved and so few come in to visit the Love of our souls. "The streets," says he, "are full, but the churches are empty. Crowds are eagerly intent on their own interests, and few come to commune with Jesus about His!"

St. Alphonsus, also, with his usual thoughtful sweetness, suggests to us how many churches there are where Jesus is obliged to dwell in filth, disorder, and neglect, and where, from week's end to week's end, no one comes to visit Him. With what childlike acts of love, ever varying, yet ever tender, may we not pour out our hearts before Him in all these deserted sanctuaries! Can we not muse on Jesus thus abandoned, until our hearts grow hot, and the tears come into our eyes? Oh, how acceptable to Him is this little offering of heartfelt sorrow! He loves to be remembered, as all lovers do; and nothing is little in His sight that is done for the love of Him, for His love transmutes and magnifies it all.

I do not say that you should faint at the bare name of sin, as saints have done: such things require a special grace and great heights of love. But you can do a little in reparation and in sorrow for the sin of the world, and out of that little, be it ever so little, God will have great glory, and we shall comfort one another's hearts.

∞

Sorrow over your own sins

Yet, as I said before, we must not forget to sorrow for our own sins also, and to sorrow for them chiefly as offenses against a God so infinitely good and loving. "If we grieve and sorrow for our sins," says St. Chrysostom, "we lessen the magnitude of our sin; what was great, we make small — nay, oftentimes we do away with it altogether." And St. Basil, commenting on those words, "Thou has turned my weeping into joy,"[62] says, "It is not everyone into whose soul God infuses joy, but into his who has deplored his sin with vehement grief, and with assiduous lamentation, as if he wept for himself dead; for such weeping turns to joy at last."

"We ought to bear our sins in mind," says St. Chrysostom again, "for not only do we extinguish them by so doing, but we become gentler and more indulgent toward others, and we serve God with greater tenderness, having from that memory of our sins a better insight into His inestimable goodness."

Scripture tells us, "Be not without fear of a forgiven sin";[63] and, indeed, such a fear will be the best security against another fall. Some saints tell us that if we knew by divine revelation that our sins were forgiven, we should still sorrow for them, as David did

[62] Ps. 29:12 (RSV = Ps. 30:11).

[63] Ecclus. 5:5 (RSV = Sir. 5:5).

when such a revelation was vouchsafed him, and St. Paul, who was confirmed in grace; for such a sorrow is continually feeding our love of God.

Yet in this sorrow we must not be excessive; we must consider our sins more in the general than in the particular, and, above all, as was revealed to St. Catherine, it should be rather a recollection of the Precious Blood, and a pondering of the divine mercy, than a dry study of our sins, according to the advice of St. Bernard: "I advise you, my friends, occasionally to draw back from the annoying and anxious scrutiny of your ways, and to go out upon the wider and serener paths of the divine benefits. Sorrow for sin is indeed necessary, but it should not be continual. We should interpolate it with the more joyous thought of God's compassion. We must mingle honey with our wormwood, or else its bitterness will not be healthy."

Life is but a very little while, compared with eternity; and throughout eternity, we shall be infinitely happy, and yet have but one occupation: to give glory to God. We shall literally nave nothing else to do. And this single task will contain in itself such treasures of bliss, that there will be nothing left that we can desire.

Why not begin this work on earth? Why not try even now to fall in love with that dear glory of God which will be our joy and worship in the life to come?

The character of God's goodness is to be communicative. He is always communicating Himself to His creatures, in nature, in grace, and in glory. We must copy this example.

There is such a thing as a selfish goodness, thinking only about our own selves and our own souls. Indeed, this does seem a great matter, when you see so many thousands around us who hardly realize that they have souls at all. Yet it is dangerous to dwell exclusively on this. And who can have the Precious Blood, and know what it is, and feel what it does, and yet not long to pass it on to other souls? I wish that we could always do all things for the sole glory of God, but this can hardly be. Yet we may all do, without effort, much more than we have done, if we will only try to sorrow over sin, over the sins of the whole world, because our blessed Lord God is so deeply offended by them.

∞

Reap the blessings of this devotion

And this devotion is not without immense blessings to our own souls. What hinders us most, when we have once set to work to serve God in good earnest, is not so much sin as worldliness and self-love. Now, see how both these miseries, which so hang about us, keep us down, and adulterate all the good we do, are kept in check by this devotion.

The characteristic of the world is that it ignores sin. Things are right or wrong as it pleases, and according to its own canons; but as to a secret stain upon the immortal soul because the invisible God is offended, this it will not hear of for a moment. It is reckoned a doctrine to unman people, an idle bugbear, a priestly superstition. A man who sees everything as sin or not sin, who seeks everywhere the secret glory of the hidden Creator, who follows unearthly standards and uses unearthly weights and measures, who strives to do the commonest actions from supernatural motives, and who can love what he does not see, until he loses the power of loving, or at least of loving vehemently, what he does see can hardly be possessed either by the spirit of worldliness or of self-love. His life is a protest against the world, and also against himself.

Yet this is only a description of what a man who took up this devotion would soon become. He who looks long and lovingly on

God will soon cease to see any loveliness in himself, and thus this practice would deliver him from the two greatest enemies he has in the spiritual life.

We should find also that this devotion would give us great power with God. Answers to prayers would begin to come more thickly upon us than before. Our words would have a weight beyond themselves, or beyond our talents, reasoning, or eloquence. What is worth anything which God has not blessed? Spiritual power is the only real power, and it follows different rules from other power.

So take up this devotion to God's offended glory, and you will see by many a sensible proof that God is with you in other more abundant and more effectual ways than He has been heretofore.

Lastly, if you wish to press on toward the prize of Christian perfection, and to become a saint, listen to this story; listen to what happens to a man who has done no more than hinder two mortal sins from being consummated in outward acts. St. Paphnutius had dwelt in the desert for many a long year, and by weary penances had toiled for his sanctification. At last a strange thought came into his mind, and he ventured to express it in prayer to God. He desired to know to whom on the earth he was equal in sanctity. He asked it in simplicity and true humility, and God vouchsafed to speak to him. He told him he was now equal to a certain piper in an Egyptian village that He named. At once the saint set forth to seek him.

When he came to the village, he asked for the piper and was told that he was piping in the tavern for the amusement of those who were drinking there. Strange, thought St. Paphnutius. However, he sought the piper out, led him aside, and spoke to him of his spiritual state. What good works had he done? "Good works?" rejoined the piper. "I know of nothing good that I have ever done;

but once, when I was a robber, I saved from violence a virgin consecrated to God; and once, also, I gave money to a poor woman, who, out of poverty, was offering herself to sin." And then Paphnutius understood how God had given to that piper graces equal to his own, because, for his Maker's glory, he had in his rough robber days hindered two mortal sins.

Be concerned with God's glory now

What is it, then, for which I am pleading? Only for this: that you should not altogether cut yourself off from the glory of God, as if it were no concern of yours, and that you and He were not in partnership! This is really all. God is going to give you His glory for your own in Heaven for all eternity. Surely you cannot altogether disclaim connection with it now; surely its interests very much concern you; its success must be your success, and its failure your failure too. You cannot stand aloof from the cause of Jesus on earth, and even keep up a sort of armed neutrality with God, when you desire as soon as ever you die, without so much as tasting the sharpness of Purgatory, to be locked in His closest embrace of unutterable love forevermore. Yet this is the plain English of the lives of most Catholics. And can anything be more unreasonable, more ungenerous, or more mean? Verily we do not look like a people who have come to kindle a fire upon the earth, nor to be pining because it is not kindled.

Ah, Jesus, these are Thy worst wounds. I think lightly of the ruddy scars of Thy hands and feet, of the bruised knee and the galled shoulder, of the head with a thousand wounds, and of the wide-open heart. But these wounds — the wounds of coldness, neglect, unpraying selfishness; the wounds of the few who were once fervid and now are tepid, of the multitudes who never were fervent and so cannot even claim the odious honors of tepidity; the wounds wherewith Thou wert wounded in the house of Thy friends — these are the wounds to be wiped with our tears, and softened with the oil of our affectionate compassion.

Blessed Lord, I can hardly believe Thou art what I know Thou art, when I see Thy people wound Thee thus! And my own wretched heart! It, too, reveals to me sad secrets about man's capability of coldness, and his infinity of ingratitude. Alas, the concluding chapters of the four Gospels read like a bitter jest upon the faithful!

O poor desolate glory of God! Thou art a foundling upon the earth! No one will claim thee, or acknowledge kindred with thee, or give thee a home! Cold as the world is, and pitiless the pelting of incessant sin, thou liest crying at our doors, and men heed thee not. Poor homeless glory! Earth was meant for thee once as much as Heaven, but there have been robbers abroad, and it is no safe traveling for thee along our roads now. But there are some few of us still who have pledged ourselves to Heaven, that from this hour we will take thee to our own homes, as John took Mary. "Henceforth our substance is thy substance, and all that we have is thine."

Chapter Four

Pray for others

Let us see what goes into the saving of a soul, and what is involved in its being saved.

In the first place, it was absolutely necessary that God should become man, in order that that soul should be saved, according to the dispensation of God. It was absolutely necessary that Jesus should be born, teach, act, pray, merit, satisfy, suffer, bleed, and die for the saving of that single soul. It was necessary that there should be a Catholic Church, Faith, sacraments, saints, the Pope, and the Sacrifice of the Mass for that one soul. It was necessary that there should be a supernatural substance or quality, a marvelous participation in the divine nature, called sanctifying grace, and that on this should be accumulated loving acts and impulses of the divine will, in the shape of manifold actual graces, preventing, accompanying, following, and efficacious, or else that soul cannot be saved. Martyrs must die, Doctors must write, popes and councils must expose and condemn heresy, missionaries must travel, and priests must be ordained for the safety of that single soul.

When all these preparations are completed, and by an act of merciful omnipotence that soul is created out of nothing, there must be a guardian angel appointed to it. All through its life, Jesus must be occupied about it. Mary must have a great deal to do with it. All the angels and saints must pray and interest themselves about it. To every good thought, pious word, and devout action — and, of course, they soon come to be innumerable — a participation in the divine nature, grace must concur. Unseen evil spirits have to be warded off from it and foiled in their attempts upon it. Hourly temptations have to cause more or less emotion among its advocates in Heaven.

Every attribute of God vouchsafes to legislate for its advantage, so that it plays upon them all like one who fingers the keys of a musical instrument. The Precious Blood has to be communicated to it through extraordinary sacraments, which are full of mystery and were instituted both as to form and matter by our Lord Himself. All sorts of things — such as water, oil, candles, ashes, beads, medals, and scapulars — have to be filled with a strange undefinable power by ecclesiastical benedictions in its behalf. The Body, Blood, Soul, and Divinity of the Incarnate Word have to be communicated to it over and over again until it becomes quite a common occurrence, although each time it is in reality a more stupendous action than the creation of the world.

It can speak up to Heaven and be heard and obeyed there. It can spend the satisfactions of Jesus as if they were its own, and can undo bolts and bars in Purgatory, and choose by its own determinate will whom it will liberate and whom it will pass over. And all the time it is so near to God, and its heart is a place so sacred and so privileged, that none but God Himself can communicate grace to it — not even the angels, nor the Mother of God herself, blessed throughout all ages.

All this goes to the salvation of a soul. To be saved, it has to be God's child, God's brother, and to participate in God's nature. Now, see what is involved in its being saved.

∞

Consider a recently judged soul

Look at that soul yonder that has just been judged. Jesus has this instant spoken; the sound of His sweet words has hardly died away; those who mourn have scarcely closed the eyes of the deserted body. Yet the judgment has come and gone; all is over. It was swift but merciful — more than merciful; there is no word to say what it was. It must be imagined. One day, please God, we shall experience it.

That soul must be very strong to bear what it is feeling now. God must support it, or it will fall back into nothingness. Life is over. How short it has all been. Death is done with. How easy was its passing sharpness. How little the trials look, how puny the sorrows, how childish the afflictions!

And now something has happened to it, which is to be forevermore. Jesus has said it. There can be no doubt about it. What is that something? Eye has not seen, nor ear heard.[64] It sees God. There is stretched before it an illimitable eternity. Darkness has melted from before it. Weakness has fallen off from it. Time has vanished, which had cramped it so. There is no ignorance. It sees God. Its understanding is inundated with unspeakable delights; it is strengthened by unimaginable glory; it abounds in that Vision next to which earthly science is an illiterate stupidity. The will is flooded with love; excessive happiness thrills through every affection. As a sponge is filled with the sea, so the soul is filled with light, beauty, bliss, ravishment, immortality, God.

These are foolish words — lighter than feathers, weaker than water. They are less than a shadow of what the soul feels. Eye has not seen; ear has not heard; heart has not conceived. There it is on

[64] Cf. 1 Cor. 2:9.

the threshold of it all — the same soul that but a moment ago was sobbing in pain, feeble as an unmanly child. There can be no mistake about it.

But not only so. There is not the slightest risk of its being forfeited. All is sure. All is its own, its very own, inalienable, and forever. Sin can never come near it. Imperfection cannot breathe upon it. It knows no change, although its variety is infinite. It knows no inequality, although its joys are multitudinous and its delights innumerable. It is crowned king, and forever. And the empire of all this magnificence — how cheaply has it been purchased! Those transient toils and cares of life, which grace turned into contentments, and love to real pleasures! And now, here is this come, the light of glory, and the beauty of the Everlasting Vision! It would appear but a dream; only that the marvelous calm of the soul tells of the power and the depth of its new life. Its ability to bear its own consciousness is the gauge of its freshness and its immortality.

And all this is involved in the saving of a soul. And there is probably never a moment in which there is not some soul in this situation, just judged, its sentence favorable, and its eyes opened on the incommunicable beauty and goodness of God.

O dull and weary, weary and dull! This is all we can say, when we turn our thoughts back to our own petty cares, teasing temptations, vexatious self-love, annoying littleness, and ungenerous shabbiness with God! That soul has gone, is judged; it is well with him! Oh how well! And we are still here. Our great risk yet to be run! O dull and weary, weary and dull!

Yet a few minutes ago, that soul was not secure. There was a desperate contest going on, a pitched battle between Heaven and Hell, and Heaven seemed at a disadvantage. The sufferer was patient enough to merit anything that could be merited. But God put the last gift, the ultimate grace, final perseverance, beyond the reach of merit, and so seemed almost to throw the victory into the hands of the enemy. It was a terrific moment. All was at stake. All that had gone to the saving of that soul, from eternity up to that hour, was on the point of being lost and frustrated forever; it is lost, it is frustrated, and forever, almost every minute, perhaps quite every minute, all the world over. All, too, that was to be involved in the saving of that soul just then ran the risk of never being attained. Can risk, even in idea, go beyond this risk?

And Jesus stood by, watching the turnings of the battle, how it would go. The beatings of His Sacred Heart might have been heard in the silence of the moment. He had suspended His own sweet and easy law, whereby, because of His merits, we can merit also. Although He Himself had merited for us the gift of final perseverance, and whosoever receives that grace receives it for the sole merits of our Lord, yet if seemed as if He had given that moment up to the sheer sovereignty of the Divine Majesty. It was thrown, so it appeared, on the great, overpowering, limitless might of the mercy of the Undivided Trinity.

∞

Assist in others' salvation

One law alone is left unfettered. It is on purpose. It is the law of prayer, intercessory prayer. You are of kith and kin to that dying man, or you are his enemy; you are his priest, or his nurse, or his benefactor; you are his neighbor, or you are a thousand miles away; you know him well, or you never heard of his existence or dreamed of his agony. It matters not.

The victory has been left to you. The matter is in your hands. His soul hangs on your prayers. Jesus has decreed that you, not He (if I may say so untrue a thing), are to help save that soul. You are to put the crown on all that has gone toward his salvation. You may never know it, or at least not until you are judged yourself. Yet, in the communion of saints, and in the unity of Jesus, you are to be the "savior" of that uncertain soul, the victory of that unsettled strife!

But what is prayer? The mystery of prayer? We have need to ask the question if it involves so great a responsibility, and can do so great a work, and if it is in truth a precept that we must pray for others as well as for ourselves.

Be mindful of your unworthiness before God

There are many things that make up a true account of prayer. First, we must consider who we are who pray. None could have a more ignoble origin. We were created out of nothing, and we came into the world with the guilt and shame of sin already on our souls, and the burden of a hideous penalty that eternal lamentation never could remit. To this, our original disgrace, we have added all manner of guilt and shame, of treason and rebellion, of irritability and disrespect, of our own. There are no words that would exaggerate our malice, no description that would convey a fair idea of our helpless ignorance. Everything about us was little to begin with, and we have made it immeasurably less. It is hard to conceive ourselves worse than we are — so much so, that it is necessary to make it a duty to be patient and forbearing with ourselves quite as much as with others.

Then we must consider who it is to whom we pray: the infinitely blessed majesty of God, next to which nothing can be conceived more good, more holy, more pure, more august, more adorable, more compassionate, more incomprehensible, or more unutterable.

The very thought of God takes away our breath. He is three living Persons. We live, and move, and breathe in Him. He can do what He wills with us. He is no further bound to us than He has graciously and piteously chosen to bind Himself. He knows everything without our telling Him or asking Him. Yet it is to Him that we pray.

Next, let us think where it is that we pray. Whether it is a consecrated place or not, it is in God Himself. We are in the midst of Him, as fish are in the sea. His immensity is our temple. His ear lies close upon our lips. It touches them. We do not feel it; if we did, we would die. It is always listening. Thoughts speak to it as loudly as words; sufferings even louder than words. His ear is never taken away. We sigh into it even while we sleep and dream.

Next, let us ask, whence comes the value of our prayers? They are fleeting words, fugitive petitions. There is nothing in us to give ground for a hearing, except the very excess of our unworthiness and, therefore, the extremity of our need. Otherwise, why should our prayers be in the Creator's ear more than the roaring of a lion, or the querulous complaining of the plover, or the cry of the suffering beast run down by the hunters? Their value comes principally from this: that God Himself has vouchsafed to become a man, has lain out upon the inclement mountains and spent the night in prayer. He mixes us up with Himself. He makes our cause His, His interests ours, and we become one with Him. So by a mysterious communion, the work of His prayers runs into our prayers; the wealth of His enriches the poverty of ours; the infinity of His touches, raises, and magnifies the wretchedness of ours.

So when we pray, it is not we who pray, but He who prays. We speak into our heavenly Father's ear, and it is not our voice, but the voice of Jesus, like His Mother's voice, that God vouchsafes to hear. Or rather, the Eternal vouchsafes to be like Isaac in his blind, old age. His younger son kneels before Him for His blessing, with license to play his elder brother's part. "The voice indeed is the voice of Jacob," and it is not he whom I will bless, "but the hands are the hands of Esau," roughened with the toil of the world's redemption. And He says with Isaac, "Come near me, and give me a kiss, my son." And immediately, as He smells the fragrant smell of His garments — for it is truly the stole of Christ — blessing him, He says, "Behold the smell of my son is as the smell of a plentiful field";[65] and so He filleth him with blessings.

And this is not an end of the inventions of His paternal love. For, we must next inquire with whom it is we pray — never alone; of this we are sure, whenever we rightly pray. There is One dwelling in us who is co-equal, co-eternal God, proceeding from the Father and the Son. He forms the word in our hearts and then puts music in our cry, when we exclaim, "Abba, Father!"[66] He is our "access to the Father."[67] He "strengthens us with might unto the inward man."[68] He makes us "speak to ourselves in psalms, and hymns, and spiritual canticles, singing and making melody in our hearts to the Lord, giving thanks always for all things, in the name of our Lord Jesus Christ, to God and the Father."[69] He is the Spirit in whom "we pray at all times, by all prayer and supplication, and watch in the same, with all instance and supplication for all the saints."[70] He is the Spirit "who helpeth our infirmities; for we know not what we should pray for as we ought; but the Spirit Himself

[65] Gen. 27:22, 26-27.

[66] Rom. 8:15.

[67] Cf. Eph. 2:18.

[68] Eph. 3:16.

[69] Eph. 5:19-20.

[70] Cf. Eph. 6:18.

asketh for us with unspeakable groanings; and He that searcheth the hearts knoweth what the Spirit desireth."[71] Oh, then, does not the mystery of prayer deepen and deepen upon us?

∞

See how easy and effective prayer is

Next, look at the incredible ease of prayer. Every time, place, and posture is fitting, for there is no time, place, or posture in and by which we cannot reverently confess the presence of God. Talent is not needed. Eloquence is out of place. Dignity is no recommendation. Our want is eloquence enough; our misery is recommendation enough. Thought is quick as lightning, and quick as lightning can it multiply effectual prayer. Actions can pray; sufferings can pray. There need be no ceremonies; there are no rubrics to keep. The whole function is expressed in a word. It is simply this: the child at his father's knee, his words stumbling over each other from very earnestness, and his wistful face pleading better than his hardly intelligible prayer.

Then consider the efficacy of prayer. We have only to pray for lawful things, to pray for them often and perseveringly, and to believe we shall receive them — and receive them, not according to the poverty of our foolish intentions, but according to the riches, wisdom, and munificence of God — and it is an infallible truth that we shall receive them. God is at our disposal. He allows us this almost unbounded influence over Him, not once or twice, not merely on feasts or great occasions, but all our lives long. Are any of the mysteries of grace sweeter than this?

We read of one saint, that so availing were her prayers supposed to be, people came from all quarters to beg her to recommend their

[71] Rom. 8:26-27.

necessities to God. She, meanwhile, heard them and forgot them. She was immersed in contemplation, saw only the divine attributes, and had no thought but for the Spouse of her soul. She was amazed, then, when crowds came continually to thank her for the answers that had come to her prayers on their behalf, and in an ecstasy she spoke her wonder in the ear of Jesus. "Daughter," replied our dearest Lord, "your will is always and only to do my will, and I will never let you vanquish me in love; and, therefore, my will is to do your will, even when you have forgotten that you ever willed it." See what manner of Lord He is with whom we have to do!

∞

Intercede for others

Then, last of all, it is not for ourselves alone that our Lord lets us pray, but for others also. Nay, He expressly commands us to make intercessory prayer. Through His apostle, He speaks with that positive and unusual form, "I desire first of all that supplications, prayers, intercessions, and thanksgivings be made by men."[72] And in the passage quoted above from the eighth chapter of the letter to the Romans, when the apostle says, "He that searcheth the hearts knoweth what the Spirit desireth," he adds, "because He asketh for the saints according to God." Thus the inestimable privilege, the mysterious gift of prayer, is given to us not merely for our own necessities, but so that we may use it for the temporal and spiritual good of others.

How strict an account we shall have to render for so great a favor, and how careful we should be that this power should not be entrusted to us in vain! Whatever other talents God may not have given to us, this one, without doubt, He has given to us. There is

[72] 1 Tim. 2:1.

no distinction of persons. Young and old, rich and poor, learned and simple, priest and religious and layperson, we are all bound to the practice of intercessory prayer. Woe unto us if we hide our talent, or venture to return it to our Judge unfruitful!

Let each one examine himself, and see what time he has given hitherto to this devotion, and whether the past is in this respect altogether what he would have it be. To pray always[73] is a hard precept and one we can come to only by time and habit, as well as by gift and grace. But the thing is to find that the older we grow, the more we pray, and the more we pray, the more our prayer takes the line of intercession for the souls of others.

Perhaps, never while we are on earth shall we realize the heavenly might of prayer, nor the exceeding riches of that treasure, which now, alas, we make so light of, seeing not how thereby God's glory is so much within our power. Oh, what might we not do by prayer! What might we not do in every remotest corner of the earth, in the cells of Purgatory, and in the open courts of Heaven!

Yet the times are against prayer; the spirit of the age is against it; the habitat of our countrymen are against it. Oh, for faith in prayer! With faith in simple prayer, the interests of Jesus shall spread like a beneficent conquest all over the world, and the glory of God shall beautifully cover the earth as the abounding waters cover the bed of the sea, and the choirs of redeemed souls shall multiply and multiply, until the arms of the Good Shepherd should be, were it possible, overladen with the sheaves of His prolific Passion!

Heaven opens sometimes and gives us a glimpse of this potency of prayer. See how it opened on St. Gertrude.[74] She was divinely

[73] Luke 18:1.

[74] *Revelations*, Bk. 4, ch. 12.

instructed that as often as the Hail Mary is devoutly recited by the faithful on earth, three efficacious streamlets proceed from the Father, the Son, and the Holy Spirit, most sweetly penetrating the Blessed Virgin's heart. Then, from her heart, again with efficacious impetuosity, they seek their fountains and break at the foot of God's throne, as a sunny wave breaks upon a rock, leaving her most powerful after the Father, most wise after the Son, and most benignant after the Holy Spirit. These streams, while the Hail Mary is being said, flow around the Blessed Virgin superabundantly, and with potent impetus, and on the other hand flow back again upon her most holy heart. So with marvelous delectation — I am using St. Gertrude's words — they seek their fountain first, and then rebounding back, bright drops of joy, and bliss, and eternal salvation are sprinkled over all the persons of the saints and angels — nay, more, over those who on earth are then commemorating that same salutation, whereby is renewed in everyone all the good that he has ever to this time received through the most salutary Incarnation.

Yet, what is easier than to say a devout Hail Mary? And if this is true of the Hail Mary, what also of the Our Father, and the Creed, and the missal prayers, and brief prayers from the Gospel? Do we know what we are doing, and where we are living, and what is all around us, and how far our influence goes, and where our responsibilities end? And have we measured our privileges, and taken the height of our dignity, and fathomed the depths of grace?

We are beset by our own greatness. We work miracles and know it not. We move the heavens, yet we ourselves are in thoughtless rest on earth. The mystery is too much for us, the problem too hard, the supernatural quite oppressive. But the comfort is that we shall do all things well, use all powers, satisfy all duties, be equal to all dignities, and exhaust all blessings, if only we will serve Jesus with pure intention and out of love. Once we go forth upon the earth, and live, move, breathe, speak, act, think, joy and sorrow, toil and rest, welcome and suffer, all for Jesus, then we need have no other thought, no other rule. No atom of what we are, or of what we have received, or of what we can effect, will then be lost. All things conscious will be for Jesus; all things unconscious will be for Jesus too. All things possible will be for Jesus; and if there were anything impossible for one in Christ, the very impossible would be all for Jesus too!

Fulfill the three aims through intercessory prayer

But let us apply our three instincts of the devout life to the practice of intercessory prayer. If we love our heavenly Father, there is a gentle constraint upon us to hunger for His glory; and souls are His honor, and sin His dishonor. Now, we may not be able to preach, or to write books, or to traverse distant lands as missionaries, or to give money to send others there. It may be little indeed that of ourselves and by our actions we can do for God's glory or the conversion of souls. But intercession reaches everywhere. Neither time nor place bounds it. Ignorance cannot keep it out, nor superstition silence it, nor sin refuse to stay within its influence. Wherever grace can come, prayer can reach, and that is wheresoever God's omnipotence extends, save and except that one place whence hope has been commanded to withdraw. Not that God is not glorified there also; but it is a glory we worship with silence, fear, and a trembling hush of heart. It is not that glory of His which we are His fellow workers in promoting.

We hear of some land where God's glory is endangered. There is some country, perhaps, where the civil power is at variance with the Holy See, which is more adverse to God's glory, more injurious to the interests of Jesus, or more fatal to the cause of souls than any other country. Or, again, we read with burning eyes and heart of the spiritual destitution of the slaves in certain countries; or of the persecutions and tiring vexations of the Catholic clergy under heretical dominion, or of the impenetrable provinces of China and Japan; or of Catholic cities of scandalous profligacy; or of the wily plots of an anti-ecclesiastical diplomacy; or of the depression of religious orders; or of idle, extravagant bishops; or of jealousy of missions and retreats; or of disedifying controversies and foolish parties and silly questions. There is no saying to what an extent God's glory is compromised by any one of these things. We may be the weakest and most obscure among the Church's children, yet we can reach all this by intercession, and reach it, too, with efficacy and power. We may work for it without interruption; our ordinary actions may go to it; we may do more than all the ambassadors and legates who ever were, and yet not for an hour be distracted from our profession or our trade. We shall never know, until it meets us at the judgment, a goodly show, a beautiful vision, how much glory we have thus gained for God, without cost, without toil, almost without advertence, yet with such infinite and eternal recompense.

In like manner also shall we by intercession advance the interests of Jesus. There is something very touching to see how our dear Lord has vouchsafed, if I may say it, to leave His work unfinished in order that our love of Him may have the joy of finishing it. St. Paul might well say that he rejoiced in his sufferings for the Colossians, because thus he "filled up those things that are wanting of the sufferings of Christ, in His flesh for the Lord's Body, which is His Church."[75] It is a great artifice of our Savior's love

[75] Cf. Col. 1:24.

that He has chosen to be so dependent upon us for the harvest of His Cross and Passion; and we must have cold hearts indeed if it does not move us.

Take any one temptation from which you suffer. How wearisomely it dogs you; how miserably it entraps you; how it is always wakeful, always fixing itself on every good work, devotion, penance, and prayer! How tired you get of resisting, how often you unhappily consent, how still more often you are teased and disquieted because you cannot make out whether you have consented or not! Yet every moment of resistance is a supernatural act, a victory of grace, an interest of Jesus. So also is every sigh of sorrow over a fall, every aspiration sent up, arrowlike, to Heaven, every naming of Jesus or Mary on the confines and in the risk of sin.

Now, how many thousands are there all the world over who are wearily fighting with the same temptation, and possibly under more disadvantageous circumstances than you are? See, then, how many interests of Jesus you can reach by intercession in this single respect; and I am purposely selecting a very trifling matter — trifling, that is, in comparison with other things where our blessed Lord is yet more concerned. Do at least as much as this: intercede for those who are being tempted with the same temptation as you are.

If we can do such an immense work for Jesus, with scarcely any trouble to ourselves, can we think we love Him if we are not doing it? How we can love Jesus and not practice intercession is unintelligible. The wonder is how, prayer being what it is, those who really believe, can ever leave off praying, can ever do anything else but pray.

∞

Recognize your place in God's family

One of the most divine and striking characteristics of the Catholic religion is the Communion of Saints, the way in which everything belongs to everybody, and nobody has any spiritual property of his own. The merits and satisfactions of our dear Lord, the joys and woes of Mary, the patience of the martyrs, the perseverance of confessors, and the purity of virgins — they all belong to all of us. Just as the blood circulates from and to the heart all over the body, so, in the Church, there is no division or separation. Heaven, Purgatory, and earth — it is all one body. We interchange our merits, we circulate our prayers, we pass on our joys, we infect with our troubles, and we use each other's satisfactions as they come to hand. We have all sorts of relations with Heaven; as to Purgatory, we have a regular science and endless practical methods for it; and on earth, kith and kin, blood and country, Jew, Greek, Scythian, bond and free[76] — it is all one.

This is what strikes heretics as so very portentous about us; there is no other word than *portentous* for it. We talk of the other world as if it were a city we were familiar with from long residence, just as we might talk of Paris, Brussels, or Berlin. We are not stopped by death. Sight is nothing to us; we go beyond it as calmly as possible. We are not separated from our dead. We know the saints a great deal better than if we had lived with them upon earth. We talk to the angels in their different choirs, as if they were — as they are — our brothers in Christ. We use beads, medals, crucifixes, holy water, indulgences, sacraments, and sacrifices for all this, as naturally as we use pen and paper, or axe and saw, or spade and rake for our earthly work. We have no sort of distrust about the matter.

We are all one household, and there is an end of it. The blessed Lord God is our Father; His dear majesty is our affair. Our elder Brother created us and has our own nature. Mary is our mother.

[76] Cf. Gal. 3:28.

The angels and the saints are all the kindest and most familiar of brothers. The air of the place is simply an intense filial love of the Father whom we all adore, so our reverence is a child's reverence, and our fear a child's fear.

How can they who live outside the household understand this? Must it not necessarily seem to them a system of human mysteries, an unscriptural fabrication? They are "strangers and foreigners"; how can they divine the ways, the feelings, and the sympathies of the "fellow citizens of the saints and the domestics of God"?[77] They can read the words, but they can know nothing of the heat and life, the strength and perception, the health and love that are in them; so a veil is over their hearts — truly over their hearts rather than their understanding — when Paul's words are read. For they who would understand the edifying of the Body of Christ must first "all meet into the unity of faith," and so needful is this right faith, that it is the truth that we must do "in charity in order that we may in all things grow up in Him who is the Head, even Christ; from whom the whole Body, being compactly and fitly joined together, by what every joint supplieth, according to the operation of the measure of every part, maketh increase of the Body, unto the edifying of itself in charity."[78]

Orlandini says of Fr. Peter Faber that he embraced in the bosom of his charity the whole human without any exception and had his hands full of business for everybody with God. The more lost and profligate a man was, the more his pity kindled toward him. And that he might put greater vehemence into his prayers, he excited and elevated them with the deepest reflections. When he prayed for people, he put them before himself, as redeemed

[77] Eph. 2:19.

[78] Eph. 4:15-16.

with the Precious Blood of Christ, as Christ's heirs, as Christ's kingdom, so that he stirred up his own affectionate zeal by thus realizing their dignity and price. At the same time he offered to God the merits of Christ and His saints the more nobly and feelingly, until at length, by this simple practice, he accustomed himself to entertain quite a magnificent opinion of everybody.

St. Catherine of Siena tells us that God said to her, "You ought with the utmost anxiety to pour forth prayers for all rational creatures, and for the Mystical Body of Holy Mother Church, and for those whom I have given over to you to love with a singular affection." St. Gertrude also was told, "Whenever someone says at least one Our Father and Hail Mary, or any psalm on behalf and in the name of the universal Church, the Son of God presently accepts it with the deepest gratitude as the fruit of His most perfect humanity, and giving thanks to God the Father for it, He blesses it, and He distributes it, multiplied by that benediction, to the universal Church, for her profit to eternal salvation."

But let us now see for whom especially these intercessions should be offered. Spiritual writers give us different recommendations: I shall follow here, as so often before, the Jesuit Lancisius.

∞

Pray for those in mortal sin

Pray for those who are in mortal sin, or out of the true Church. Thus the eternal Father said to St. Catherine of Siena, "I affectionately entreat you to pray assiduously for the salvation of sinners, for whom I ask of you wrestlings and tearful prayers, so that I may satisfy my longing to show them grace and mercy." When she heard these words she was greatly inflamed with divine love, and being, as it were, intoxicated and unable to contain herself, she cried out, "O Divine Mercy and Eternal Goodness, it is no wonder to me that Thou sayest to converted sinners returning unto Thee, 'I will remember no more the injuries you have done unto me'; but that Thou shouldst say so to the stiff-necked who persecute Thee daily with their iniquities, that Thou shouldst say, 'I will that you should affectionately pray for them; I long to show them mercy' — this is indeed a wonder."

Again, God said to her, "You shall delight in the Cross . . . to the glory and praise of my holy name, continually moaning with anxious heart over the death of the human race, because you see it brought down to such misery as your tongue cannot express. For it is by moaning and wailing of my friends that I make dispositions for showing mercy to the world. And this is what I am continually asking of you, and of my other friends; and this will be the sign that you love me truly, and I, on my side, promise never to neglect your holy desires."

Again, God complained to her thus: "See, my daughter, with what sins they strike me, especially with self-love, whence every evil proceeds. Self-love has infected the world, as if it drunk poison; it comes from pride, and holds every sort of evil in itself. Do you, therefore, my servants, prepare yourselves with mercy, supplications, and anxious desires, grieving over the offenses committed against me, and also over the damnation of the sinners themselves, and so you will mitigate the wrath of my divine judgment." Here, you see, is another practice hinted to us — prayer against self-love in all souls throughout the world. If you suffer from it yourself, pray for the deliverance of others from it. This is an artifice of the spiritual life that never fails.

We read in the life of St. Clare of Montefalco, that she once prayed for a certain person who was laden with the guilt of great crimes and had delayed his conversion to the last years of his life. Twice when she began to pray, she felt herself repelled from prayer by a hidden violence, and she heard an interior voice telling her not to pray for that wretch, as she would not be heard. She returned, however, a third time to her prayer, and obtained his conversion in the following manner. She placed herself before Christ the Judge, as if she herself were laden with all this man's sins, and, as so laden, she obliged herself to make satisfaction for him, and to bear all the punishment that the order of Divine Justice should desire and exact, until the Divine Goodness should deign to convert that soul. This act so pleased our Lord that the obstinate sinner was suddenly converted and led a good life from that time forth.

St. Teresa gives this as a reason for founding her convents: that, as there are so many who offend God, nuns ought to pray for their conversion, and with especial assiduity for the defenders of the Church, and particularly for preachers, and other learned men who maintain its truth. Diego de Yepes tells us in his life of her, that she spent whole nights praying and weeping for the conversion of souls, especially those infected with heresy, and that she would have given a thousand lives to convert one soul. The whole forty years during which she thus exercised herself in prayer, she asked nothing so much of God as the spread of His glory and the augmentation of the Church; and she was willing to remain ever so long in Purgatory, if only she could make God better known and loved by men.

∞

Pray for lukewarm souls

Those who are lukewarm or tepid are on the very verge of great sins, and yet they are in a state of grace at present. Their necessity is great, and so they claim our charity. Their renewal to favor, if they fall, is very difficult — more so than the conversion of sinners — and so it is a great glory of God. Jesus has given them the first grace: He has converted them. And now He is on the point of losing them; His interests are in danger.

As God has been pleased to reveal to us His special distaste for the lukewarm, so would it be very acceptable to Him if we made prayer and penance for the lukewarm one of our special devotions.

Our dear Lord! How He seems to suffer in them! And, if they be lost, what graces will have been in vain, what sacraments wasted, what a triumph for our Lord's enemy! I beg of you to think of this, and when you think of it, to think of me. It is a devotion of much love and of many graces.

∞

Pray for the multiplication of saints

The glory of God, the good of souls, and the interests of Jesus are implicated, in so many and in such great ways, in the multiplication of saints and in their final perseverance. One saint is worth a million common Catholics. Our Lord said even a stronger thing to St. Teresa: that one soul, not a saint, but seeking perfection, was more precious to Him than thousands living common lives.

It is astonishing how unsupernatural we are, even in our devotions, and how we let natural principles and natural activity carry us away even in spiritual things and when we are doing God's work. I remember a good religious telling me some years ago that in a town in the east of England, he and his people had picked out certain influential Protestants of public notoriety and prayed to God most earnestly for their conversion. However, no answer came. At last it struck him that there might be a little too much forcing of man's will upon God in the matter. He proposed, therefore, that they should change their prayers, and pray for those whom God saw fittest for grace; and all at once their mission bore fruit.

∞

Pray for those in need and in tribulation

Pray for all those the world over who are in various necessities and tribulations, whether spiritual or temporal. Orlandini says of Fr. Peter Faber that it increased the grief and sorrow of this tender-hearted man that the majority of people do not know how to refer their affairs and miseries to God, but rely upon human helps while they neglect divine ones. This vehemently stimulated his compassion, so that he himself laid before God the cares and calamities of all men and became a suppliant for them in all their straits, troubles, misfortunes, and necessities until at last he passionately desired, like another Moses, to have his hands always lifted up on high, to carry help and consolation to so many who were battling with suffering and sorrow, whether dead or living. He had pictured to himself the various vexations, calamities, diseases, pains, hunger, despair, want, and all the countless evils to which men are subject, and as a good and sedulous priest, to borrow the simile of St. Chrysostom, he pleaded all their causes with God, as if he had been appointed in some special way the common father of the whole world. It is quite incredible with what zeal he burned to be the minister of our dear Redeemer, and by Him to aid everyone in all his griefs; nay, if it may be said, he yearned, in spite of his humility, to do miracles to relieve those evils whose cure is beyond the bounds of nature.

∞

Pray for the necessities of your benefactors

We should pray for the necessities of our benefactors, among whom are to be reckoned our enemies, because they give us occasions of merit and help us on the road to Heaven. St. Agnes said to St. Bridget, "Nothing is more lovely, or more acceptable with

God, than to love those who injure us, and to pray for our persecutors." St. Chrysostom, speaking of David and Saul, tells us, "It is reckoned to us as martyrdom, if we count our enemy our benefactor, and do not cease to pray for him."

It was revealed to Fr. Giulio Mancinelli, who was especially devoted to intercessory prayer, that he was one of seven, then (about 1603) in the Church Militant who above others, so as to be thus distinguished in the sight of God, prayed for all men. It was once given him in a vision to see the glory of St. Lawrence the martyr,[79] and among other lights that he then received, this was one: that we ought earnestly pray for our benefactors, not only because of the gifts and temporal goods conferred upon us, but because of the affection of charity with which they were given, and which is of greater esteem than the gifts themselves.

Both are to be repaid — the gifts by labor and assiduity in prayer; the affection of charity by loving our benefactors and getting them grace from God. We must also in our gratitude respond to their intention for the divine honor and love, for our benefactors bestowed their favors upon us with a view to God. So we, in like manner, to recompense their reverence, love, and tenderness toward God in the giving of alms, must wish them well and beg of God that they may be promoted to serve God more and more by works of charity.

∞

For those in pursuit of Christian perfection

Pray for all those who are seriously occupied in the pursuit of Christian perfection, and for whatever they desire toward that

[79] St. Lawrence (d. 258), deacon who was martyred in the persecution under Valerian.

end, although it may involve pain and suffering. For this is the common appetite of the saints, and it is lawful to ask it for them if they are rightly asking it for themselves, because it is good for God's glory, for the interests of Jesus, and for the bringing to penance multitudes of souls.

Thus St. Francis Xavier, when St. Jerome[80] showed him in a vision at Bologna all he was to suffer, cried out, "More, O Lord, more!"

Thus St. Teresa said, "Either to suffer or to die," and St. Mary Magdalene de' Pazzi, "Neither to suffer as now, nor yet to die, but to suffer more."

Thus David exclaimed, "Prove me, O Lord, and try me; burn my reins and my heart";[81] and Jeremiah prayed with natural shrinking, yet with supernatural trust, "Correct me, O Lord, but yet with judgment, and not in Thy fury, lest Thou bring me to nothing."[82]

St. Paul said, "I please myself in my infirmities, in reproaches, in necessities, in persecutions, in distresses, for Christ."[83]

And how unapproachably beautiful are the words of Job: "Can an unsavory thing be eaten that is not seasoned with salt? Or can a man taste that which when tasted bringeth death? The things which before my soul would not touch, now, through anguish, are my meats. Who will grant that my request may come, and that God may give me what I look for? And that He that hath begun may destroy me, that He may let loose His hand and cut me off? And that this may be my comfort, that, afflicting me with sorrow,

[80] St. Francis Xavier (1506-1552), Jesuit missionary known as the Apostle of the Indies; St. Jerome (c. 342-420), biblical scholar.

[81] Ps. 25:2 (RSV = Ps. 26:2).

[82] Jer. 10:24.

[83] 2 Cor. 12:10.

He spare not, nor I contradict the words of the Holy One. In what is my strength that I can hold out? Or what is my end that I should keep patience? My strength is not the strength of stones, nor is my flesh of brass."[84]

∞

Pray for an increase in the accidental glory of the blessed

It may be added here that some writers recommend prayer for the increase of the accidental glory of the blessed in Heaven. For instance, when a religious prays that those of his order may live holily, or that some of them may come to be canonized, the founder (seeing it in God, or God making it known to him) gains an increase of accidental glory.

Thus Innocent III says, "Many, or rather most, think it not unworthy that the glory of the saints should be capable of increase up to the day of judgment and, therefore, that the Church may lawfully desire for them this increase of their glorification."[85] Our Lady is said to have revealed to St. Thomas of Canterbury[86] that her glory is always receiving new increments in Heaven, that is, from the good works of those devoted to her. So also men may pray for the increase of devotion to particular saints; and it was revealed to St. Gertrude that the blessed receive fresh accidental glory every time Communion is received on earth. I merely mention this practice to show how far the power and prerogatives of intercessory prayer extend.

[84] Job 6:6-12.

[85] Innocent III (1160-1216; Pope from 1198), *De Celeb. Miss.*

[86] St. Thomas Becket (c. 1118-1170), Archbishop of Canterbury and martyr.

∞

Pray for the rich

Another intercessory devotion is to be found in the life of Marie-Denise de Martignat, one of the first religious of the Visitation. She spent almost the first fifty years of her life in the courts of France and Savoy, but the spirit of the world never passed upon her heart, any more than the smell of fire upon the garments of the three children in the fiery furnace.[87]

Her soul was visited by such abundant lights as to the misery of this world, and the unsatisfactoriness of its honors and pleasures, that she had continually in her mouth the words of Solomon: "Vanity of vanities, all things under the sun are vanity!"[88] She used to say that if a hermit had uttered these words, they would have been taken for the exaggeration of a contemplative; but that God, having put them into the mouth of one of the greatest, richest, and most peaceable of kings, they caused in her such a profound compassion for great people, because of the risk of their salvation, that she took the rich, highborn, and prosperous as the matter for a special devotion and desired to communicate the same devotion to everyone she met.

"Ah!" she exclaimed, "they are hemmed round with no common misery; they go down to Hell without thinking of it, because their staircase thither is of gold and porphyry. Great in this world, they let themselves have no leisure to reflect that soon they will be very little; having the habit of commanding others, they presume upon themselves and live as if God, Heaven, and the angels are under their obedience, as well as earth and men. How they will be disenchanted, when, in a moment, they shall discover themselves

[87] Cf. Dan. 3:94.

[88] Cf. Eccles. 1:2, 14.

to have been, and now be forever, slaves of the Devil; or if God shows them mercy, what a surprise to them to find themselves in the kingdom of Heaven far below the poor and vile whom on earth they would not allow to come near them!"

Hence, during her whole life, she possessed this enlightened compassion for the rich, and made special intercession for them. She said it was a greater charity to pray for them than for those who were languishing in hospitals and prisons. She declared that nothing should at once humble and encourage Christians more than heroic sanctity of great people who have kept humility in the midst of glory, and have used this world as though they used it not.

It is in harmony with this special devotion of hers that we read, toward the conclusion of her life, that one day when the superioress asked her if it was worthwhile to ask a certain favor of a person of very high rank, she replied, "Yes, my dear mother, do it. I assure you, it is a very great charity to princes and great people to make them do good works. The world, the flesh, and the Devil make them do so many bad ones that they will one day return more thanks to us who have been the cause of their giving alms, than we gave them for the alms we procured from them."

Another time, when she saw the superioress writing to a princess, she said, "My dear mother, please always put something in your letters to great people about the holy fear of God, or the sovereignty of the Divine Majesty, or the greatness of eternity and the shortness of this life. For there are always so many flattering these poor great ones, and a day will come when they will wish it had not been so."

When she heard of the death of Louis XIII, she said, "Alas! I saw that monarch born, I saw him baptized, I saw him crowned, I saw him married, I saw him reigning, and now he is no more!" Somebody asked her whether she would pray much for him, and she said, "Yes, more than people would believe; for, however well he lived, and however well he died, he may possibly have something still to satisfy for to the equitable justice of the King of kings. He is gone into a kingdom that is conquered only by the humble of heart. No one goes in there scepter in hand."

∞

Practice intercessory prayer in different ways

As to the time, place, and method of intercession, these may be left to everyone's choice. Following are suggestions:

- Have particular days in the week for particular intentions, such as for the Pope, for the clergy and religious orders, for all in mortal sin, for all in their agony, for the lukewarm, for those in sorrow, for those for whom God wishes us especially to pray. Or have a scheme of thirty intentions for the days of the month.

- Note down your intentions in writing, and keep them in a missal or prayer book.

- Visit the Blessed Sacrament, and go through these intentions meditatively, exciting affections of zeal for the divine honor and of loving solicitude for the interests of Jesus.

- Resolve to take some word, or aspiration, or offering that shall stand for all your intentions, and use it at Mass and Communion, in your thanksgiving, before and after meditation, Rosary, examination of conscience, etc.

- If you are sleepless at night, or from any cause have short intervals of unexpected leisure in your ordinary occupations, have recourse to intercession.

These practices might be multiplied almost infinitely. The best will be those which are the most simple, come naturally, and rise out of our usual devotional exercises.

∞

Find joy and humility in intercessory prayer

Oh, the unfathomable sweetness of this mystery of prayer! One of the ends for which we came into the world was to make intercession. One of the ends for which our blessed Savior shed His Precious Blood was that we might make acceptable and efficacious intercession. One of the things that God is waiting for us to do now is make intercession. Yet how much time do we habitually spend in the delightful exercise of this great privilege!

How we talk of popes and cardinals, of bishops, priests, and religious orders! How we overflow with the prattle of devotional or ecclesiastical gossip! We have a criticism for everybody's conduct in everything. We could teach them better. We could show them the right way. We take higher views and burn with hotter zeal. We get an easy character for piety by talking much and fluently about God, and by making ourselves very tiresome to others by our fidgets about ecclesiastical plans and the interests of Catholicism — conversational fidgets, for the most part, and stopping there; we are not to the fore, when doing — tedious doing — is required. The Corinthians could not come near us in the variety of our wisdoms and our gifts; we could beat them down; we could surprise St. Paul; so exuberant, so oracular, so necessary to God, His Pope, and His church, does our talk show us to be, or at least show that we think ourselves to be!

Now, I wonder how much we pray. I wonder what proportion our secret intercession bears to our open criticism. I fear it is very little, for I cannot help fancying that if we prayed more, we would feel that we prayed so little, that we should not dare, for shame's sake, to talk at all. I have a great notion of the spirit of concealment being something like two-thirds of practical Christianity. I will be bound our praying people lie hid among those who never tell us how deeply they are interested in Catholic affairs. The eye that is quick to see a fault, and the ear that loves to listen to criticism, and the tongue that brags: these will be the signs of a praying soul — when the rainbow comes to be the emblem of despair, and not before!

The whole duty of intercessory prayer, and our own discharge of it, may help us to one of those occasional revelations which are so profitable to our souls. Our spiritual life seems to be going on all safely and smoothly. We do not imagine ourselves to be saints. But we feel we are taking pains. We manage to keep ourselves in a state of grace. Nay, we have made distinct sacrifices for God, either in being converted to the Faith, or in entering religion, or in embracing the ecclesiastical state, or in some way or other; and although we do not actually rest upon the meritoriousness of these sacrifices as though our predestination were finally and happily fulfilled by them, yet we never forget them, and the thought of them is a continual support to us. These are beginnings of something very bad. But our Lord comes to our rescue, and without any apparent cause, a supernatural light is poured into our souls, illuminating every corner and hiding place, and revealing to us, in a most startling way, how very little, after all, we have done for God. It is like the light of the particular judgment, which lays all our life with its actions and motives clearly before us in one moment, so that God may be justified, and we pass a fair sentence on ourselves.

Oh, how blessed are these little revelations! For out of them come humility, and freshness, and strength, and joy in Jesus, and abandonment of self into the arms of God. We could not believe we did so little for God, if this gracious light did not flash it upon us in such a way that we cannot refuse to see, or doubt that we have seen it. Think of intercession, and see whether it may not bring you now another of these affectionate revelations.

It is difficult to have the better of our Lord in the strife of liberality and love. Of all the fruits of the Holy Spirit, none seems more desirable, because none is less earthly or more heavenly, than joy; and it is just this fruit which our blessed Lord bestows on such as devote themselves to intercession. This is very observable. There is a certain sunniness and lightheartedness about them for which there seems no ordinary cause, except that it is like the sweet lightening of the spirit which comes after a kind and unselfish action.

This may partly be the reason. But there is another also. We see not the fruit of our intercession; the spirit of prayer escapes out upon the earth, and is everywhere like the hidden omnipresence of God. It is out of our sight. It is not like a series of distinguishable works. We hardly remember how much intercession we have made. Who can count the sighs he has sent up to God, or the wishes without words that his heart has told into the ear of Jesus? And so from the fruit's being hidden, vainglory attaches itself to it less than to almost any other devotion.

However this may be, sweetness and consolation, submissively desired, are beyond all doubt great helps to holiness. And whosoever desires to joy in God, and to abound in all joy and consolation in the Lord, to be cheerful and prompt in serving Jesus, to be patient with life, and to be equable in all things, which is not far from being holy in all things, let him throw away himself and his own ends and, wedding the dear interests of Jesus and of souls, betake himself to intercession, as if it were his trade or he had as much to do with it as his guardian angel has to do with him. Joy is the especial recompense of intercession. It is part of His joy, who rejoices in the harvest of His Passion. What stirs in our hearts has come to us from His! It was first in His, before it was in ours, and an angel's presence would be less desirable than is that little task of the Redeemer's joy.

Chapter Five

Make use of the many riches God gives you

If we are in earnest about our souls, with a quiet fidelity to those duties, practices, and devotions which obedience sanctions to us, our love of God increases without our knowing or feeling it. It is only now and then, in certain temptations, or on great feasts, or sometimes without apparent cause, that God allows us to perceive that we have really made some progress, and that we care more for Him and less for anything else but Him, than we used to do.

One sign to us of this increase of love is the growing sense of our own unworthiness and of the extreme littleness of everything we do. It becomes a pain to us that we have so little to offer to God and that our service of Him is, after all, so wretched and ungenerous. The more we know Him, and the more we approach to thoughts at least a little more worthy of His blessed majesty, the more this feeling increases upon us and, as I say, becomes a pain.

It is this which drives the saints to yearn for suffering and to pray for crosses. The common cares and the ordinary weariness of life are not enough to satisfy them, because they do not give them room for their heroic love. They want — a vain yet loving strife! — to keep pace with the generosity of Jesus. Why should they do so little for Him? Why should they be thus imprisoned and kept in by the littleness of everything around them? If sin was once a misery to them, now their inability to love God royally and magnificently, to spend themselves and to be spent for Him in glorious sacrifices — this has become a greater misery to them. Like Areuna, they would give to their King as kings give, with full hands and prodigal expenditure.[89] When God Himself gives them quiet times, and multiplies their joy and peace, they turn against Him, so to speak, with amorous complaint, "Nay, but I will buy it of thee at a price, and I will not offer to the Lord my holocaust free of cost."[90] Then they say strange things that sound undoctrinal, about their being ready to endure all the pains of Hell to all eternity, if only they can thereby promote God's glory one little degree; and they talk of disinterested love until they almost seem to incur the censures of condemned propositions.

These thoughts are not for us. They would be unreal in us. But we, too, in our measure, feel this pain. We want to do more for Jesus, and our own cowardice, when we come to the point, is a keen misery and a sensible shame to us. "Copious redemption," says the psalmist, "there is with God,"[91] and it is this copiousness of our redemption that at once stimulates our love and makes it discontented with itself. All that Jesus has done for us has been done with such unnecessary abundance, with such outpouring of affection, with such supernatural profuseness of mercy and compassion, that it is plain at every step, in each separate mystery of the Incarnation, that what He wants is not our salvation only, but our love also.

[89] Cf. 2 Kings 24:22-23 (RSV = 2 Sam. 24:22-23).

[90] Cf. 2 Kings 24:24 (RSV = 2 Sam. 24:24).

[91] Cf. Ps. 129:7 (RSV = Ps. 130:7).

The same longing and luxury to be with the children of men, His creatures, which would have led Him, if man had never fallen, to come to us in an impassible[92] body, and of the same Virgin Mother, now that we have fallen and He has had to come to us as a passible Redeemer, seems only to run riot all the more in the depths of its own tenderness and love. He cannot pardon without at the same time adopting as sons. He cannot cleanse us from sin without making us heirs of Heaven. He cannot absolve us from the past without at the same time storing us with grace for the future. Every gift He gives is double, treble, or a hundredfold. One drop of blood would have done, and He shed every drop. Grace would have sufficed for His sacrament of love, but He must give Himself — Body, Blood, Soul, and Divinity. The Blessed Sacrament is a superfluous mercy, an unnecessary love. Only to show the most love and to get the most love — this was what was intended. This is His way. And as we get to know Him and to love Him more, we want it to be our way also. And the little we can do seems so little, so very little!

Rely on the means God
provides for you to glorify Him

Now, from what we know of Him, we may be sure He would never leave us in this predicament. He desires nothing so much as our love. He would never leave us without adequate means of loving Him. If an earthly father knew that his child was longing to make him a present, but had not the means, with what prompt hand and overflowing heart would he furnish him with the means! Will Jesus do less? That at least is not His way.

[92] That is, beyond the reach of suffering or harm.

Look at what He did for His Mother at the Presentation.[93] No creature, nor all creatures put together, ever loved God as she did at that hour. And never yet had that ever-blessed and most dear Majesty been worshiped with an adequate act of worship. The angels, with all the varied powers and faculties and manifold affections of their nine choirs, had been casting their gifts before the throne with fiery love and burning songs of praise these thousands of years, and the Divine Complacency had mercifully stooped to feed itself upon them. Mary herself, the lowly and the chaste, was a more sweet act of worship to the Most High, and all the everlasting praise of the heavenly hierarchies would fill up but a little corner in her Immaculate Heart. Yet even she fell short, and oh, how far short! Sweet Mother! She knew this well; none knew it better; and if ever love could have run wild in the blessed and worshipful calmness of her immense virtue, as it did with her children the saints, and their weaker grace, she might have wished to be annihilated, if so she could have worshiped God with a sufficient love.

But Jesus came to the rescue of her love. He put Himself into her arms and said to her, "Offer me! I am equal to my Father! I am a gift, not only worthy but of the selfsame price and value, infinite, unutterable as Him!" Now for the first shall the most Holy Trinity have an act of fitting worship. Every attribute shall be glorified, every perfection crowned with a crown of love and adoration, every mercy recompensed; every debt and duty of every creature shall be satisfied; nay, the love and worship of all possible creatures shall be by one act outrun and overpassed forever!

Oh, joy, exceeding joy, to those who love our most dear God — a joy beyond all other joys! And Heaven was silent, and the angels with spirits gushing with love looked down adoringly, and on this

[93] Cf. Luke 2:22 ff.

earth of ours in Sion's temple, Mary took her Baby into her arms, and held Him up, and gave Him with all the might and impetus of self-sacrifice to the eternal Father. And so she, the first of all creatures who did so, worshiped God aright, and gave due glory to the Eternal.

And now, oh mysterious love, whereby our dear Lord will persist in making Himself so common! There is not a moment, day or night, on this round globe, that the same Child, the living Host, is not being elevated by mortal hands between earth and Heaven!

Thus, also, does He come to the rescue of our love. He can do so in two ways: first, by giving to the littleness of our actions an immensity of value by uniting them to His own, and letting the worth of His own flow into them; and second, by treating us as He treated Mary, giving us Himself and all that belongs to Him to do with what he will, and to offer to God, as and when we please. And it is of these riches of our poverty that I am going to speak at present.

∞

See that all things are yours in Christ

It is really very difficult to believe our own greatness and nobility in Christ. The catalogue of our privileges always seems to be only a sort of devout exaggeration. Take yourself at any given moment, whether of pain and weariness, or of satisfaction and sensible devotion, and you will see how difficult it is, not so much to hope, as to believe that someday you will really be saved, dead, judged, crowned, in Heaven, and with eternity before you. It is not so much that you fear the opposite, as that the greatness of the reward, the infinity of the bliss, and the contrast with your present misery and lowness, are more than you can take in. You meditate on Heaven, and then you think, "Will there be a moment, or an hour, while men on earth are going on as usual, and I shall be thus, in the fixed possession and enjoyment of all this?" And you smile, not exactly with incredulity, but as Sara smiled when she heard the angel say that she would have a son.[94] So, in its measure, is it with the inheritance we have in Christ even when on earth. It seems too much.

Yet St. Paul says to the Corinthians, "All things are yours . . . whether it be the world, or life, or death, or things present, or things to come; for all are yours, and you are Christ's, and Christ is God's."[95] And again to the Hebrews, he says, not that you shall hereafter, but that you have already, "come to the mountain, and to the city of the living God, the heavenly Jerusalem, and to the company of many thousands of angels, and to the church of the firstborn who are written in the heavens, and to God, the judge of all, and to the spirits of the just made perfect, and to Jesus, the Mediator of the New Testament, and to the sprinkling of blood, which speaketh better than that of Abel."[96]

When Mary rules with her sweet scepter of ever-granted prayer over the empire of the Sacred Heart, it is our kingdom over which she is the queen. All it is and all it has is ours, for "all things are ours, and we are Christ's, and Christ is God's." For these are our treasures, which He has given us, having won them for us with His blood: His own sacred humanity, body and soul, His childhood, hidden life, ministry, Passion, Blessed Sacrament, and session at the Father's right hand; His Mother, all that she is or has; His countless angels, beautiful and strong; all the good works and penances of earth; all the Masses that are said; the countless sufferings

[94] Cf. Gen. 18:12.

[95] 1 Cor. 3:22-23.

[96] Heb. 12:22-24.

of those in Purgatory; the graces that the lost had and did not correspond to; the sanctity of the saints — Joseph, John the Baptist, the Apostles, and the rest; all the praise of birds and beasts and the orderly elements; all that creatures could do; God's past mercies, through the Old Testament history downward; and the love that the Three Divine Persons bear to each other, and the incommunicable love wherewith God loves Himself eternally.

These things are ours in Christ. Oh, surely a fair and magnificent domain! These things He puts into our hands, just as He put Himself into Mary's hands at the Presentation, that we may be able to satisfy our love. What blessed occupation for our time! What Heaven begun on earth! Every one of these things we can use as freely as if it were our own, for three distinct purposes, and we can merit by them all, as by our own actions, for the oblation of them is our own. He gives us them to be offered. First, we may use them to make acts of love, and second, to make acts of thanksgiving. Of these two uses I shall speak hereafter. And third, we may use them for intercession, and this is what we have to do with at present.

If we have laid well to heart the lessons of the last chapter, we shall feel so drawn to the blessed practice of intercession that we shall be discontented with our own means of interceding. We shall feel that our dry, bald petitions, our cold words, and our slovenly devotions, what with the distraction of our employments, and the hardness of our hearts, can never satisfy our loving desires to promote by intercession the glory of God, the interests of Jesus, and the good of souls.

See then! Jesus puts all these things into our hands as weapons of intercession. As there are no bounds to His love of us, so does He seem bent that there shall be almost no bounds to our possibilities of loving Him. Love would not be love if, having these treasures, it did not use them.

When, therefore, we desire to intercede with God for something that is to His greater glory, we can offer to Him any of these things, presenting to Him the actions themselves, so that they may appease His anger and stir His compassion toward us. The mere offering, with a devout intention, is a great thing and avails much, just as the silent presence in Heaven of the five wounds that our Lord deigned to keep after His Resurrection is said by theologians to be our Lord's intercession, continually pleading with the Father, although our Lord no longer prays for us as He did on earth.

But we ought not to stop here with the actions only. We should endeavor to unite ourselves with the dispositions in which Jesus, Mary, the angels, or the saints did the particular action in question. This will make our intercession still more efficacious and still more meritorious. We may also, if we please, wish the action could be multiplied a thousand times, so that God would have more and more accidental glory thereby. Oh, it is astonishing how the conversion of sinners will come in upon us, how quickly scandal will be abated, how the dews of grace will become heavy rains and fructify in the Church, if we devote ourselves to this practice! And we shall not be, as in past years we have so often been, like Gedeon's fleece, dry — almost miraculously dry — when all was wet around it![97]

∞

Offer to God the sacred humanity of Jesus

Take the sacred humanity of our dearest Lord. We may offer to God the perfections and powers of His human soul — the abysses of grace, science, and glory, which are in it; the love with which it

[97] Cf. Judg. 6:36-40.

loves God at this moment, and all the love with which it will ever love Him, to all eternity. We may ask for the conversion of a sin-stained soul, by the beauty and brightness of His soul, which at this hour is so lighting up the heavenly Jerusalem that "it needs neither sun nor moon to light it, for the Lamb is the light thereof."[98] We may ask health and strength for the preachers and missionaries of our Lord by all the perfections of His glorified body at this hour.

Or, leaving Heaven, we may come down to earth, and offer to the Father all the unspeakable worship that our Lord's mystical life in the Blessed Sacrament is offering Him from a thousand, thousand tabernacles: the poverty, the humiliation, the obedience to His priests, the zeal for souls, the refraining of His senses, the endurance of sacrileges, the patient love, and the miraculous manifestations of that hidden life.

Or, again, we may draw upon the past. There is the act of love in the moment of the Incarnation, the imprisonment for nine long months in Mary's blessed womb, the virtues practiced there, and the world governed from there. There is the Nativity, and the mysteries of the first twelve years: Bethlehem, Egypt, Nazareth, and Jerusalem, and all they mean and contain of the unfathomable humiliations of the Incarnate Word, and of His inexpressible love for Mary and for men. There is the hidden life at Nazareth, the hiddenness of the Omnipresent, the obedience of the Omnipotent, the poverty of the All-Rich, the fatigue of the Great Creator, the prayer of God, the love for Joseph, the sanctification of Mary, the merits and the satisfactions, and the complacency of angels, Mary, and of God in the wonders and virtues of those eighteen years. There is the three years' ministry, the baptism by John, and

[98] Apoc. 21:23 (RSV = Rev. 21:23).

the fasting in the wilderness, His way with His disciples, and His way with sinners, the contradictions He encountered, the sermons He preached, the miracles He wrought, the weariness He endured. Then we come to the shore of the illimitable sea of His most dear Passion. And beyond that, we have the risen life, the various apparitions, especially that first one to His Mother, the forty days of secret legislation for the matter and form of the sacraments and for the Church, all the beauty, charity, and hiddenness of those days, the words spoken, the wonders done, the graces given, the blessings imparted, and then the admirable pomp of His Ascension.

When will this fountain have run dry? When, if we never repeated the same thing twice over, shall we have exhausted these marvelous infinite acts, infinite not in themselves, but by their union with His divine Person, and which have such unlimited power with God? All these are at our disposal for intercession; and we may well believe they will have especial efficacy when suited to the sacred seasons of the year, all except the Passion, which has all seasons for its own.

Offer to God Christ's Passion

Now, let us speak of the intercessory use we may make of the Passion. We should naturally expect to find that as the work of our redemption was principally achieved through the mysteries of our blessed Lord's Passion, He should desire those mysteries to be especially in our remembrance, and should allow them to prevail with His Sacred Heart over all others, when offered to Him in love, thanksgiving, or intercession. St. Bernard declares that the mere thought of our Lord's Passion is a spiritual Communion. Fr. Balthazar Alvarez not only made it the ordinary subject of his meditations, but he used to say to his novices, "We must not think we have done anything until we have reached this point, that we never in our hearts forget Christ crucified."

Our Lord Himself said to St. Mary Magdalene de' Pazzi, "If, every Friday, you will pay attention to the hour in which I expired upon the Cross, you will at once receive particular graces from my spirit, which I then returned to the eternal Father; and although you do not feel this grace, it shall always rest upon you." And the great bell of the Duomo still calls the faithful of Florence to this sacred remembrance.

St. Clare of Montefalco had the Passion so perpetually in her thoughts, that everything she saw became instantly an ingenious memorial of something connected with our blessed Savior's sufferings. Our Lord said to the Bl. Veronica,[99] "I wish all men to do their best to sorrow in their hearts through veneration for my Passion, as if compassionating me. If they shed one little tear over it, they may be sure they have done a great thing; for the tongue of man cannot tell what joy and satisfaction that one little tear causes me."

The angels revealed to Bl. Joanna of the Cross that the Divine Majesty took such complacency in sorrow for the Passion of Christ, and that such sorrow was so grateful a sacrifice, that it was reckoned equal to the shedding of our blood, or the endurance of great afflictions. St. Theodore Studita cautions us that even though Easter has come, we must on no account let the memory of the Passion fade away, but keep the life-giving wounds, the Cross, and sepulcher always before our eyes.

Orlandini tells us of a saying of Fr. Peter Faber, that as the Passion was Christ's road to glory, so compassion for the Passion is

[99] Possibly Bl. Veronica of Binasco (d. 1497), Augustinian nun. — Ed.

ours. Our Lord said to St. Gertrude, "Everyone, even though he should feel himself weighed to the ground with great sins, may breathe freely with the hope of pardon, if he will only offer to God the Father my most innocent Passion and death; let him be sure that by this he shall receive the saving fruit of indulgence, for there is no remedy on earth so efficacious against sin, as a devout recollection of my Passion, joined with true repentance and a right faith." St. Albertus Magnus used to say that a single tear shed over our Lord's Passion, was better than a year's fast on bread and water.

St. Mary Magdalene revealed to a certain holy Dominican that when she retired into the wilderness to do penance after our Lord's Ascension, she desired to know from Jesus how she was to occupy herself. And our Lord sent St. Michael to her with a most beautiful cross which he planted at the door of her cell, so that she might spend her days in incessant meditation on the Passion. Once, when St. Gertrude was meditating on the Passion, she understood by a light from Heaven that to ruminate on the sufferings of Christ is an exercise of infinitely greater efficacy than all others. Lastly, St. Augustine says, "What kindles, urges, inflames and drives me to love Thee more than anything else, and to make Thee lovely above everything else, is the most ignominious and bitter death, which Thou, O good Jesus, didst endure for the work of our redemption. This alone, this altogether, easily claims for itself all our life, all our labor, all our devotion, and, finally, all our love. This, I say, best excites, most sweetly seeks, most amply multiplies our devotion."[100]

With what sweet artifices of love our Lord can repay this devotion is most beautifully shown in the life of St. Gertrude. One

[100] Conf. 2, 16.

Friday, when it was now near evening, she cast her eyes upon a crucifix, and, moved with compunction, she cried out, "Ah, my sweetest Creator and Lover, what and how great things didst Thou bear for my salvation today! And I — oh, so unfaithful! — have made no account of them, and the day has gone by while I have been occupied with other things. Alas! I have not devoutly called to mind hour after hour that Thou, dear Life that giveth life to all, for the love of my love, hast died!" The Lord from the crucifix answered her, "What you neglected I have supplied for you; for every hour I gathered into my heart what you ought to have collected in yours; and this has made my heart swell with such an excessive fullness that I have waited for this hour with great desire so that this intention might be made to me on your part. And now with this intention which you have just made, I will offer to God my Father all that I through the day have supplied for you, because without your own intention, it could not be so salutary for you!" "In this we may remark," says St. Gertrude, "the most faithful love of Jesus for man, which, solely on account of that intention by which He grieves over what he has neglected, amends it all with God the Father, and supplies for all deficiency in such a most lofty way."

Once also, when the saint was handling a crucifix very devoutly, she understood by a supernatural light that when anyone looked with devotion on a crucifix, he was looked upon by God with such benignant mercy that his soul, like a shining mirror, received from divine love such an exceedingly delectable image that all the heavenly hosts are delighted with it; and for as often as he shall have done this on earth, he shall have these images for so many increases of eternal glory in Heaven.

And this is not a mere devotion of feeling. "Ah!" said St. Gertrude once. "My only hope, and the salvation of my soul, tell me how I can do Thee at least a little good, then, for this Thy Passion, to Thee so bitter, to me so salutary." And this was our Lord's answer: "When a man follows another's interests in preference to his own, he repays me the captivity which I endured in the morning, when I was taken, pinioned, and grievously tormented for men's salvation. When he humbly acknowledges himself to be at fault about anything, he recompenses me for the judgment that I underwent at the first hour, when I was accused by false witnesses and sentenced to death. When he refrains his senses from things that delight him, he repays me for the scourging I endured at the third hour. When he obeys an ill-natured superior, he relieves the pain of my crown of thorns. When he is the injured party, but asks pardon first, he compensates for my carrying of the Cross. When he almost goes beyond what he can do in extending charity to others, he repays me for that extension which I so sharply endured when distended on the Cross at the sixth hour. When, to hinder a sin, he does not mind sorrow or reproach, he repays me for my death, which I suffered for the salvation of the world at the ninth hour. When he is reproached and answers humbly, he, as it were, takes me down from the Cross. When he prefers his neighbor to himself and thinks him more worthy of honor, or any other good thing, than himself, he pays me for my burial."

On another occasion, a similar revelation was made to the same saint. She said to our Lord, "Ah, Lord, tell me how I can laudably venerate Thy Passion." He replied, "By more frequently revolving in your mind that anxiety by which I, your Creator and Lord, when in my agony, prayed the more intensely, and through the excessive vehemence of my solicitude, desire, and love, I moistened the ground with my bloody sweat. Then you must commend to me all you do, and all that has to be done about you, in union with that subjection wherewith I, for the same reason, said to the Father, 'Not my will, but Thine, be done.' So you must receive all prosperous or adverse things with the same love with which I send them all to you for your salvation. You must receive prosperous things with gratitude, in union with that love by which I am your lover, and condescending to your frailty, I procure them for you, that by them you may learn to hope for eternal prosperity. You must receive adverse things in union with that love with which, out of the affection of my paternal fidelity, I send them to you, so that by them you may earn for yourself an everlasting good."

Our Lord said to St. Bridget,[101] "I counsel you to have always two thoughts in your heart: first, the remembrance of what I have done for you in suffering and dying; this thought will excite love of God; second, the consideration of my justice and the future judgment; this will strike fear into your soul." When He speaks to her of the praises of good Christians, He counts, as one, that the whole of their thoughts go to His Passion. This, too, was the great devotion of our Blessed Lady, as she herself revealed to St. Bridget: "My thoughts and my heart were always in the sepulcher of my Son"; and again, she bade the saint always to be considering His Passion.

When Bl. Angela of Foligno asked God what she could do to please Him more, He vouchsafed to appear to her several times, both sleeping and waking, always as crucified on the Cross. He told her to look at His wounds and then showed her, in a marvelous manner, how He had endured all those things for her. Lastly, He said, "What, then, can you do for me that would be enough?" Another time, as the Bollandists[102] relate, He appeared to her, and said, "Whosoever wishes to find grace, let him never take his eyes

[101] St. Bridget of Sweden (c. 1303-1373), founder of the Order of Brigittines.

[102] A small group of Jesuit scholars of the seventeenth century who edited the *Acta Sanctorum*, a collection of lives of saints.

from the Cross, whether my Providence is visiting him with sorrow or with joy."

No wonder, then, that the same Angela should have heard from our Lord that these were the benedictions that He would multiply upon those who were devoted to His Passion, and upon those who imitate it, and upon those who compassionate it. "Blessed are you of my Father who compassionate me, and who are sorrowing with me, and who, walking my road, have merited to wash your stoles in my blood. Blessed are you who compassionate me crucified for you, and afflicted with immense griefs, that I might satisfy for you and redeem you from immense and eternal pains; for compassionating me in my poverty, sorrow, and contempt borne for you, you have been found worthy. Blessed are you who shall be mindfully and devoutly compassionate toward my Passion, which is the miracle of all ages, the salvation and life of the lost, and the sole refuge of sinners; for you shall be truly partakers with me of the kingdom, and glory, and Resurrection which I have acquired by it, and coheirs with me forever and ever. Blessed are you of my Father, and of the Holy Spirit, and truly blessed with the benediction that I shall give in the last judgment, because, when I came unto my own, you have not repulsed me, as my persecutors did; but, by your compassion, have received me, a desolate stranger, into the home and hospitality of your heart. You have compassionated me, stretched naked on the Cross, hungering, thirsting, weak, nailed, and dying. You have willed to be my companions, and in this you have truly fulfilled the works of mercy. Therefore, shall you hear in that terrible hour, 'Come, you blessed of my Father, receive the kingdom which was prepared for you before the foundation of the world.' For I was hungry on the Cross, and, at least by compassion, you gave me to eat. Oh, happy you, truly happy, and blessed altogether, for if upon the Cross I prayed to my Father with tears and weeping for my crucifiers and torturers, and excused them, saying, 'Father, forgive them, for they know not what they do,' what shall I say for you who have compassionated me, and been my devout partners, when, not upon the Cross, but all blissful in my glory, I shall judge the world?"

Now, what do these examples and revelations show, except that our Lord has been pleased to give us His Passion as if it were really more utterly and completely our own, to do with it what we willed, than the pains we ourselves suffer, or the afflictions we have to bear?

But to come to the use of the Passion in intercession, which is our immediate subject, Lancisius tells us, "The offering of the Blood of Christ, or of His Passion and death, to the eternal Father, or to Christ Himself, in order to appease Him for the sins of the world, is of boundless efficacy." This practice was taught by God to St. Mary Magdalene de' Pazzi, when he vouchsafed to complain to her that there were so few in the world who made any effort to appease His anger against sinners. In consequence of this, many times in the day, she offered up the blood of Christ for sinners of all classes, and her ordinary practice was daily to offer it fifty times for the living and the dead. She did this with so much fervor that God repeatedly showed her multitudes of souls whose conversion she had thus obtained, as well as multitudes released from Purgatory.

Once in a rapture she cried out, "As often as the creature offers this blood, by which it is redeemed, it offers a gift which has no price, that it can be paid back. Nay, the gift is so great that the eternal Father reckons Himself under obligation to His creature; for He sees it in its misery, which His infinite goodness desires to compassionate, and compassionating to communicate Himself to it; and thus this offering is the cause of His communicating now, and forever continuing to communicate, His goodness to His creature."

"This devotion," says Lancisius, "glorifies and recreates God with the most excellent and noble of all offerings. It asks, or rather in a certain sense exacts, for our past sins remission, preservation from sin in time to come, the conversion of sinners and heretics, and freedom from the temporal pains due to sin. It avails, also, as a thanksgiving for all public personal blessings, for the impetration of the divine assistance, and for the relief of the numberless necessities both of the living and the dead."

∞

Honor God through Mary

Persons often wish to know how much devotion they ought to have to our Blessed Lady, and where their love ought to stop. They are dissatisfied if they are told that they can never have enough devotion to her, that, so far as degree is concerned, there is no possibility of excess, and that there is no limit at which their love need stop. True as this is, it does content them. They think it a sort of pious exaggeration, which is true in a sense, but no real answer to their question, or solution to their difficulty.

But they would hardly be able to object, if it was said to them, "You are to love Mary as much as Jesus loved her, and you are to have as great a devotion to her as Jesus wishes you to have, and you can have no scruple in praying to Jesus for this devotion according to His will."

It is impossible to know Jesus, much more to love Him, if we have not a warm devotion to His ever-blessed Mother. Neither can we conceive of any devotion to her more sure to move the Heart of Jesus to listen to our intercessions than the offering to Him of those graces which He Himself bestowed upon her, those acts of love by which the Three Persons of the Most Holy Trinity adorned her as their choice trophy of compassion, and those mysteries in which she corresponded to these graces and merited so unspeakably. She is so bound up with the glory of God that every act of homage to her is a plain act of love of God. She is herself so completely the choice of interest of Jesus that He has none on earth to compare to the defense and propagation of her honor! For, if His Sacred Heart is mercifully bent upon the salvation of souls, He has chosen Mary as the refuge of sinners and the advocate of souls. If all God's works praise Him, and if, when He looked upon the earth that He had made, He was moved to pronounce it very good, while the morning stars sang together and the angels shouted for joy, how much more do His own works and gifts in Mary praise Him everlastingly, while she furnishes an unending theme for the songs of angels and of men!

Oh, for the sake of Jesus, we must learn to increase our love of Mary. It must be a devotion growing in us like a grace, becoming strong like a habit of virtue, and waxing more and more fervent and tender until the hour when she shall come to help us to die well and to pass safely through the risk of doom.

Do we think sufficiently of this — that devotion to our Blessed Lady is not a thing that, like the possession of a book or a rosary, we have once for all, final and complete? It would be no less untrue to say that when we have received from God the grace of humility, we have simply to hold fast what we have and never dream of getting more, than to say that devotion to Mary is an ungrowing thing. I repeat, it must grow like a virtue, and become strong like a habit, or it is worth nothing at all. Nay, it is worse than worth nothing, as a little thought will show you.

Love of Mary is but another form — and a divinely appointed one — of love of Jesus; and, therefore, if love of Him must grow, so also must love of her. If a person were to say, "You must not mingle prayer to Mary with prayer to Jesus," he would show that he had no true idea of this devotion, and that he was already on the brink of a very dangerous error. Yet people sometimes thoughtlessly speak as if devotion to the Mother were a little trifle allowably cut off from devotion to the Son; that it is something surrendered by Jesus to Mary; that Jesus is one thing and Mary is another; and that devotion to the two is to be divided between them in proportion to their respective dignities — say a pound to Him and an ounce to her. If such persons really saw what they mean, which they do not, they would perceive that they were talking impiety.

Love of Mary is an intrinsic part of love of Jesus, and to imagine that the interests of the two can be opposed is to show that we do not understand Jesus, or the devotion due to Him. If devotion to Mary is not already, and in itself, devotion to Jesus, then when we show devotion to her, we are consciously subtracting something from Him, and so actually robbing God, which is sacrilege. So that when people tell us to keep within bounds, to moderate our devotion, and not to go too far, or to do too much for Mary, they are not, as they fancy, securing to Jesus His rightful honor, but they are making the horrible confession that they themselves do take something from Jesus to give to Mary, although they are careful that it should not be very much.

How dreadful this sounds, when put in plain words! Devotion to Mary, can get wrong in kind; it can never err in degree. If love of Mary is not love of Jesus, if devotion to Mary is not one of His own appointed devotions to Himself — and the chief one, too — then my theology, as well as my love, tells me that I can have no room for Mary at all, for my heart cannot adequately hold Jesus as it is.

Dearest Mother, how little I would know of you, if I could think of you so dishonorably! And what a poor, low notion would I have of God Himself! I might as well think grace kept me from God, or sacraments enabled me to do without Jesus, as imagine that you did anything else but gloriously magnify His love of me and wonderfully intensify my love of Him!

Now see what materials the life of our Blessed Lady presents to us, that we may offer them again to God! Is there any disclosure of His love to a simple creature, or to all creatures together, equal to the grace of her Immaculate Conception, or of her election to the Divine Maternity? Whether we go through her life by the mysteries of which it is composed, or sum it up in what theologians call her three sanctifications — at her Immaculate Conception, the moment of the Incarnation, and the descent of the Holy Spirit at Pentecost — it furnishes us with innumerable motives most dear and persuasive to the Heart of Jesus. Every act is full of His grace and of her heroic love; every one is more pleasing to Him than all the heroism of His saints; and out of every one of them, because of the supreme love that was in her soul, God gains more glory than out of all the services of three hierarchies of Heaven.

The two devotions, to her dolors and her joys, might furnish illustrations of this. Passing over the devotion to her dolors[103] as better known, I will speak only of the devotion to her joys, which may be called the Franciscan devotion.

It was the practice of St. Thomas of Canterbury to say the Hail Mary three times a day, in honor of our Lady's seven earthly joys: the Annunciation, the Visitation, the Nativity, the Epiphany, the finding in the Temple, the Resurrection, and the Ascension. One day our Blessed Mother appeared to him and said, "Thomas, your devotion is most acceptable to me; but why do you call to mind

[103] The seven dolors, or sorrows, of Mary are the prophecy of Simeon, the flight into Egypt, the loss of the child Jesus in the Temple, Jesus' carrying the Cross, Jesus' death on the Cross, the taking down of Jesus from the Cross, and the burial of Jesus.

only the joys that I had on earth? Henceforth remember those also which I now enjoy in Heaven, for everyone who honors both of these I will console, exhilarate, and present to my most dear Son at the hour of death." St. Thomas felt his heart filled with a marvelous exultation, and he cried out, "And how, my sweetest lady, can I do this, when I do not so much as know what these joys are?" Our Blessed Lady then told him that he was to honor with seven Hail Marys the following joys: first, that the Most Holy Trinity honors her above all creatures; second, that her virginity has set her above all angels and saints; third, that the great light of her glory illuminates the heavens; fourth, that all the blessed worship her as the Mother of God; fifth, that her Son grants her whatever she asks; sixth, for the grace given her on earth and the glory prepared in Heaven for those devoted to her; and seventh, that her accidental glory goes on increasing to the day of doom.

But it is not only to our blessed Lord that we may offer the sorrows and the joys, the gifts, graces, and greatness of His Mother, but to herself also. One day, when St. Gertrude was invoking her with the *Salve Regina*,[104] she saw our dear Mother, as if drawn by ropes, incline toward her. By this she understood that as often as anyone names Mary his advocate with devotion, her motherly tenderness is so much moved by the name, that she is, as it were, unable to prevent herself from granting his prayers. At the words, "Thine eyes of mercy," our Lady gently touched her Son, and

[104] "Hail, Holy Queen, Mother of mercy, our life, our sweetness, and our hope. To thee do we cry, poor banished children of Eve; to thee do we send up our sighs, mourning, and weeping in this valley of tears. Turn, then, most gracious advocate, thine eyes of mercy toward us, and after this our exile, show unto us the blessed fruit of thy womb, Jesus. O clement, O loving, O sweet Virgin Mary! Pray for us, O holy Mother of God, that we may be made worthy of the promises of Christ."

turned Him toward the earth, saying to St. Gertrude, "These [meaning the eyes of Jesus] are those most merciful eyes of mine, which I can incline to the salvation of all who invoke me, from which they receive the most rich fruit of eternal salvation." Hence, she learned from our Lord at least once a day to invoke that most kind Mother with these words: "Turn, then, most gracious advocate, thine eyes of mercy toward us," and she was assured by Him that she would thus secure for herself no little consolation in the hour of death.[105]

St. Bernard tells us to offer all our offerings to God through the hands of Mary; and although the passage is so well known, I must not omit it here. "Whatever you are going to offer, remember to commend it to Mary, so that grace may return to the Giver of grace through the same channel whereby it flowed into you. Not that God was unable to infuse grace as He willed, without this aqueduct, but He chose to provide a channel for you. For your hands, perhaps, are filled with blood, or soiled with gifts, which you have not altogether shaken off from them; therefore that little which you are going to offer, take care, if you do not wish to be repulsed, to give it to Mary to offer with those most worthy and acceptable hands of hers. For those hands are as whitest lilies, and the lover of lilies will never reprove as not found among the lilies what is found in Mary's hands."[106]

∞

Offer God the worship of the angels

The beautiful life of the angels, God's eldest-born, may also furnish us with most ample materials for intercession. And our Lord

[105] *Revelations*, Bk. 4.

[106] *De Aquæductu*.

seems to call our attention to it, when He bids us pray, "Thy will be done on earth as it is in Heaven."

Scripture teaches us a great deal about the angels, their worship of God, their ministries toward other creatures, their individual characters — as in the case of Michael, Gabriel, and Raphael — their multitude, and their nine choirs by name. Some theologians have taught that each angel is a species of himself, which would indeed open out quite an overwhelming view of the magnificence of God. Others, with more show of reason, make twenty-seven species, three in each choir, as there are three choirs in each hierarchy;[107] and even this gives us amazing ideas of the court of Heaven, when we remember how hard it is for us to conceive of any further specific division of reasonable creatures than into those with bodies and those purely spiritual. Others, without entering into the question of species, tell us that the grace of each angel is something quite different in beauty and excellence from the grace of his fellows; and if we follow out this thought also, it will be a joy to us to think of all the perfection of sweet worship that God is receiving in Heaven while we are serving Him so meanly upon earth.

Sr. Minima of Gesu Nazzareno, a Carmelite nun of Vetralla, who lived at the time of the French invasion of Italy and spent a life of incessant and wonderful intercession, used to offer continually to the Divine Majesty the love of the first choir of seraphim, in reparation for all the outrages then going on in the world. So also we are supplied with fresh materials for intercession by the

[107] St. Thomas Aquinas divides the nine orders of angels into three hierarchies, based on their proximity to God. In the first hierarchy are the seraphim, cherubim, and thrones; in the second, the dominations, virtues, and powers; and in the third, the principalities, archangels, and angels; cf. *Summa Theologica*, I, Q. 108, art. 6.

various magnificence of worship which the different orders of saints are at this hour, and every hour, offering to God in Heaven, a worship and a glory that is increasing constantly as fresh souls from earth or Purgatory attain to bliss.

And in all this, we satisfy our love, while we are with gentle efficacy influencing the Sacred Heart to grant our prayers.

∞

Offer God all the works and worship of creation on earth

Then, again, if we descend to earth, even there we find sweet bundles of fragrant incense wherewith to appease the just anger of God and to win a loving answer to our prayers. All that the saints have ever done in past centuries, the wonders of Joseph's hidden sanctity, the solitary austerities of the Baptist, every weary step the Apostles took along the Roman roads, every pang the martyrs suffered; or — farther back into the Old Testament times — the raptures of the prophets, the fidelity of the Maccabees, the marvels of David's godlike heart, the fights of Joshua, the meekness of Moses, the purity of Joseph, the simplicity of Jacob, the meditations of Isaac, the faith of Abraham, the priesthood of Melchisedech, the building of Noah, the blood of Abel, and the long nights and toilsome days of Adam's nine hundred years of diligent, heroic, and accepted penance: all these we may offer humbly and confidently, as if the sweetness and freshness of yesterday were upon them.

But there is the present, as well as the past. Earth brings forth its glad harvest for God's glory at every hour. Out upon its hills and plains and valleys this day, in the convents and in the world, how many supernatural acts are rising up to God, how many acts of faith, breathings of hope, sighs of love and holy sorrow, how many penances, how much conformity in pain to His most blessed will!

How many Masses are being said, how many Communions made, absolutions given, Anointings of the Sick received, and each hour how many dear although silent victories are the waters of Baptism achieving for the glory of the ever-blessed Trinity! All these belong to us; all these may we gather at our will and put them on the live coals of our devotion in the thuribles of our hearts, and offer incense to the Most High.

The inferior creatures are all praising God, by answering the end of their creation: the beasts of the field, the birds of the air, and the fishes of the sea, the woods and flowers, the winds and dews; and these, as they strike upon our eye or ear, we can offer in grateful love to the majesty of God.

There are, too, God's own works, from the creation of the world to the present hour of His manifold Providence; His forbearance with sin, or His judgments on it; His voices and visions and revelations; His interpretations in behalf of His Church; His visible protection of His ark in old times, and of the Holy See in our own. By all these, He is willing to be entreated. All these He gives us as weapons for the armory of prayer.

The inventive love of the saints and holy men has gone even further than this. They have offered to God in the fervor of their hearts all the homage that all creatures could offer to Him; so that they might come, or rather, might seem to come, as near to His infinity as possible. They have dared to conceive of those three abysses — the power of the Father, the wisdom of the Son, and the love of the Holy Spirit — as pouring forth in order and beauty all possible worlds, and have offered up these countless systems as an act of love and a plea of intercession. They have offered up, too, the manifold and unknown sufferings of Purgatory, which they one day expect themselves to feel, as beautiful in their perfections, holy in their dread functions, and further sanctified by contact with the holy souls, and so as a sweet oblation to the justice and purity of God.

∞

Offer the infinite perfections of the Trinity

But holy men have gone further even than this: "All things are Christ's, and Christ is God's."[108] They have felt how unequal to the majesty of God are all the praises of creatures; and therefore, when they have desired to implore of God some more-than-common grace, they have offered to Him His own infinite perfections, and the glory He receives from those attributes which are Himself. They have pleaded by the eternal generation of the Son, and by the double procession of the Holy Spirit. They have offered to God the knowledge and love whereby He knows and loves Himself, and the incommunicable complacency of the Three Divine Persons in each other.

And they have found, not only an answer to their prayers, but an increase of divine love in their souls, which they would hardly have conceived to be possible. They have found the technical terms of dogmas and definitions to be, not mere words and sounds, but flames from Heaven itself.

It is difficult to keep to our subject — that of intercession — when we are quoting so many things that run away with us and cause us to speak of love. But let us review all these riches of our poverty, all these our possessions in Christ, and see if we have not indeed an abundance of sacrifices with which to approach God in continual and fervent intercessions.

Through what fields of delightful meditation do they not lead us all the while! What liberty of spirit they impart to us! How easy

[108] Cf. 1 Cor. 3:23.

it is to make this a service of love, where all so breathes of love that it almost causes us to forget our intercession!

Take the case of invalids, of persons, not so much suffering from the pain of serious illness, as beneath the continual pressure of ailing health. They, too, desire to devote themselves to the glory of God, to the interests of Jesus, and to the saving of souls; yet they can do nothing, so far as external activity is concerned, and perhaps they have not the means to help good works with alms. Direct intercession, direct asking of God in so many words for grace for such-and-such a person, is soon exhausted. There is nothing in it to beguile the weariness of infirm health or to lead the spirit on.

But to wander through these treasuries of holy offerings — countless, various, and beautiful as they are — is a placid occupation of the spirit. It renews the flagging devotion and thus enables us to keep up and perpetuate our affectionate and reverential communion with God, while we are in reality doing great and solid work for His glory and the advancement of His Church.

And not to invalids only, but to all, it is an easy, because interesting, practice of the presence of God — interesting to the affections as well as to the mind. The more our ideas about God are multiplied and the more various our thoughts, images, and recollections of things that have to do with Him, of course the more our minds and hearts are engrossed with Him, and so it becomes easier to live all day in His sensible presence.

And we should not omit to mention the unworldly temper this method of intercession would produce in us. The world's strong point is its multiplicity. Its objects of interest are so numerous. It addresses so many sides of our nature. It lays hold of us in such a variety of ways; whereas, religion is to many people so intellectually uninteresting, so dry and barren, so uniform and monotonous.

They know so little about it; and they cannot always keep to one thing. And thus spirituality is at a disadvantage.

It is true that there is a very lofty and sublime state of the soul in contemplation where the bare thought of God is its perfection. But these things are not for us. We, and such as we, need all the interest that variety and beauty can give to devotion, and even then we tire of it before long. And thus, the more interesting and various our religious knowledge is, the easier we find it to cast out of our souls the miserable spirit of the world and to become engrossed with the interests of Jesus.

And what consolation, too, is there not in all these riches of our poverty, when low spirits are upon us, or an overdepressing sense of sin, or the thwartings of men, or the failure of good works, or the unsatisfactoriness of life and of the world? Downcast as we may be, after all, we want nothing so much as that God should be loved, and Jesus have that which is rightfully His. And so weary with work or foiled with disappointment, when the dark night is closing in, bringing with it to our sick spirits a sense of imprisonment, and when the dismal rain curtains us round, and we fret to be at liberty and at large, there is the very freedom of a sovereign to a soul traversing this boundless empire of God and Jesus, of Mary, angels, saints, men, and the blameless creatures, and rejoicing in that never-ceasing sacrifice of praise which is rising up from every nook and corner of creation to the dear majesty of our most loving God and Father.

Chapter Six

Learn to grow holier in every moment and instance

God is the center of everything and the value of everything. As everything comes from Him, so everything returns to Him. Even the rebellious creature, which refuses to repose in the embraces of His love, falls into the hands of His justice. Nothing is worth anything, except insofar as God chooses to have to do with it. The enlightened mind or the loving heart can respect nothing, except under its relation, true or supposed, to Almighty God. There is but one view of things that is true, and that is God's view of them.

It seems hardly worthwhile to say such very obvious things. Yet the misery is that even Catholics find difficulty in getting these truths into their minds, to say nothing of the further difficulty of acting upon them when received. Many men are shocked at the external signs of oblivion of God, which are so distressingly obvious in a heretical country. And yet they themselves in their own subject matter do not really let God have that which is rightfully His.

Look how Catholics act when mixed up with a political party or a scientific institute, and at once you will see conduct that, implicitly at least, supposes that God is very well in His own place, but that He has limits, and that to intrude Him — and religious considerations that have to do with Him — into certain discussions, actions, or interests is either an impertinence or a narrow-mindedness, or at least a tolerated idiosyncrasy. There are many good people who, from the best of motives, fall into this, and they deem they are going to win God some glory, and His Church some prosperity, from thus playing the civil to the world and its principles. Alas, they wake up one day and find that, while their own devotion has become dull, their prayers distracted, their piety merely exterior, and their principles insensibly lowered to the level around them, they have not drawn to God one single soul or, in any one nook of the world, increased the love of our dear Lord.

At this time, men must have a very clear view of God, or else they are quite sure in a hundred ways not to let Him have that which is rightfully His. It is very obvious to say that if we always knew what God wished, it would be a great help to us in serving Him. We would not surely throw ourselves into open rebellion against the express will of God. Yet practically, in by far the greatest number of our actions, we do know this; and in all of them, if we do not know what He would have us do, we know at least the motive from which He would have us act, whenever we act at all. "Whatever you do, whether you eat or drink, or whatever you do, do all for the glory of God."[109]

∞

Recognize how God enables you to love Him

St. John tells us that God is charity.[110] Thus in the whole of the almost infinite and complicated system in which we live, God has contrived all things, quite wonderfully, for these two ends: He has

[109] 1 Cor. 10:31.

[110] 1 John 4:8, 16.

arranged everything, first, so that He may be loved and, second, so as to enable us to love Him. If we may dare thus to speak of the Almighty, He seems to have no other end in view at all; and He manages things by artifices of almighty power in order to bring this about. This is His rule by which He has done everything. The hearts of His creatures are the only treasures He will condescend to accept from His own creation.

It is remarkable, when we come to think of it, that neither angels nor men were created in a state of nature, but in a state of grace, and were thus able at once to love God and to merit eternal life, which is nothing else than eternal society with Him. Grace was a better position than nature for loving God. By grace He could communicate Himself to us. By it He at once got more love from us, and made us more able to love Him.

Then came redemption, and the same end is visible there. He could have forgiven sin without the Incarnation; but it was the most loving way and more sweetly constrained us to love Him. When our dear Lord came, one tear was enough to redeem countless worlds; but blood was more loving. One drop of blood was enough, but to shed it all, and to shed it variously, in the garden, at the pillar, during the Way of the Cross, and on Calvary, was more loving, more likely to call out man's love. When Jesus went, and the work of redemption was to go on operating through all ages, common grace would have done; but that Jesus should come back to us invisibly in the transcending wonder of the Blessed Sacrament was more loving, more personal, and more constraining to our affections. We might be eternally happy in a sinless immortality, spent in a world of beautified nature; but His delight is to be with the children of men,[111] and that they should be with Him to

[111] Cf. Prov. 8:31.

all eternity, and that nothing short of His own dear and adorable Self should be their enjoyment.

You see, everything our heavenly Father does is for love. He vouchsafes to long for our love. He makes us so that we can be happy only in loving Him; and then, looking compassionately on our intense desire to love Him more, He does all that we will let Him do to enable us to love Him more and more worthily and fervently. Thus, all is love from first to last: there is no other measure; there is no other principle.

Oh, that we had the hearts to take this in, and all that it involves! If we are to come to weights and measures with Infinite Goodness, surely His love of us should be our measure of love of Him, a measure to which we must never cease to aspire, although we shall never attain it. If our hearts are not at once touched, melted, and carried away by the very thought and name of God, reflection must at least convince us that all religion is a matter of love, and that without some love we can never see God.

All through, God takes the lower place in His own world. He stoops to plead when we should expect Him to command. He makes as though we were laying under an obligation Him who created us out of nothing, and from whom alone all that is good proceeds. He woos our souls with blandishments which no churlishness of ours seems ever to repel. He is continually giving way, continually waiving His rights, putting Himself in our position and us in His. The Incarnation is itself a figure of the whole conduct of the Creator to His unworthy creatures. The mystery of the Blessed Sacrament is simply in harmony with the way and conduct of the Almighty in His own world.

And, alas, we are not touched! We are as hard, dry, ungracious, and mean as ever — as though it were some great honor to us to show off the might of our free will, and that while God was contriving everything to get love from us, we could manage, in spite of Him, to make religion as nearly as possible a shopkeeper's bargain or a convict's grudging obedience. Oh, until we got to know our own hearts, Hell might have seemed a severity; but truly a little self-knowledge shows that it is almost the chiefest, because the most indispensable, of the divine mercies.

Well might St. Francis run about the woods in the valley of Spoleto, exclaiming, "Oh, God not known and not loved!" Well might St. Bruno[112] cause the mountain solitudes to echo with his one lifelong cry: "Oh, Goodness! Goodness! Goodness!" Well might our dearest Lord appear to St. Gertrude, pale, weary, bleeding and dirt-stained, and say, "Open your heart, my daughter, for I want to go in and lie down; I am weary of these days of sin!"

Develop a spirit of oblation

But at last, as we grow in the knowledge of God, we grow in His love also. We come at length to feel pain and anguish because we do not love our blessed God more, and because others do not love Him also. Here, too, He is ready to meet us. He not only arranges all things so as to get love, but with this, He arranges so as to enable us to love Him in all manner of supernatural ways. First, He gives us all that is His, and lets us offer it to Him again as if it were all our own; these are the riches of our poverty, which we then considered. Second, He magnifies our own poor actions and gives them an immense value by uniting them to His, and enabling us to do them from supernatural motives and in union with Him.

It is this last method of putting it in our power to love Him more worthily that we are to consider now. We are to meditate on

[112] St. Bruno (c. 1032-1101), founder of the Carthusian Order.

the treasure of our common actions, and on the Catholic devotion of perpetually offering them up to God united with the actions of Jesus. This is the second manner in which God mercifully rescues us from the littleness and worthlessness of our own selves.

There is not a single thing we do all the day long that may not, and quite easily, be made to advance the glory of God, the interests of Jesus, and the salvation of souls — no matter how completely the world may have set its seal upon it, or how utterly it seems to be an affair of temporal business or a trivial concern belonging only to the misery of human life. The heavenly motive enters into it; in that moment it is all filled with God, and becomes a jewel of almost infinite price, with which the Divine Majesty condescends to be well pleased. The hours pass, one following the other; each one is filled with actions belonging to our state. We write, or read, or keep accounts, or buy, or sell, or speak, or think, or suffer; and all the while, if we choose it, we are minting money, heavenly money that can merit eternal life. Only the act or intention of oblation, by which our actions touch those of God made man, is needed to confer this value upon every single thing we do.

Pious people sometimes complain of the distractions of worldly occupations; they think it will be the peculiar business of Heaven to worship God with an unintermitting worship; in fact, they complain that earth is not Heaven. Yet surely, in this respect at least, it need not be so very unlike it. If ours is a service of love, every one of these so-called distractions is in truth a precious oblation. Every action is Host and incense and song and sacrifice all the day long, if we choose that it should be so ourselves. Now, if we have really at heart God's glory, the interests of Jesus, and the saving of souls, if we would fain be occupied in these things at all hours, we must not neglect to profit by this treasure of our common actions.

The spirit of oblation is essentially Catholic. It springs from the doctrine of the Mass, which is the center and fountain of all true devotion. It belongs to a religion of sacrifice, such as the Gospel is in every way. Our dear Lord redeemed us by the oblation and sacrifice of Himself; and hence, oblation and sacrifice enter into every minutest detail of our religion. No wonder they should give a shape and form, a genius and spirit, to Catholic devotion.

This is so obvious, it need not be dwelt upon. But what I want you to observe is that here also is the same contrivance for love, the same sweet parental spirit, that God vouchsafes to show us everywhere. It would seem as if prayer was a privilege that could not possibly be exceeded even by infinite compassion, and that a creature could look for nothing more than the privilege of making his wants known to his merciful Creator.

Yet oblation is something beyond prayer. In prayer we receive from God. In oblation, it is He who vouchsafes to receive, and we are allowed to give. To make presents is not only a sign of love, but of some sort of equality; and thus from oblation there springs a more familiar, tender, and affectionate familiarity with God than could arise from petition only. The childlike freedom of the saints comes in great measure from this spirit of oblation.

∞

Follow the saints' examples

Let us now see what the practices of the saints have been with regard to the oblation of their own daily actions to God. We must remember throughout that our position is this. We are longing for God's glory, for the interests of Jesus, and for the good of souls. We see an overwhelming amount of work to be done, little time to do it in, and small means with which to do it. We must be covetous of all we have, greedy of grace, and greedy of everything that grace can make its own. Our dear Lord! It is for Him we are working, so we must work hard, and always. We have something to do, and we do it, and there the action stops. But if we do the same thing with devout attention, offering it to Jesus in union with something similar which He condescended to do on earth, it becomes a sweet sacrifice of immense power with God.

What miser but would be minting money all the day if he could? Yet this is just what we can do — and, through the stupendous mystery of the Incarnation, in a most real way, and effectual to the obtaining of eternal life.

St. Thomas teaches that the work of a just man becomes more meritorious in proportion to the excellence of the supernatural motive for which the work is done, and that as love — the love of benevolence, as it is called — is more excellent than any other, so works done for that motive are the most meritorious of all. Furthermore he teaches that works done to God as our Father are more meritorious than those done for Him as our Creator, because the motive is more excellent.

God revealed to St. Matilda[113] that it was most pleasing to Him that we should offer Him all our actions in union with those of Christ, and our Lord Himself taught the same to St. Gertrude and also to St. Mary Magdalene de' Pazzi. Thus St. Thomas says, "Christ is signified by the double altar of holocausts and incense; because by Him we ought to offer to God all the works of virtue by which we afflict our flesh, and these are offered on the altar of holocausts; and that we should offer to Him also all those which we do with a greater perfection of mind, by the spiritual desires of the perfect, and these are offered on the altar of incense."[114] Thus, St.

[113] St. Matilda (c. 1241-1298), Benedictine nun.

[114] *Summa Theologica*, I-II, Q.102, art. 4.

Ignatius in his rule says, "All his children are to have a right intention, not only as to their state of life, but as to all details, always in all of them seeking to act only so as to please the Divine Goodness for His own sake." And St. Teresa says, "Everyone will gain the desired end of his prayers more efficaciously, if he will but offer his actions to the eternal Father in union with the merits of our Lord."

In order to avoid weariness and the straining of the mind, Lancisius recommends that this offering should be made by single words — either, "I will [or 'I offer,' or 'I do,' or, 'I say'] this for Thy sake, my heavenly Father!" — and that we may either keep to the same words or vary them, according as we find our devotion is most excited.

The same spiritual writer recommends also that we should offer to God the particular circumstances of our actions, as well as the actions themselves. For example, on rising in the morning, he would have us say, "O most holy and beloved Father, I now desire to rise because of Thee, and in union with the merits, and all the works of my dear Lord, without delay, so as promptly to obey the call of holy obedience, and to dress myself with all modesty, and as quickly as I can, so that I may begin all the sooner to work for Thy glory." And he says that this variation of the material circumstances of our actions at once increases the merit of the offering, and prevents weariness and oppression of spirit. Yet this might act differently on different persons, or on the same persons at different times.

He recommends also, as an act of greater love and merit, that we should make the offering of our actions for several supernatural ends, subordinate to the great one of God alone. And he gives the following examples, not that we should necessarily think of them all in all our actions, but in order to furnish variety for different tastes and devotional inclinations: for the supernatural goodness there is in the act of virtue itself; to fulfill the precepts of God and the Church; to obey our superiors; to overcome and mortify self; to satisfy for the sins of another person, for, in order to satisfy for our own sins, it is not necessary to make a distinct oblation of our actions — for, every supernatural work of a just man satisfies for his sins of itself, if it is not offered for others; that by this work we may worship, glorify, and please God in the highest degree; that we may show Him our gratitude for all His gifts to us and to others, to the sacred humanity of our blessed Lord, to our dear Lady, the angels, the saints, and even the unhappy ones who are lost; that we may give good example and edification; that by this action or word we may increase the habits of virtue that make us dear to God; that we may become more like God; that we may thus adorn our soul, and make it a more fitting temple for the Holy Spirit and a more chaste member of Jesus Christ; that we may so spread more widely the glory of Christ and the efficacy of His Precious Blood by thus multiplying supernatural actions in ourselves; that we may gladden the Church Triumphant; that we may adorn the Church Militant; that we may confound the evil spirits; that we may call down more grace upon all the Body of Christ; that we may thus before men and angels exhibit the efficacy of the Blessed Eucharist; that we may fulfill thereby our vows, or desires, or resolutions; that we may be faithful to divine inspirations; that we may imitate Christ and the saints; and that we may thereby do honor to our dear Lady, our guardian angel, or our patron saint.

And all these intentions will apply as well to the suffering of evil as to the doing of good.

Thus, in the secret laboratory of intention, the dress of our commonest actions is daily turned into the finest gold; and we may learn, to our great consolation, of what value these actions become in our Lord's sight, from His own revelation to St. Gertrude.

"As a covetous usurer," said He, "would not willingly miss the opportunity of making a single penny, much more unwillingly would I allow one thought or one movement of your little finger made for my sake to perish, without my turning it to my own great praise and your eternal salvation." On another occasion, when she was suffering one night from weakness, she ate some grapes, with the mental intention of refreshing our Lord in herself. He, on His part, took this as a royal gift, and said to her, "In this I confess that you have recompensed me for the bitter potion which I for your sake took upon the Cross; for now I suck unspeakable sweetness out of your heart; for with how much greater purity of intention you recreate your body for my glory, with so much the more sweetness do I acknowledge myself recreated in your soul." Another time our Lord said to her, "My tenderness will accept one step, or one lifting of a straw from the ground, or one word, or one courteous gesture, or one *Requiem aeternam* for the dead, or one word for sinners, or even for the just, if there be a pious intention along with it."

But it was not simply because Gertrude was a saint that our Lord took such pleasure in this oblation of her ordinary actions. Once when the whole community were bowing at the words, "The Word was made flesh," out of reverence for our Lord's Incarnation, she understood our Lord to say, "Whenever anyone with devout gratitude bows at these words, giving me thanks because, for the love of him, I deigned to become man, so often, impelled by the spur of my own tenderness, do I condescendingly bow to him in return; and with the most intimate affection of my Heart, I make a double offering to God the Father of all the fruit of my most blessed humanity, in augmentation of that man's eternal bliss."

See, also, how He speaks of comforts. "Whosoever," said He to St. Gertrude, "shall study to take all his recreations and use his comforts, in drinking, eating, sleeping, and the like, with this intention in his heart or mouth: 'Lord, I take this food — or whatever it may be — in union with that love wherewith Thou didst sanctify Thyself, when, in Thy most sacred humanity, Thou didst use like comforts, to the glory of the Father, and the salvation of the whole human race, so that, in union with Thy divine love, it may increase the consolation of those in Heaven, on earth, and in Purgatory,' he, each time he does so, is, as it were, a most firm shield in front of me, against the many vexations with which worldly people persecute me, and I look upon him as my protector and defender."

∞

Recognize Jesus as a gentle Master

Once, on the Thursday before a carnival, Gertrude heard some servants in a neighboring house making a noise in the kitchen, preparing their breakfast. She sighed, and exclaimed, "Alas, my Lord, how early men rise in the morning to persecute Thee with their feasting!" But our Lord, smiling a little at her, replied, "Nay, dearest daughter! There is no need for sighing. They who are making the noise are not of the number who rage against me with their gluttony; for by this breakfast, they are incited to their daily toil. Wherefore I delight in their feeding, as a man rejoices when he sees his beast feed heartily, because it will serve him better."

O gentle Lord, why do not our hearts melt when we read these things of Thee?

It is no taskmaster with whom we have to do! Such little toils and such great rewards! Such a profusion of mercies, and graces, and caresses! If the dog loves his master, and shows that he appreciates his kindness and attentions, much more should we serve, and all for love, so dear a Master as our compassionate Lord! Yet, alas, we persist in having such hard notions of our wonderful God.

We go on imitating the ungracious ways of the servant who hid his one talent in a napkin for fear of his Lord's austerity,[115] and we will not own God for what He is: our almost incredibly indulgent Father.

And how He feels this rude perversity! "Hear, O ye heavens! and give ear, O earth! I have brought up children, and exalted them; but they have despised me. The ox knoweth his owner, and the ass his master's crib; but Israel hath not known me, and my people hath not understood."[116]

Yet while we will not show Him the gratitude of beasts, He still covenants to be to us more than a mother to her child. When Sion said, "The Lord hath forsaken me, and the Lord hath forgotten me," He answered the cry: "Can a woman forget her infant, so as not to have pity on the son of her womb? And if she should forget, yet will not I forget Thee."[117]

What is more necessary to true worship than a deep and calm reverence? Nay, what is more sweet to fervent love than to be hushed and awe-smitten in the presence of the refulgent attributes of God? Familiarity in religion would be a simple impertinence if reverence did not mingle with it. What more familiar than the relation between father and son, yet what love more reverent than filial love? Yet it was no true reverence that made Peter tell his Master to depart from him because he was a sinful man,[118] or which made the craven men of Gadara beseech Jesus to withdraw His importunate blessings from their coast.[119] But it was reverence that

[115] Cf. Luke 19:20-21.

[116] Isa. 1:2-3.

[117] Isa. 49:14-15.

[118] Luke 5:8.

[119] Matt. 8:34.

made Magdalene strive to hold the risen Jesus by His feet, although it was not His will to suffer it.[120]

Too often, alas, we mistake coldness for reverence, and stiffness for respect. How sweetly did Jesus reprove that spirit when St. Gertrude complained to Him of one of her nuns who, out of reverence, as she fancied, kept away from a community Communion. "What would you have me do?" said our blessed Lord. "These good people tie the bandage of their own unworthiness so tightly over their eyes that they cannot see the tenderness of my paternal Heart."[121]

The spirit of St. Gertrude was so eminently a spirit of oblation and of familiarity, that when Lancisius wrote his *Treatise on the Presence of God*, he devoted an entire chapter to the methods observed by her in oblation of her ordinary actions. Sometimes she offered her actions in union with the mutual love of the Three Divine Persons of the adorable Trinity. Sometimes she offered the pains and tears of Jesus for the negligences of her actions. Sometimes she made her oblation in union with the efficacious prayer of Jesus, and in the virtue of the Holy Spirit, for the emendation of her sins and the supply of her omissions. Sometimes in gratitude for blessings, she offered with her thanks "that sweetness which in the supercelestial treasury of the Divinity, beyond all sense, and with infinite pleasure, the Divine Persons communicate to each other." Another of her offerings was all the Passion of God's dear Son from the hour when He first wept as He was laid upon the straw in the manger, to the hour when He bowed His head upon the Cross, and with a loud cry gave up the ghost. This was for her sins.

[120] John 20:17.

[121] *Revelations*, Bk. 3, ch. 10.

Then, in reparation for her negligences, she offered to the Father all the most holy conversation of His Son, which was faultlessly perfect in all thoughts, words, and deeds, from the hour when He was sent into the world, to the hour when He presented to His Father the glory of His victorious flesh. In union with her thanksgiving she offered back to God what He had given, and using the Sacred Heart of Jesus as a sweet-thrilling organ, she sounded it in the virtue of the Paraclete, and accompanying it with her songs, she sang to God praises on behalf of all the creatures in Heaven, on earth, and beneath the earth, which have been, are, or ever shall be.

At other times, she made her offerings in union with the divine perfections; and our Lord Himself taught her to offer some actions to Him in union with the love by which God was made man. Once when she was offering to the Father all the holy conversation of His Only-Begotten, it seemed to her as if all the gems with which our Lord's vestments were adorned, moved in them, and gave out a most ravishing melody in praise of the eternal Father, by which she knew how acceptable to God was this particular method of oblation.

At other times, she made her offering in this way: "O Lord, I offer this work to Thee by Thine only Son, in the virtue of the Holy Spirit, to Thine eternal praise." It was then given her to see that by this intention, her works were ennobled, and made magnificent beyond all human estimation; for, just as a thing looks green that is looked at through a green glass, or red through a red glass, so is everything most pleasing and acceptable to God the Father that is offered through His Only-Begotten Son.

Sometimes she prayed that our Lord would deign to offer for her all the perfections that He had on the day of His Ascension. At other times, she offered her heart to God, to His eternal praise, to fulfill in both her body and her soul all His good pleasure. At this offering, Jesus was pleased to show Himself so touched, that with great joy, and the utmost sweetness, He stooped from the Cross and, embracing her with unspeakable exultation, gently pressed her to the wound of His most holy side, and said, "Welcome, my dearest daughter! You are the most soothing ointment of my wounds, and the most sweet alleviation of my pains."

Our Lord taught her also to say, "Alleluia," to praise God in union with all the heavenly citizens, who incessantly praise Him by that word in Heaven. Sometimes she offered to God all the holy conversation of Jesus to supply for her deficiency since the hour of her Baptism, not affording such a Guest a worthy mansion in her soul. Or, at the elevation of the Host, she made the offering for all her want of correspondence to the inspirations of the Holy Spirit.

Or, again, in union the most spotless limbs of our blessed Lord, she commended to Him, as He Himself had taught her to do, all the limbs of her body, with every movement of them, so that from that time, they should never move except for His love, and to His praise and glory. When she did this, she beheld a golden belt issue from the Heart of God, and clasp her soul, so as to unite it in indissoluble love with our Lord.

These are given as specimens of St. Gertrude's method and spirit, which may be suggestive to ourselves; not as recommending any of them particularly as fitting for ourselves. What a different idea we would have of our dearest Lord if we practiced anything of this sort! How would all our thoughts, and loves, and wishes be quickly brought into subjection to Him! And does not this at least show us how the driest and most secular occupation may, with ease and sweetness, be turned into a perpetual service of divine love?

∞

Sanctify your recreation and free time

Besides these ordinary actions belonging to our state and calling in life, our recreation and free time should be filled with meritorious actions, so that Jesus may always be reaping a harvest of glory and of love in our hearts.

Mariano Sozzini, a father of the Roman Oratory, mentions that one of the fathers in his day, as he went daily from the refectory to the recreation room, used to pray for the four first fruits of the Holy Spirit — charity, joy, peace, and patience — because, to make recreation at once general and useful, these four gifts were required. Some have attained to such a practice of the presence of God, that when out walking, and engaged in conversation, they have contrived to say to God in their hearts at nearly every step they took, "For Thy sake, for Thy sake"; and the same while helping themselves at table, and at nearly all their gestures during meals.

St. Mary Magdalene de' Pazzi told her novices to offer to God's glory, if it were possible, the very blinking of their eyes, and the slightest motions of their limbs. In order to get this practice more deeply rooted in them, she often asked, first one, and then another, quite unexpectedly, and whatever they were doing, with what intention they were acting. If someone gave her no answer at once, she gathered that she had begun her work without a previous intention, and reproved her for losing an occasion of merit, and taking away a pleasure from God.

It is mentioned as a marvel in the life of Gregory Lopez that, for three years, he had said in his heart at every respiration, "Thy will be done on earth as it is in Heaven"; and the habit was so formed in him that if he awoke during the night, he began to do the same.

We cannot do these things, but it makes us love God more to know that He has raised up men who could. Blessed be the Most

Holy Trinity for all grace that has ever been in the spirits of angels, and the hearts of men!

∞

Look for opportunities for holiness during illness

There are many who desire to be all for God, and are fain to practice some such bodily austerities as they read of in the lives of the saints; but either their health is ailing and uncertain, or they have not the courage to do penance, or, which is most common of all, their health and courage both are wanting. We need a treatise on perfection for valetudinarians. People in ailing health can do both more and less than those in a downright illness; and the more and the less need distinguishing and explaining.

Now, if such persons are really honest with themselves, they should look out for penances that neither give them bodily pain they cannot bear, nor interfere with their infirmities. It is plain that to be scrupulous about the use of our time is just such a penance as this. We can promise God that we will never willingly waste our time in occupations by which we cannot merit. Now, this resolution is by no means easy to keep in these days; it will often be felt as a yoke, interfering with our natural liberty. Yet if we keep it, we shall really be doing penance, and at the same time reaping an immense harvest for the glory of God, the interests of Jesus, and the good of souls.

∞

Grow holy even through play

This does not by any means forbid recreations. You may remember the story of St. Charles Borromeo[122] and his game of

[122] St. Charles Borromeo (1538-1584), Archbishop of Milan.

chess. When others were saying what they would forthwith begin to do if they knew they would die within an hour, the saint said he would go on with his chess, for he had begun it simply for God's glory, and he desired nothing better than to be called away in the midst of an action begun for the glory of God.

It is easy to merit at play, for almost all pastimes are full of opportunities for the practice of virtues. But it is not easy to merit my idling about, by purposeless lounging, by wishing the time away and voting things a bore, and by many kinds of frivolous, gossiping conversation. Religious people are, for the most part, not so scrupulous about the use of their time as they should be; yet, surely if, as we believe, St. Charles is a degree higher in Heaven for his game of chess, it is a sad thing to miss so many opportunities of meriting, and so many occasions of advancing the interests of Jesus.

∞

Use your time to gain merit

Really, the exact use of our time might almost be to many of us an index of the coolness or the fervor of our love. If an active practical man were allowed a certain number of hours in a rich gold-digging, where the dirt was cleared away and there was nothing to do but to pick out the pure ore, he would think a man mad who would suggest to him to suspend his toil, unless fatigue really compelled him to do so. And this is just our case with the ordinary actions of our life, and even with our recreations. The real toil has been done by our blessed Lord; the stones and the mud were His share. For us there is nothing left, if we choose, but the precious ore; and the hours for our gold-digging are numbered, and we know not how near death we are.

Alas, we shall never know the value of time, until it has slipped from us and left us in eternity. *Dearest Lord, will it leave us with Thee?*

St. Gertrude once told our Lord that she wished to build Him a spiritual ark, and she asked Him how she was to do it. He answered her as follows: "It is commonly said among you that the ark of Noah had three stories, and that the birds were in the upper one, men in the middle, and the beasts below. Now, take this for your model, and divide all your days upon this plan. From early morning to the hour of noon, you shall offer me praises and thanks on behalf of the whole Church, with the warmest affection, for all the benefits I have ever conferred on men since creation, and especially for that adorable compassion which causes me to let myself be sacrificed on the altar in the Holy Mass . . . to the eternal Father for men's salvation. While men make light of all this, and give themselves to pleasure and feasting, ungratefully forgetful of me, do you in their stead, offer me continual praises, and so will you seem to catch the volatile birds, and shut them up in the higher chamber of the ark.

"From noon to evening, be zealous daily to exercise yourself devoutly in good works, in union with the most holy intention wherewith all the works of my sacred humanity were done, to make up for the negligences of the rest of the world. And this will be to congregate men in the middle chamber of the ark.

"From evening to dawn . . . protest against men's impiety, whereby they not only refuse me gratitude for what I have done, but provoke me to anger by all manner of sins. And offer for their repentance the pain and bitterness of my most innocent Passion and death, and thus will you gather the beasts into the lower chamber of the ark." Yet, while our dear Lord thus traced out for St. Gertrude the way in which she was to spend her day, He knew of all her toils and cares, and that by obedience to her rule, she must, with her spiritual daughters, take her daily recreations, as well as discharge the minute duties of monastic government.

∞

Offer up your solitude for a holy death

There is another and most profitable practice: to do for your solitude what you do for your occupations. When you are alone, or awake in the night, offer up your solitude in union with the solitude of Jesus in the sepulcher and in the tabernacle. And do this to impetrate for yourself and for those you love the grace of a good death: that you may die in the grace of God, and with great merit, so as to glorify God all the more in Heaven, and having had great fruit in helping to save the souls for whom Christ died and was buried; that you may die without fame and glory, as Jesus died without honor between two thieves; that you may die without any obligation of going to Purgatory, and leaving behind you a great treasure of satisfactions that you do not need yourself and which can be added to the treasures out of which the Church grants indulgences; and that you may glorify God on earth even when you are dead, by the memory of your good works, by salutary advices given, or devout books written, or the abiding fruit of your prayers.

∞

Let all things remind you of God

Through the practice of oblation, we can merit by the commonest things, if we are in a state of grace. Every time we merit, we give God a distinct glory, the interests of Jesus a distinct advancement, and the souls of men almost innumerable benefits through the Communion of Saints.

Now, here is another way of meriting by common things: rising to God by the sight of creatures. This, as you know, has been one of the commonest and most fervent practices of the saints. Lancisius says, "You go out of your house, and you see some people talking; pray that they may say no idle words for which they will have to give account. You hear the howling of the wind; pray for those who are at sea. You pass by a tavern and hear the noise of those within; pray that they may not offend God, and that those who have done so may go to Confession."

When St. Athanasius sent for St. Pambo[123] to leave the desert and come to Alexandria, the holy abbot saw a gaily dressed actress in the streets, whereupon he began to weep. When he was asked why he did so, he answered, "Two things move me; one is the damnation of that woman; and another is that I do not take as much pains to please God as she does to please wicked men." You see, even sinful things were steps to God for him.

When you hear the pattering of the rain, thank God for it, and desire to offer Him as many good acts of faith, hope, charity, contrition, thanksgiving, humility, adoration, and petition as there are drops in that shower. Ask for the continual influx of the helps of grace in good measure, heaped up, shaken together, and running over,[124] by which you and others may always act in the most perfect manner, and glorify God in the greatest possible degree.

When you pass any village or town, or the house of some great man, ask God, by the merits of those who dwell there, to have mercy upon you; give Him thanks for all His blessings, past, present, and future, on the inhabitants; commend to Him all their necessities, and beg Him to hear their prayers; grieve for all the sins committed there, and ask for the remission of them; commend to God the souls of those departed there.

Surius tells us, in the life of St. Fulgentius, that when the saint went to Rome, and beheld all the palaces of the nobility, he cried

[123] St. Pambo (d. c. 390), one of the founders of the Nitrian group of monasteries in Egypt.

[124] Cf. Luke 6:38.

out, "How beautiful must be the heavenly Jerusalem, if the earthly Rome shines thus! And if such dignity is given in this world to those who love vanity, what must be the glory of the saints who contemplate the truth!"

St. Paul of the Cross[125] was passing through the wood of Fossanova, and having come into a thicket, he began to cry out to his companion impetuously, "Oh, do you not hear how these trees and leaves are crying out, 'Love God, love God'? And then kindling more and more with divine love, his face began to dart out bright rays, and he kept exclaiming, "Oh, how is it you do not love God? How is it you do not love God?" And when they had gotten back again onto the Roman road, he said to everyone he met, "My brother, love God, love God, who deserves it so much! Do you not hear the very leaves of the trees crying out to us to love God? O love of God! Love of God!" And he spoke with such unction that the passersby burst into tears.

We read of him in another place that everything served to remind him of God, and he used to imagine that all creatures cried out to entreat the love of man for Him who made them. He was often observed, when walking in the fields, to gaze earnestly at the flowers as he went along and to touch them with his stick, saying, "Hold your tongues; hold your tongues!" And he used to tell his religious that the flowers were always calling upon them to lift up their hearts in love and adoration toward their heavenly Creator.

∞

Do not overburden yourself with devotions

There is a great difference between having a variety of mental devotions and loading ourselves with an indiscreet number of

[125] St. Paul of the Cross (1694-1775), founder of the Passionists.

vocal prayers; and what spiritual writers say of the one case does not always apply equally to the other. Yet, there is no mistake more common than to confound the two.

Now, the loading of ourselves with an immense number of vocal prayers is not always (for there is no *always* in spiritual science, except where sin is in question), but almost always, a simple evil. How many are there who began their fight well, but soon grew weak and weary on the wing, and at last fell to the earth, entangled in litanies, overloaded with *Memorares*,[126] encumbered with Rosaries, or helplessly pinioned by the obligations of a score of Third Orders and Confraternities! They have ruined themselves with holy things.

Having a great variety of mental devotions may often be an evil, but it is a different thing from this; and the unqualified censure that some rigorous authors pass upon all such variety is certainly not in keeping either with the practice of the saints, or with milder teaching of their works. There is nothing a man so soon becomes attached to as a system of spiritual direction, and so completely does his own one favorite way seem to him the sole safe way, that he can hardly realize the diversity of God's operations, or give the Holy Spirit liberty in the hearts of those whom he is training.

We know well enough that solid mortification and persevering self-abjection are the real roads to the highest sanctity; but are

[126] "Remember, O most gracious Virgin Mary, that never was it known that anyone who fled to thy protection, implored thy help, or sought thy intercession was left unaided. Inspired with this confidence, I fly unto thee, O Virgin of virgins, my Mother. To thee I come, before thee I stand, sinful and sorrowful. O Mother of the Word Incarnate, despise not my petitions, but in thy mercy, hear and answer me."

persons to sit down weeping by the low wayside of the most ordinary attainments, unless they have the heart to scale the rugged heights? Are there no other paths of love that lie higher on the mountain breast, above the plain, although lower far than those ambitious pinnacles? Ah, how many are sent low, held low, and forced lower, by being unwisely forced too high! "A good superior," said St. Jane Frances de Chantal,[127] "must learn to fly low as well as to fly high"; and the first is a harder duty than the last; for, mark the words, it is not to be low, or to rest low, but to fly low.

Now, it may be quite true that the shortest and most direct road to high sanctity is found in keeping to one thing, one subject of meditation, one exercise of devotion, and that this painful unity should be kept up for some years without a change, as a celebrated writer recommends. Yet who is sufficient for these things? How are people in the world to do these things without the helps of a religious house, with no novitiate, no set penances in community, but with a thousand necessary distracting duties, and the unavoidable diversions of social interchange? Yet they have a call to love; they will not be kept down. They must either have a process for withering their souls, or they must fill them with the dews of Heaven.

Hence it is we so often see those spiritual anomalies of a devout life, half filled with the practices of the demure cloister, and half with the appurtenances of a London season. And what comes of these fitful vagaries? Unhappiness, failure, and vehement self-abandonment to worldly pleasures, as if in revenge for past strictness, and a lower lowness of the Christian life, which I hardly like to think of. Anything can come of these experiments except high sanctity, or low sanctity either. They result in no sanctity at all.

[127] St. Jane Frances de Chantal (1572-1641), foundress of the Visitation Order.

See how God is calling souls, and lead them by the gentlest and most winning ways, unless there is a clear vocation to the hard and rough. Many are lost, because they are forced too high, and many more, because they are made to fear sensible devotion, and to believe that dryness is solidity. Oh, do anything, I beseech you, rather than tire people of their good, compassionate God! Rather, interest them in Him, if you can, and all you can.

∞

Make use of brief, spontaneous prayers

Another method of glorifying God by little and common things is the practice of saying brief, spontaneous prayers. St. Francis de Sales says, "The great fabric of devotion leans upon this exercise, which can supply the defects of all other prayers, and all other prayers cannot supply the defect of it."

When Fr. Brandano was going to Portugal, he asked St. Ignatius in what devotions the scholastics of society were to be exercised. The saint replied that besides the usual formal devotions, they were to exercise themselves in seeking our Lord's presence in all things, in talking, walking, looking about them, listening, thinking, and everything, as it is certain that the Divine Majesty is in all things in at least three ways: by essence, presence, and power. He said that this exercise of finding God in everything is less laborious than meditations on abstract matters, and causes God to visit us in wonderful ways, even for one brief prayer.

Thus we may sigh for God's glory, send up to Heaven one arrow-like word about the interests of Jesus in the streets of our city, or breathe a little prayer for souls, wherever we are. Without any constraint, we may make scores of them in a day; and each one is more to God than a battle gained, or a scientific discovery, or a crystal palace, or a change of ministry, or a political revolution.

Many such brief prayers are indulgenced, and thus the same little brief sentence will gain merit, impetrate grace, satisfy for sin, glorify God, honor Jesus and His Mother, convert sinners, and soothe with substantial indulgence the holy souls in Purgatory.

But in order to attain all these ends, it is not enough that these prayers should be uttered in a slovenly, offhand way, or without an inward attention.

Can we do nothing more for Jesus in this respect than we have done hitherto? O *Love! Love! You yourself must tell us, and teach us how, and remind us when we forget.*

∞

See how God longs for your love

It is as good to repent that we may thus offer, in union with the merits of our dear Lord, and all those sublime supernatural treasures that we considered in the last chapter, not only our ordinary actions, but everything also that happens to us. Every one of our little sufferings, pains, contradictions, and our weariness may thus be made missionaries to spread the Faith, apostles to convert sinners, and angels to praise the majesty of God. Our little mortifications, too, few and cowardly as they may be, with the stripes and thorns, the lance and the nails touching them, can draw the Heart of Jesus toward us and others with tremendous power. The grace we have received during the day may be doubled by being offered up at night in union with His grace from whom ours came. Thus does Jesus help us to love Him; thus does He make us kings and priests already.

If we truly mourn because He is offended, if we truly thirst after the glory of our merciful Father, if we are touched with pity for poor, graceless, or tempted souls, see what marvels we can do without so much as turning out of our way, or distracting ourselves from our business, or even, so our dear Lord has contrived, omitting our pastimes and recreations.

Verily, all things are meant for Jesus; and when we see what we can do, and, alas, what we have not done, we may begin to think that there is no corner of earth where the harvest of God's glory is scantier or less thriving than in our own poor hearts.

Is there not a myth of someone who turned to gold whatever he touched, and was soon embarrassed by his marvelous gift? This is our case under the Gospel, under the law of grace. All we touch turns to gold, by intention or oblation. Yet our gift need never embarrass us. We shall never fill God with glory, nor Heaven with merits. But it will be a sad thing at the end of life to look back upon the millions of wasted opportunities.

But, someone may say, how are we to note them, and to remember them now, as they come before us in such multitudes, and so incessantly? I answer, not by any rule that can be given, nor by any formal method that can be devised. You must love. There is no other way. There is no help for it. Love will teach you everything and tell you the secrets of Jesus. Love will make things easy and sweet. Love will be a new nature to you. There is nothing you want that love will not do for you, or get for you, and nothing else but love can do it. You must love.

I wish we could really see and feel what it is to be allowed to please God. If we saved the life of the queen's child, we would not easily forget the grateful look of the royal mother's face; it would be long before her burning words of thanks died away in our ears; a sovereign's tears, and those tears of joy, are not things to be readily forgotten. But what a very unimportant thing this is compared with being allowed — were it but once in our lives — to please God! The thought really grows upon us until it overshadows our spirits.

Think what we are, our origin, our rebellion, our natural infirmities, our personal vileness, our horrible guilt, our despicable unloveliness. And then there is God — the invisible, all-holy, incomprehensible God — and He stoops to be pleased with us. He longs for us to try to please Him, and He contrives all nature so that by grace we may please Him more, and He gives us numerous supernatural ways and powers of pleasing Him! The immensity of this condescension is simply inexpressible. Oh, that our dearest Lord would enlarge our hearts, that we might take it in!

But why talk of taking in one of His condescensions? Why, He makes our hearts large enough to take Him in — Body, Blood, Soul, and Divinity! Thus our thoughts run off to another condescension, another love. This is always the way: one tops another. There is no end; climb one height, and there are higher heights. And all is love!

Dear God! St. Gertrude said we might call Him so, and what else can we call Him? Oh, why do we not love Him? Most dear God! So dear beyond word or thought!

If we think of these three things — God, ourselves, and the supernaturalness of the system in which we are — we shall surely at length come to see that the capabilities that we, who are neither saints, nor like saints, nor in sight of being saints, have of glorifying God are positively awful and frightening.

First, if we unite our actions with those of Jesus, they gain almost an infinite value. What we have to offer to God is something like infinite. Nay, we can offer Jesus, who is infinite. We can offer God His Equal — and that in everything we do, say, think, or suffer.

Next, consider the multiplicity of our actions. There is no reckoning them. They run ahead of our figures almost at once. Two men are advised to get up early in the morning to make half an hour's meditation. One does, and the other does not. The one who does merits, and so glorifies God more, unspeakably more than all physical science or art unions have glorified Him since the Flood, by the mortification of rising early; by his modesty in dressing; by his act of the presence of God; by his Sign of the Cross; by his preparatory prayers; by his meditations; by the penance of his posture, weariness or distraction; by his resolutions at the end; by each prayer all through it; and by the obedience of the whole duty. It would be more correct to say that each of these ten merits were bundles of many merits. But put them at ten. This one little practice would give the following results: in each year, he would glorify God 3,650 times by that one action, and each of these times he would please God. And to be allowed to do so once in all eternity would be an unspeakable condescension, and each time he would glorify Him more than all physical science has ever done, because he would glorify Him supernaturally.

After the multiplicity of our actions, consider the ease of this devotion of offering them up to God in union with the merits of His Son. One glance at Jesus, and it is done. No word, sigh, or train of thought is needed. Love looks to Jesus, and all is accomplished.

Then remember, each merit implies a new degree of grace, and each degree of grace a corresponding degree of eternal glory, if we die with the gift of perseverance. Eye has not seen, nor ear heard, nor heart conceived one single degree of beatific glory;[128] and then we have to multiply all this millions and millions of times.

And if we fell into deadly sin, and then had the grace to ask — just to ask contritely, and in our Lord's own easy way — for the Precious Blood, Jesus thinks it nothing merely to forgive us, but He must also put back to our account all this formidable sum of

[128] Cf. 1 Cor. 2:9.

merits. So passionately does He long to have us with Him in Heaven forever!

And yet there are such things as lukewarm Catholics!

My Jesus, how patiently Thou bearest with them! Thou hast covered the whole earth with a net of love, which Thou hast been busily devising from all eternity! We break it all to pieces, and what dost Thou do, sweetest, dearest, kindest Lord? Thou settest to work with the most unconquerable love to net a new one of merciful precept and cheerful fear, and catchest in that the foolish souls who would not be caught by love!

Oh, how sweet it is to be saved by Jesus! It seems as if it were better than if we had never fallen. It is such a joy to owe everything to Jesus. Such a joy not to be able to do without Him for one moment! Such a joy to find Him everywhere, and always to find Him laying us under new obligations, and binding us with fresh chains of love! Oh, that we were bound so fast to Him that we could never get loose from Him!

But this is the heavenliness of Purgatory, that we are His, His own, His very own, unalterably, forever! Surely Adam's nine hundred years of penance among the brambles of the lonely world would be worth living, if only we might be allowed to make one heart love Jesus a single degree more! And yet here we are in His blessed Church, where the beginning, middle, and end of our whole religion is that all things are ours, and we are Christ's, and Christ is God's!

If there is one thing more inexpressibly touching than another, it is God, the Everlasting Holiness, begging glory of His creatures on His own earth. It is like a father suffering martyrdom for his guilty child. And then to see Him, the suppliant Creator, the almighty Mendicant, refused the alms He asks! Does it not make us wild — wild with love? And who refuses Him so often as we? Alas, who will give to our eyes rivers of tears to weep day and night for this? Verily it is more inconceivable that men should not love God than that there should be Three Persons in One God! And yet, what can be more winning than God, or more fatherly than God? He asks glory of us, such as we are! Why do we not love Him? What more can He do? He asked that Himself ages ago: "What can I do that I have not done?" Yes, what can He do more?

Oh, look children of God, look! He is in His own world, behaving and arranging all — blessed be His most dear majesty — as if we, not He, were the final cause of all creation!

Chapter Seven

Offer thanks to God

It is plain that what has been insisted upon in the foregoing chapters comes to this: the Gospel being altogether a law of love, it is not enough simply to save our own souls; or to be more accurate, it is very much against our saving our own souls, if we do not try to do something for the souls of others, whether by action or by prayer. And furthermore, the Gospel being a law of love, our religion must be as much as possible a service of love, and consequently we run a great risk of being lost if we treat this life as simply an opportunity of getting to Heaven on the easiest terms and by the barest observance of necessary precepts, putting aside the glory of God, the interests of Jesus, and the saving of souls as things that do not concern us.

I have not asked much of you. I have not put before you either bodily austerities or retirement from the world. I have not told you to aim at heights of supernatural prayer, or at the love of suffering, or at any difficult lifelong strain after interior recollection and the sensible presence of God. I have done no more than put before you practices and counsels of the saints by which you may occupy yourselves more with God, and do so easily and lovingly. I have not even said, "You shall at least do so much as this," or, "This you must certainly not omit." I have left it to you and to your own love. I am not making rules; I would fain persuade someone — one would be enough — to love God a little more for His own dear sake.

And the order of my subject naturally leads me now to the subject of thanksgiving. We have seen that in order to practice intercession, our blessed Lord, in His unspeakable love, first gives us all His own treasures so that we may offer them back to Him with amazing efficacy, and then, besides that, He allows us to make our own most trivial actions almost infinite by uniting them to His merits and intentions. But these two things are not available for intercession only; they serve equally for thanksgiving and for praise and desire.

I will speak in this chapter of thanksgiving; and then praise and desire in the next.

Do not neglect to thank God

If we had to name any one thing that seems unaccountably to have fallen out of most men's practical religion altogether, it would be the duty of thanksgiving. It would not be easy to exaggerate the common neglect of this duty. There is little enough of prayer, but there is still less thanksgiving. For every million Our Fathers and Hail Marys that rise up from earth to avert evils or to ask graces, how many do you suppose are followed by thanksgiving for the evils averted or the graces given?

Alas, it is not hard to find the reason for this. Our own interests drive us obviously to prayer, but it is love alone which leads to thanksgiving. A man who wants only to avoid Hell knows that he must pray; he has no such strong instinct impelling him to thanksgiving. It is the old story.

Never did prayer come more from the heart than the piteous cry of those ten lepers who beheld Jesus entering into a town. Their desire to be heard made them courteous and considerate. They stood afar off, lest He should be angry if they with their foul disease came too near Him. Alas, they did not truly know that dear Lord, nor how He had lowered Himself to be counted as a leper for the sons of men. They lifted up their voice, saying, "Jesus, Master, have mercy on us." When the miracle was wrought, the nine went on in selfish joy to show themselves to the priest; but one, one only, and he an outcast Samaritan, when he saw that he was made clean, went back, with a loud voice glorifying God, and he fell on his face before our Savior's feet, giving thanks. Even the Sacred Heart of Jesus was distressed and, as it were, astonished, and He said, "Were not ten made clean? And where are the nine? There is no one found to return and give glory to God, but this stranger?"[129]

How many a time have we not caused the same sad surprise to the Sacred Heart!

When the neglect of a duty is so shocking as is surely the neglect of thanksgiving, it is desirable to show the amount of obligation that rests upon us in the matter; and this can best be done by the authority of Scripture. St. Paul tells the Ephesians that we are to be "giving thanks always for all things, in the name of our Lord Jesus Christ, to God and the Father."[130] Again, we are "to abound unto all simplicity, which worketh through us thanksgiving to God."[131] The Philippians are admonished, "Be not solicitous; but in everything, by prayer and supplication with thanksgiving, let

[129] Luke 17:12-18.

[130] Eph. 5:20.

[131] 2 Cor. 9:11.

your petitions be made known to God."[132] To the Colossians, the apostle says, "As ye have received Jesus Christ the Lord, walk ye in Him, rooted and built up in Him, and confirmed in the faith, as also you have learned, abounding in Him with thanksgiving."[133] Again, "Be instant in prayer, watching in it in thanksgiving."[134] Creatures are said to be created to be received with thanksgiving by the faithful and by them who have known the truth; "for every creature of God is good, and nothing to be rejected, that is received with thanksgiving."[135] And it was the very characteristic of heathen that "when they knew God, they glorified Him not as God, nor gave thanks."[136]

∞

Prepare for Heaven by offering thanks

What is our life on earth but a preparation for our real life in Heaven? And yet praise and thanksgiving are the very occupations of our life in Heaven. What is the language of the angels, ancients, and living creatures of the book of Revelation, but, "Amen! Benediction and glory, and wisdom, and thanksgiving, honor and power, and strength to our God forever and ever. Amen"?[137]

We are constantly invoking our Blessed Lady, the angels, and the saints, and we know and are sure that they are always praying for us in Heaven; yet am I not right in saying that when we make pictures of Heaven in our own minds, it is not so often prayer we

[132] Cf. Phil. 4:6.

[133] Col. 2:6-7.

[134] Col. 4:2.

[135] 1 Tim. 4:4.

[136] Rom. 1:21.

[137] Apoc. 7:12 (RSV = Rev. 7:12).

picture, as praise and thanksgiving? Nay, sometimes when death has been at hand, the life of Heaven has cast its light forward over God's servants; they have seemed almost to forget prayer, and, as if they were already in hearing of the angelic songs, and had caught the note, they occupy with thanksgiving those awful hours that most of all in life seem to need petition and struggling prayer.

Thus, when St. Paul of the Cross was lying dangerously ill, he passed his days in the utterance of thanksgiving and praise, often repeating with particular devotion those words from the *Gloria:* "We give thanks to Thee for Thy great glory!" This had always been his favorite short prayer, and he had frequently exhorted his religious to use it whenever they had any particular undertaking in hand, saying, with particular earnestness, "For the great glory of God."

Now, the Church on earth reflects the Church in Heaven; the worship of the one is the echo of the worship of the other. If the life in Heaven is one of praise and thanksgiving, so, in its measure, must be the life on earth. The very center of all our worship is the Eucharist; that is, as the word imports, a sacrifice of thanksgiving. Everything catches its tone from this. Everything in the Church radiates out from the Blessed Sacrament. The spirit of the Eucharist must be found everywhere.

Let us suppose that the true idea of worship was the one implied in the common practice of most men; that it was simply a matter of prayer to a superior Being. What relation does this put us in with God? He is our King, our Superior, a keeper of treasures, Himself infinite wealth. We go to Him to ask for something. He is to us what a rich man is to a beggar. Our own interest is the prominent part of the matter. Or we are afraid of justice. We desire to be let off our punishment and have our sins forgiven. He is compassionate and will hear us if we are importunate.

Taking prayer only as the whole of worship, we can rise no higher than this. It is all very true, and very necessary besides. Prayer can teach us to depend on God, and answered prayer to trust in Him. But Infinite Goodness will not let us rest on such terms with Him. We are to be with Him to all eternity; He is to be our everlasting joy; to know Him and to love Him is life; and love of Him is the joyful praise of Him forever.

Let thanksgiving lead you closer to God

As the spirit of oblation — the permission to make God presents — at once brings in a dearer and more familiar relation with God, so also does the spirit of thanksgiving. To thank a benefactor simply to get more from him is not thanksgiving, but a flattering form of petition. We thank God because we love Him, because His love of us touches us, surprises us, melts us, and wins us. Indeed, so much is thanksgiving a matter of love, that we shall thank Him most of all in Heaven, when He has given us His crowning gift of the Beatific Vision; when He has given us all of Himself we can contain, and so there is nothing left for us to receive. Thanksgiving is, therefore, of the very essence of Catholic worship; and as the practice of it increases our love, so does the neglect of it betoken how little love we have.

Ah, if we have reason to pity God — if we may dare so to speak with St. Alphonsus — because men sin against His loving majesty, still more reason have we to do so when we see how scanty and how cold are the thanksgivings offered up to Him. Nothing is so odious among men as ingratitude, yet it is the daily and hourly portion of Almighty God. There is no telling what He has done for men; there is no exhausting the mines of His abundant mercy implied by each one of his titles: Creator, King, Redeemer, Father,

Shepherd. He loves to be thanked, because all He wants of us is love, and that He should please to want it is itself an infinite act of love. He had chosen to put His glory upon our gratitude; and yet we will not give it to Him!

What is worst of all, this affront does not come, like open sin, from those who are His enemies, and in whose conversion His compassion can gain such glory among men; but it comes from His own people, from those who frequent the sacraments and make a profession of piety, from those whom He is daily loading with the special and intimate gifts of His Holy Spirit. Many of us are shocked with sin and sacrilege; scandal makes us smart; heresy is positive suffering, a pungent bitterness, like smoke in our eyes. It is well. Yet we, too, go on refusing God His glory by our neglect of thanksgiving. We could glorify Him so chiefly, and yet it hardly comes into our thoughts. Can we then be said to love Him truly and really?

What have we to do — how often shall I say it? To love God, and to get Him glory. God forbid we should so much as dream that we had anything else to do. Let us, then, go about the world seeking these neglected pearls of our heavenly Father's glory and offering them to Him. How is it that we have the heart to wish to do anything but this? Some of His servants have even desired not to die, so that they might stay on earth to glorify Him by more suffering. Such wishes are not for us; but they may do us good, for they help to show us how little love we have. And I must think that to find this out is everything. I can believe that men are deceived and think they love God when they do not love Him, or that they wish to love Him and do not know how. But can anyone know how little he loves God, and how easily he can love Him more, and not wish to do so? Jesus died to prevent the possibility of this, and can He have died in vain?

We do not find fault with sinners who are living out of the grace of God, and away from the sacraments, because they do not make thanksgiving. They have something else to do. They have to do penance, and reconcile themselves with God, and wash their souls afresh in the Precious Blood of Jesus. The neglect of thanksgiving is an ingratitude that our dear Lord has to impute to His own forgiven children, who are living in His peace, and in the enjoyment of all His privileges.

Now, this deserves to be especially noted. I do not know if you will agree with me, but, to my mind, the faults of good people — I do not mean slips and infirmities, but cold, heartless faults — have something specially odious about them. A sin is not so shocking a thing to look at, for all its intrinsic deadliness; and this may be the reason why, in the book of Revelation, God breaks out with such unusual and vivid language about lukewarmness and tepidity.[138] When the angels asked our Lord as He ascended, "What are those wounds in Thy hands?" how much is insinuated in His reply: "The wounds wherewith I was wounded in the house of my friends!"[139]

See the many ways God reveals Himself to you

The Bible is a revelation of love, but it is not the only one. There is to each one of us a special and personal revelation of divine love in the retrospect of that fatherly Providence that has watched over us through our lives. Who can look back on the long chain of graces of which his life has been composed since the hour

[138] Cf. Apoc. 3:16 (RSV = Rev. 3:16).

[139] Cf. Zech. 13:6.

of his Baptism, without a feeling of surprise at the unweariedness and minuteness of God's love? Consider the way in which things have been arranged for his happiness or his welfare, obstacles disappearing as he drew nigh to them — and, just when they seemed most insurmountable — temptations turning to good, and what seemed chastisements as he faced them, changing to love when he looked back upon them. Each sorrow has found its place in his life, and he would have been a loser if he had been without it. Chance acquaintances have had their meaning and done their work; and somehow it seems as if foreseeing love itself could not have woven his web of life differently from what it is, even if it had woven it of love alone.

He did not feel it at the time. He did not know God was so much with him, for what is more unostentatious than a Father's love? When Jacob made his pillow of the cold stones and lay down to sleep, where he had his vision of the ladder, he saw nothing uncommon in the place; but when he awoke out of sleep, he said, "Indeed, the Lord is in this place, and I knew it not."[140] When Moses desired to see God, the Lord set him in a hole of the rock, and protected him with his right hand while His intolerable glory was passing by, and he said, "I will take away my hand, and thou shalt see my back; but my face thou canst not see."[141]

This is ever God's way. He is with us, tender, loving, considerate, and forgiving. Our hearts burn within us, as did the hearts of the two disciples as they walked and talked with Jesus on the road to Emmaus; but it is not until He vanishes from our sight that we know of a truth that it was our dear Lord Himself.[142]

[140] Gen. 28:16.

[141] Exod. 33:23.

[142] Cf. Luke 24:31.

Thus it is that we can come to know God only by meditation. We must ponder things as Mary did. We must muse and be pensive as Isaac was. We must treasure up God's mercies, and make much of them, and set store by them, as did Jacob and David. Jacob was always looking back on his adventurous life; God was to him the God of Bethel, the God of Abraham, the Fear of Isaac. And what is David's reproach to his people but that "they forgot God who had . . . done great things in Egypt, wondrous works in the land of Cham, and terrible things in the Red Sea?"[143]

The blessings that we know of are more than enough to kindle the most fervent love. And yet we shall never know the half until the day of judgment. Who are we that God should have been thus legislating for us, and laying Himself out to please us? Has He had no world to govern? Has He had no creatures but our own poor selves, or none wiser, holier, or lovelier?

And yet we tease ourselves about predestination and eternal punishment. We reason harshly about what we cannot alter and do not understand. I must think this is most unreasonable. For look how the case stands. We know an immense deal about God, yet little or nothing beyond what He has been pleased Himself to reveal to us. Hence, when we argue against Him, our arguments are in reality founded, not so much upon what we see, as upon what He has been so good as to tell us about Himself.

Now, here we ought to observe — and people for the most part do not observe it — that God has chiefly illuminated for us His mercy and condescension. His severity is the dark side of His most dread majesty, not only because of its fearfulness, but also because He has told us so little about it. When love is in question, He has been copious, explicit, and minute. He explains, He repeats, He

[143] Ps. 105:21-22 (RSV = Ps. 106:21-22).

gives reasons, He argues, He persuades, He complains, He invites, He allures, and He magnifies. Of His rigor He drops but a word now and then. He puts it out as fact and leaves it. He startles by an abrupt disclosure, but as He startled only out of love, He is at no pains to explain, to soften, and to harmonize. Nay, the startling expressions about His judgments are outbursts from His astonished creatures — Job, Peter, or Paul — than revelations from Himself.

This very fact is itself a fresh instance of His love. Can we not take the hint that His merciful wisdom vouchsafes to give us by this method of proceeding? As we see but one side of the moon, so we see but one side of God; and what can we know of what we do not see? There is no end to the variety of the disclosures of His goodness, the inventions of His compassion, and the strangeness of His yearning over His own creatures.

He has striven to fix our gaze upon these, but we will not have it so. We are busiest with what He wishes us to think least of. And we neglect to ponder all those numberless signs of our heavenly Father's love, which are personal things between Him and us; positive and sensible touches of His unutterable affection! Oh, while God is turning everything to love, and contriving everything for love, how perversely are we trying to thwart His tenderness and long-suffering!

Consider what it is to be blessed by God. Put yourself into the scales, and weigh yourself against Him; and then see what it is to be thought of by Him, to occupy His attention, to try His patience, to call out His love! Truly, the very thought of God is a bed on which we can lie down and rest whenever we choose. The remembrance of His uncontrolled sovereignty is a joy to us greater than the vision of an angel, brighter than Mary's face, even when it shall smile its "Welcome to Heaven" on our purified and forgiven souls. That He is such a God as He is, is more, far more than rest; it is joy and bliss. That He has loved us with an eternal love, and is our own dearest Father, is joy that has no name. It is Heaven begun already upon earth!

Is it not, then, one of the wonders of the world that there should be so little thanksgiving, a greater wonder even than that there should be so little prayer, and almost as great a wonder as that God should love us so unutterably?

Let thanksgiving prepare your soul to receive blessings

A spirit of thanksgiving has been in all ages the characteristic of the saints. Thanksgiving has been their favorite prayer; and when their love has been grieved because men were unthankful, they have called on the animals, and even on inanimate creatures, to bless God for His goodness.

St. Lawrence Justinian has a beautiful passage on thanksgiving in his *Treatise on Obedience*: "Whosoever shall try to lay open all God's blessings to the full, would be like a man trying to confine in a little vase the mighty currents of the wide ocean; for that were an easier work than to publish with human eloquence the innumerable gifts of God. Yet although these are unspeakable from their multitude, their magnitude, and their incomprehensibility, they are by no means to be concealed in silence, or left without commemoration, even though it be impossible to commemorate them adequately. They are to be confessed with the mouth, revered in the heart, and religiously worshiped, as far as the littleness of man can do so. For although we cannot explain them in words, we can make acknowledgment of them in the pious and enlarged affection of our hearts. Indeed, the immense mercy of our eternal

Creator condescends to approve not only what man can do, but what he would desire to do; for the merits of the just are counted up by the Most High, not only in the doing of the work, but in the desire of the will."[144]

In one of the revelations of St. Catherine of Siena, God the Father tells her that thanksgiving makes the soul incessantly delight in Him, that it frees men from negligence and lukewarmness altogether, and makes them eager to please Him more and more in all things.

Our Lord gives the increase of thanksgiving as a reason to St. Bridget for the Sacrifice of the Mass. "My Body," says He, "is daily immolated on the altar, so that men may love me so much the more, and more frequently try to call to mind my blessings."

"Happy is he," says St. Bernard, "who, at every grace he receives, returns in thought to Him in whom is the fullness of all graces; for if we show ourselves not ungrateful for what He has given us, we may make room for still further graces in ourselves." And in another place he says, "Speak to God in thanksgiving, and you will get graces more and more abundantly." So St. Lawrence Justinian says, "Only let God see you are thankful for what He has given you, and He will bestow more upon you, and better gifts." St. Mary Magdalene de' Pazzi also received a revelation in which she was told that thanksgiving prepared the soul for the boundless liberality of the Eternal Word.

Now stop, dear reader, and meditate for a few minutes on the Eternal Word; remember which of the Three Divine Persons He is: the Second Person, the eternally begotten Word of the Father, the splendor of His Majesty, uncreated Wisdom, the same Person who was incarnate and crucified for us, the same who sent us the

[144] Ch. 28.

Holy Spirit, who gave us Mary, who gives us Himself in the Blessed Sacrament, in whose mind revolve at this moment the countless lusters of all possible creations. Then think what His liberalities must be — no bound or measure to them. We cannot count their number, nor exhaust their freshness, nor understand their excellence, nor hold their fullness, nor give intelligible human names to their kinds, inventions, varieties, and wonders.

Oh, that we had more especial devotion to the Person of the Eternal Word, that we would read the wonders the Church can tell us about Him, and then meditate and make acts of love on what we read! This is the true way to increase our devotion to His most dear humanity, and to learn how to watch at His crib, to weep over His Cross, to worship at His tabernacle, and to nestle in His Sacred Heart. Ask St. Michael, St. John the Evangelist, and St. Athanasius to get you this devotion; they have a specialty for it; and see how you will run the way of God, when its heat has made a furnace of your heart.

And then remember that He Himself has told us, through this revelation to His servant, that thanksgiving prepares the soul for His amazing liberalities. You see, you must begin this day and hour quite a new and more royal sort of thanksgiving than those mere infrequent, formal, respectful civilities by which you have heretofore been content to acknowledge your cumulated obligations to our dearest Lord. Now, promise Him this, and then with a more fervent heart read on.

St. Bonaventure, or rather the author of the meditations on the life of Christ, tells us that our Blessed Lady gave thanks to God without intermission, and lest in common greetings she should be distracted from the praises of God, she used to reply, when anyone saluted her, "Thanks be to God!" And from her example, several saints have adopted the same practice.

There was a beautiful tradition among the Jews that Lancisius quotes from Philo.[145] When God had created the world, He asked the angels what they thought of this work of His hands. One of them replied that it was so vast and so perfect that only one thing was wanting to it — namely, that there should be created a clear, mighty, and harmonious voice that should fill all the quarters of the world incessantly with its sweet sound; thus day and night to offer thanksgiving to its Maker for His incomparable blessings. Ah, they knew not how much more than that the Blessed Sacrament was one day to be! Thus our thanksgiving should not be an exercise of devotion practiced now and then. It should be incessant — the voice of a love that is ever living and fresh in our hearts.

It will be a great practical help to us in thanksgiving to classify the different blessings for which we are bound continually to thank God; and I propose that we should in this, as in so many other matters, follow the order and method proposed by Fr. Lancisius.

∞

Give thanks for the blessings common to all

First of all, we should thank God for the blessings that are common to the whole human race. St. Chrysostom is very strong upon this point. And our Lord called the practice of thanksgiving for these blessings the necklace of His spouse; for, after He had been pleased to espouse St. Bridget, and was instructing her how she should spiritually adorn herself, He said, "The spouse ought to have the signs of her Bridegroom upon her breast; that is, the memory of the favors I have shown thee — namely, how nobly I have created thee, giving thee both a body and a soul, how nobly I have

[145] Philo (c. 20 B.C.-c. 50), Jewish thinker and exegete.

endowed thee with health and temporal blessings, how sweetly I have brought thee back from thy wanderings, by dying for thee and, if thou wilt have it, restoring to thee thine inheritance."

Orlandini mentions this as one of the characteristics of Fr. Peter Faber. He was always gratefully mindful, not only of God's private blessings, but of those common to all mankind. He never forgot that thanks were due to the divine liberality, not less for these common blessings, than for special ones; and it was a source of grief to him that men generally paid no attention to them, but took them as matters of course. He mourned because men rarely blessed that sweet will and boundless charity of God, by which He had first created the world, and then redeemed it, and after that, prepared for us eternal glory, and that in all this, He had vouchsafed to think specially and distinctly of each one of us. Under this heading of common blessings must be reckoned all the graces of the sacred humanity of Jesus, the glorious privileges of the Mother of God, and all the splendor of the angels and the saints.

Among other promises that God made to St. Gertrude, this was one: "Whenever anyone devoutly praises God, and gives Him thanks for the blessings conferred upon Gertrude, the Almighty mercifully wills to enrich him with as many spiritual graces as he offers thanksgivings, if not at the present time, at least on some fitting occasion."

Orlandini tells us that Peter Faber used to be continually congratulating the angels and the blessed on their gifts, assiduously pondering the particular graces God had given them, and then, naming those he could, he gave God thanks for them on their behalf. He reckoned that this was in the highest degree delightful to those inhabitants of Heaven, as well as immeasurably profitable to us, as in Heaven the blessed see how the debt of gratitude they owe to God is simply oppressive, and never can be paid.

Peter Faber practiced this devotion, until at last he came to feel as if there was not a single token of the divine goodness shown to anyone, for which he was personally a debtor. He made himself a kind of vicar for everyone who had any sort of happiness or success, and no sooner did he perceive it than he set work to bless God and to give thanks. There was nothing joyous, nothing prosperous, that he saw or heard of without at once becoming its voice of praise and thanksgiving to the Lord. Nay, fair cities, fruitful fields, beautiful olive-grounds, delightful vineyards — he looked around upon them with exulting eye, and because they could not speak for themselves, he spoke for them, and thanked the Lord of all for their beauty and, in the name of their owners and possessors, for the dominion He had given them thereof.

How wonderful must have been the interior of this holy father's soul, decked with such various and surpassing gifts, enriched with such very peculiar and, so to speak, private graces, and, above all, with a dower of interior dispositions, which was his special characteristic treasure, and wherein hardly any canonized saint seemed to surpass him. Blessed be the Most Holy Trinity for every gift and grace that ever beautified his soul, and for all the treasures of grace that God has given to His saints, and now keeps hidden in Himself, so that we cannot glorify Him for them!

∞

Give thanks for the blessings God has given you

The second class of the divine mercies, for which we are bound to offer continual thanksgivings is obviously the multitude of personal blessings that we have received from the unmerited goodness of God. How beautifully St. Bernard expresses this in his first sermon on the Canticles. In the wars and conflicts, says he, that at no hour are wanting to those who live devoutly in Christ, whether from the flesh, the world, or the Devil — for man's life is a warfare on the earth, as you have experienced yourself — we must daily renew our songs of gratitude for the victories already obtained. As often as a temptation is overcome, or a vice subdued, or an imminent danger avoided, or a snare of the evil one discovered in time, or an inveterate passion of the soul healed, or a virtue long coveted and prayed for, and at length by the gift of God granted to us, what must we do, but, according to the prophet, utter the voice of praise and thanksgiving, and bless God at each single blessing for all His gifts? Or else, when the last day comes, we will be reckoned among the ungrateful, who cannot say, "Thy justifications were the subject of my song in the place of my pilgrimage."[146] Nay, at every advance we make, according to the ascensions has disposed in his heart, so many separate songs must we sing to the praise and glory of Him who has thus promoted us.

Fr. Lancisius says, "I would urge all who serve God fervently and faithfully to return Him thanks with peculiar affection and zealous gratitude, at least four times in the day, for all the personal blessings He has been pleased to confer upon us: first, in the morning at meditation; second, in the middle of the day, or before dinner; third, in the examination of conscience; and fourth, at bedtime. And the first rank among these personal blessings should be held by the grace that has called us either from heresy to the Catholic faith, or from neglecting the sacraments to a good life, or from relapses into sin to a real conversion."

Our Lord said once to St. Bridget, "The bride should be ready, with fair and clean adornments, when the Bridegroom comes to the nuptials, and then are your ornaments clean when you think with gratitude about your sins, how I cleansed you in Baptism

[146] Ps. 118:54 (RSV = Ps. 119:54).

from the sin of Adam, and how, when you fell, I have so often borne with you, and when else you would have fallen, I have held you up."

Among our personal blessings, we must thank God for the continuance of health and life, whereby we can daily amass huge treasures of merits and glorify the dear majesty of God by numerous acts of love. We must thank Him also for past and present humiliations, for calumnies, for unkind interpretations of our words, deeds, omissions, or intentions, for the detractions we have suffered from, and for everything that has ever happened to mortify our self-love. For if we consider the true interests of our soul, it is a real blessing to be humbled and kept down, not only because it helps us to advance in the way of perfection, but also because of the innumerable opportunities it gives us of glorifying God and acquiring merit, and of being so much higher in Heaven. Indeed, there is hardly anything by which we can glorify God more effectually than by the exercise of virtues while we are under humiliations. So, if we are in a condition or state of life in which we do not attract the notice or the praise of men, we ought to thank God most warmly for it, considering the danger there would be to our souls in a more elevated and honorable state.

The patience and long-suffering of God should be another subject of continual thanksgiving. Is it not wonderful how He has borne with us, and we so miserably perverse all the while? How many absolutions have we not had, our lost merits restored to us, and fresh graces given us! What a miracle of patience God has been! Can we not well enter into the spirit of that Spanish lady of whom Fr. Rho said that "if she had to build a church in honor of the attributes of God, she would dedicate it to the divine patience!" How beautiful her soul must have been, and how many deep and intimate things must have passed between her and God!

Again, how many sins have we been in the way of committing, or near to committing, and by grace have not done so? And how many temptations have proved fatal to others, which never so much as came our way? Even the heathen Emperor Antoninus thanked God for the occasions of sin to which he had never been exposed. This, then, is another personal blessing for which we must always be giving thanks.

Again, there are three blessings that a Catholic ought to remember at every time: the Divine Election, which made him a Catholic; the Divine Providence, which has been his shield and buckler ever since he was born; and the Divine Liberality, which has loaded him with such a profusion of gifts and graces, not absolutely necessary for his salvation, but either to adorn his soul or to increase his joy in Christ.

St. Chrysostom also would have us remember with special gratitude the hidden and unknown blessings that God has heaped upon us. God, he says, is an overrunning fountain of clemency, flowing upon us, and round about us, even when we know it not. Orlandini tells us that in this matter also Fr. Peter Faber was remarkable. He used to say there were hardly any blessings we ought more scrupulously to thank God for than those we never asked for and those that come to us without our knowing it. It is not unlikely, in the case of many of us, that these hidden blessings may turn out at the last day to have been the very hinges on which our lives turned, and that, through them, our predestination has been worked out, and our eternal rest secured.

Give thanks for sufferings

We must not think that too much is being asked of us when spiritual writers tell us we ought to return thanks to God for afflictions and tribulations, both those that have passed and those that we may be suffering from at the present time. This is, of course, not the place to enter into the uses and merciful purposes of affliction. But they will readily suggest themselves to everyone. John of Avila[147] used to say that one "Thanks be to God" in adversity was worth six thousand in prosperity.

But we must again refer to Orlandini in his description of the special gift of thanksgiving that Peter Faber possessed. He thought it was not enough that men should humble themselves under the hand of God in the time of public calamities, but that they should give God hearty thanks for them, for famine and scarcity, for wars, floods, pestilences, and all the other scourges of Heaven, and it was a subject of "vehement" sorrow to him that men did not openly acknowledge God's merciful intentions in these things. When he grieved over the misfortunes of others, what stirred his sorrow most was that men did not see how much gentleness there was in the visitation; for that is not perfect gratitude which is fed by favors only.

"We cannot tell," says St. Antiochus, "who is really grateful, until we see whether he gives God hearty and sincere thanks in the midst of calamities." And St. Chrysostom, in his homilies on the letter to the Ephesians, says we ought to thank God for Hell itself, and for all the pains and punishments that are there, because they are such an effectual bridle to our inordinate passions.

∞

Give thanks even for "trifling" blessings

It is also a very important devotion to thank God for what we call trifling blessings. Not, of course, that any goodness of God is

[147] St. John of Avila (1500-1569), Spanish mystic.

trifling to such as we are; but mercies may be little by comparison. St. Bernard applies to this devotion our Lord's injunction to His disciples to gather up the fragments so that nothing would be lost.[148]

In the life of Bl. Baptista Varani,[149] we read that our dear Lord once said to her, "If you were never to sin again, and you alone were to do more penances than all the blessed in Heaven have ever done, and if you were to shed as many tears as would fill all the seas, and suffer as many pains as you are capable of suffering, that would not be enough to thank me for the very least blessing I have ever bestowed upon you." Another time, Baptista said that God had given her to understand that the glorious Mother of God, and all men and angels with their perfections, could not adequately thank the Divine Love for the creation of one least field-flower on the earth, which He has made for our use, in respect of the infinite gulf there is between His excellence and our vileness.

Orlandini tells us that Peter Faber excelled in this devotion also and that he used to say that in every gift of God, no matter how trifling, three things were to be considered: the giver, the gift, and the affection with which it was given; and that if we pondered these three points, we should see that there could be no such things as little mercies. And doubtless this was the reason, says the biographer, why that blessed mind was always overflowing with the abundance of divine gifts. For, as God is an inexhaustible ocean of goodness, the fountain of His liberality cannot be dried up where He meets with a considerate and thankful mind into which He can pour Himself.

[148] John 6:12.

[149] Bl. Baptista Varani (1458-1527), Poor Clare and ascetical writer.

So Thomas à Kempis observes that if we look at the dignity of the Giver, no gift is small that comes from God.[150] Our Lord taught St. Gertrude to give thanks even for future blessings not yet received. So acceptable is thanksgiving before God!

∞

Thank God for graces you impeded

St. Ignatius used to say that there were very few — perhaps not one person in the world — who thoroughly understood what an impediment we are to God, who wishes to work great things in our souls; for it is hardly credible what God would do, if we would only let Him. Hence, holy people have made a special devotion of thanking the Divine Majesty for all the blessings He would in His munificence have conferred upon them, if they themselves had not hindered Him.

Others, again, have been touched with sensible gratitude for blessings for which they were not thankful at the time they received them. Peter Faber used to say Masses, or have them said, in expiation of his own and others' ungrateful inconsiderateness when receiving blessings from God; and whenever he saw a rich or fortunate man, he used to make acts of reparation for his possible forgetfulness of his Divine Benefactor. Others have felt strongly about blessings, for which they thanked God at the time, but it now seems to them not so much as they might have done, nor so affectionately. St. Lawrence Justinian tells us that this feeling enters into the thanksgivings of the blessed in Heaven.

Then there are blessings we have abused or made light of, and St. Bernard tells us these should certainly be made the subject of

[150] Cf. Thomas à Kempis (c. 1380-1471; ascetical writer), *Imitation of Christ*, Bk. 2, ch. 10.

special thanksgiving. Others, again, have exercised devotion in thanking God for blessings that others were preparing for them, or that were growing, or that happened while they were asleep. This at least shows the ingenious love of grateful hearts.

But there is another practice recorded by Orlandini of Peter Faber that must by no means be omitted. It is well worth our imitation. It is to give God special thanks for preventing innumerable words and deeds of ours from giving scandal, when in themselves they are calculated to do so. What can be a greater mercy than this?

∞

Give thanks on behalf of creatures that cannot do so

Another practice of holy men has been to thank God on behalf of the irrational creatures, a devotion acceptable to Him as the wise Creator of the world. It has also the further advantage of a most excellent practice of the presence of God, enabling us everywhere, and at all times, to rise to Him by means of His creatures.

But we must not in this think so much of the dominion or use that God has given us out of His bounty over these creatures, as of the love that He had toward us in creating them, as He Himself said to St. Catherine of Siena: "The soul which has arrived at the state of perfect love, when it receives gifts and graces from me, does not look so much at my gift, as at the affection of charity that moved me to confer the gift upon it."

∞

Thank God for His blessings on your enemies and on lost souls

We shall also glorify God by thanking Him for all the blessings conferred upon our enemies. This devotion will be the more acceptable to Him because it is a great exercise of brotherly love; for it is impossible to practice it long without all coldness and uncomfortable feeling giving way to gentleness and tenderness, even toward those who have wronged us most, or who show the greatest dislike of us.

But, as my chief aim in this treatise is nothing but to accumulate an abundance of affectionate contrivances to get our dearest Lord a little more glory; as it is the wrongs of God and the injured interests of Jesus on behalf of which I want to move my readers, there are some other methods of thanksgiving that are very much to my purpose.

Look at the lost souls! There is not one whom God has not loaded with blessings, and pursued with tenderest graces, and striven to win with the divine caresses of His Holy Spirit. And there are no thanks there. Justice has its harvest there, but not love. Hence it is that De Ponte, in the preface to his *Meditations*,[151] recommends to us the practice of thanking God for all the blessings of nature and grace that have been bestowed on those who have lost themselves by their own willfulness. There have been some so jealous of God's glory, so afraid that some nook of His creation would not thank Him for His goodness, that they have loved to praise Him because even the lost are for His love's sake punished less than they deserve.

How prodigal has God been of His goodness! Could figures tell the number of His gifts to the multitude of the reprobate? Then add the infidels and heretics now on earth, who leave Him without thanksgiving, and bad Catholics living in mortal sin and trampling the sacraments beneath their feet, crucifying our dearest

[151] Luis de la Puente (1554-1624; Spanish Jesuit, also known as De Ponte), *Meditations on the Mysteries of Our Holy Faith*.

Lord afresh and putting Him to an open shame! Blessed be God for every one of the gifts of every one of these! May the Blessed Sacrament praise Him this hour for them all in every tabernacle!

Oh, that the number of hearts might daily increase which would love Jesus more and would mourn that He is loved so little! What is life, what is death, if God only be loved, and be loved more and more?

Sweet Jesus, where is the fire Thou camest on earth to kindle? Why is it not kindled in our hearts? Dearest Lord, if we love Thee so little, we can at least hate ourselves that we do not love Thee more!

∞

Give thanks for the angels and saints

Another practice of thanksgiving, and one that leads us to the confines of the next chapter, is to thank our blessed Lord, with the utmost fervor and simplicity of joy, for the immense multitude of angels and saints who fill the choirs of Heaven, adoring Him as their Head and thanking Him as the Author of all grace and the Giver of all gifts. For, if we sincerely love Him, it is our chief sorrow that we cannot love Him worthily, and, therefore, it is really a blessing bestowed upon us that He would have been pleased to create creatures who can love Him so much more, so unspeakably more, than we do.

To this some have added thanksgivings for all the worship and adoration our Lord is receiving at this moment throughout the earth and in Purgatory, all the sacrifices that are being offered, all the prayers that are made in churches, the vows by which fervent men are binding themselves, and all the increases of divine love that are going on in the hearts of those who are in a state of grace.

Others again have been drawn to continual thanksgiving to Jesus for the glorious mysteries of His life, as contrasted with the joyful and the sorrowful, thanking Him for them daily, for the glory He Himself had in them, and for the glory they gave His Father, as well as the benefits we derive from them. Thus, those who have had a special devotion to our Lord's Resurrection have almost always coupled it with an equally special attraction to thanksgiving.

Thank God for the gift of faith

Others have been distinguished by a deep and lifelong feeling of gratitude for the gift of faith and for all the supernatural wonders of our holy religion. These form two very distinct sources of devotion. By the latter (to speak of that first), men are led to rejoice in the absolute sovereignty of God and the unlimited supremacy of His most dear majesty, and in their own vileness and nothingness. They think they can never thank God sufficiently that they are so completely and helplessly in His hands. They would not for the world have it otherwise. They can hardly understand those who do not feel as they do. They bless God for His promises, but their habit of mind is to trust rather in His love. They do not care about merit; what they care about is His glory. In low spirits, it is the thought of God's sovereignty, rather than of His faithfulness, that is the bed of their repose. These are the persons who are always so happy in religion, except when God withdraws for a while this blessed confidence, for their greater sanctification. And even then, their language is that of Job: "Though He slay me, yet will I trust in Him."[152]

Men with this attraction seem to have a special gift of unselfishness and unworldliness. They delight in the spiritual plans and

[152] Job 13:15.

successes of other men. It is a joy to them that all the arrangements about merit, satisfaction, remission, infused habits, and indulgences, are so thoroughly supernatural. They have a profound reverence for all the benedictions of the Church, for her sacramentals, forms, and manipulations, and for the rubrics of her ceremonies, which seem to be rather gleams of Heaven than the marshaling of earthly pomps. They glory in the principles of the Gospel and the vitality of the Church being opposed to all the calculations and principles of the world. They revel in the strength of weakness, in the exaltation of holy poverty, in the splendor of abasement, in the mightiness of suffering, and in the victory of defeat. These things are to them like the odors of the spice islands wafted out to the weary navigator. They are fragrant of Heaven and of God.

It is a peculiar delight to them that men are converted by unaccountable grace rather than by controversy, and that God so often seems to take matters into His own hands, and to work of Himself, without making use of us. They have no heartaching difficulties about God and nature, because they do not look upon men as the center of the system, or the reason of creation, or the standard God measures by. They think this would narrow their spiritual views as much as believing the earth to be the center of the solar system, or the solar system the center of the universe, would narrow a man's views of nature. They look on Jesus as the center of all things, as the reason of creation, as the standard God uses, as He vouchsafes to speak of Himself as working, who is self-sufficient bliss and rest.

The predestination of Jesus, in their view, explains everything, harmonizes everything, controls everything, and is the fountain of everything that lies outside the unity of the Most Holy Trinity; and Mary's predestination is part of His. They are only here in His train, and they have no consequence or importance except the one dear dignity of being loved by Him. As the little stars go out when the great sun shines, so faith's hard facts, the permission of evil, and the eternity of punishment men cannot see because of the blessed and exhilarating dazzle of the predestination of Jesus.

∞

Give thanks for Christ's presence in the Mass and in His Church

But there is one practice of thanksgiving that must enter into all others and be joined to them — thanksgiving, if it might be so, of tears rather than of words: gratitude for the adorable Sacrifice of the Mass, and the personal presence of Jesus with His Church. It is not only the inestimable blessings of the sacrifice that must call out these incessant thanksgivings, nor is it the unspeakable love and condescension involved in it. But it is the joy that now at least thanks are offered to God that are equal to Him. We need no longer sit by the waysides of the world, downcast and weeping, because His blessed majesty is not worshiped, praised, and thanked, as it ought to be. One Mass is infinite praise, and there are Masses at nearly every moment. The Blessed Sacrament is in crowded or neglected churches all over the earth; and wheresoever He is, there is infinite praise, unspeakable worship, and unfathomable thanksgiving! And the especial function of the Holy Mass is the Eucharist, the worship of thanksgiving. Even the mere creature, by means of the Blessed Sacrament, can attain himself to a higher act of worship than he could ever else have dreamed of; for the creature can pay no higher homage to his Creator than by receiving Him in the overwhelming reality of the Blessed Sacrament.

What repose there is in the thought of all this! How many inward complaints can we hush by it! How much unhumble disquietude with our own littleness, our own vile attainments, our own impossibilities of loving God as we feel we ought to love Him!

Ah, blessed Jesus! He is all things to us. Whatever we want, it comes to us in the shape of Him, in the strangest of places and the most unaccountable of ways! Shall we not say, then, that we love God worthily and worship Him abundantly, for Jesus is our love and our worship too? How happy with an abounding, inexhaustible happiness this makes us!

And meanwhile, thanks, a thousand times thanks, to Jesus! God gets His praise, His worship, and His thanks — deep, beautiful, and infinite as Himself.

∞

Give thanks after Holy Communion

Now, this perhaps will enable us to judge how far we are truly grateful to our blessed Lord and how far we have really discharged the duty of thanksgiving. Whatever may be thought of particular methods of this devotion, practiced by the saints or suggested by spiritual writers, the whole Church is agreed on the duty and fitness of a special thanksgiving after Holy Communion. If ever there is a time for thanks too deep for words, it is when the Creator has been pleased to overwhelm His creature with this stupendous gift of Himself, and when He is actually within us.

Hence it is that spiritual writers tell us, for a while at least, not to open a book, but to commune with Jesus in our own hearts. We must surely have something to say to Him then, or at least He will say something to us in the deep silence of our hearts, if only we will listen.

Yet how stands the case in reality? Why, if we may take the fervor and regularity with which we make our thanksgiving after Communion as an index of our love of Jesus, nothing can well be more disheartening. To most of us, there is hardly a quarter of an hour in our lives more tedious, idle, aimless, or unsatisfactory than what we call our thanksgiving. We have nothing to say. Our hearts do not run over. We never can receive a greater gift in this world. With each Communion, it grows more wonderful; so much does our lukewarmness and ingratitude make the continuance of His love a stranger marvel. He who is to be our joy for all eternity has come, and we have nothing to say to Him. We tire of His company. It is a relief to us when we may believe that He has gone. We have been civil to Him. We have asked His blessing as our superior. But it has been little more than civility; at the most, it was only respect.

Alas, it is useless to ask men to adopt various practices of thanksgiving, when our Lord's own visit can hardly force one upon them. It is as if thanksgiving had but one fixed home left on earth, and that its tenure even of that was continually becoming more and more precarious. However, it will be something if these bad, lazy, listless thanksgivings bring home to us how very, very little in reality we care for Jesus, and that if we could only have His grace without Him, it would be just the religion to our mind.

Ah, dearest Lord, knowing all this, Thou abidest in the tabernacle!

∞

Examine how faithfully you offer thanks to God

But we must ask ourselves the important question: What has been our own practice hitherto with regard to the duty of thanksgiving in general? What is our habitual feeling about God's numberless blessings to us? How long have we ever spent in summing up God's blessings to us, even when we have been in retreat?

St. Ignatius wisely tells us to commence our examination of conscience every day with counting up the mercies of God and thanking Him for them. Have we so much as kept faithfully to this little practice? Many of us have regular times in the day for different spiritual duties; have we any time specially set apart for thanksgiving? Many of us, again, keep in our prayer books a little note of things and persons to pray for; have we any similar memento of the blessings for which we desire daily to thank our heavenly Father? How often have we besieged the Throne of grace for weeks and weeks with Our Fathers, Hail Marys, *Misereres*,[153] *Memorares*, Rosaries, Communions, and even penances for something we desired; and when at last our dear Lord condescended to our importunity, what proportion did our thanksgiving bear to our supplication? How long did it last? In what did it consist? With what fervor and increase of love was it accompanied? Was it a single *Te Deum*,[154] a hurried "Thanks be to God"? Did we take with an ungraceful eagerness what God held out to us, almost as if it were our wages, and then, beyond a general vague feeling of gratitude, think nothing more about it?

Alas! I fear we have all great need to take shame to ourselves in this respect. So far from having an abiding spirit of thanksgiving, or a keen lifelong recollection of God's mercies, and a loving regularity in the worship and sacrifice of thanksgiving, we go on letting the Holy Spirit Himself touch our hearts with an intimate sense of our obligations to God and our dependence upon Him, waiting until He does do so, and then feebly responding to His call. We let Him, as it were, ask for our thanks, rather than paying them with a free heart and out of an abounding love. We would be quick enough to see the wretchedness of all this if a fellow creature did it to us. But answer these questions honestly, and then say if you

[153] Ps. 50 (RSV = Ps. 51).

[154] The prayer that begins, "You are God: we praise You."

think I exaggerated when I said that the disproportion of thanksgiving to prayer was one of the wonders of the world, and one of its saddest wonders, too.

∞

Remember that God is your loving Father

And what is the cause of all this? I do not care if I write it again and again, until you are weary of reading it, if only that would ensure your remembering it. It comes from your perverse refusal to look at God as your Father. Independent of open sin, there is scarcely a misery that does not come from these hard, dry, churlish views of God. That is the root of the evil. You must lay the axe there, if you really desire to be other than you are. No schemes for self-improvement will stand in the stead of it. You may meditate and examine your conscience and pray your Rosary, and little enough will come of it, as you have so often found already. Oh, how wonderfully people can be regular in making their daily meditation, and yet it never melts into them! Not a passion is subdued, not an unloveliness smoothed away! They have the custom of prayer, without the gift of it. You may do penances, and they will harden your heart in a delusion of vainglorious humility, rather than melt into simple genuine love. The very sacraments will work only like machines out of order.

Whether it is stunted growth in the spiritual life which you deplore, or the absence of all sensible devotion, or incapacity to make or keep generous resolutions, or teasing relapses into unworthy imperfections, or want of reverence in prayer, or lack of sweetness with others — in almost every case, the mischief may be traced to an unaffectionate view of God.

You must get clear of this. You must cultivate a filial feeling toward Him. You must pray to the Holy Spirit for His gift of piety, whose special office it is to produce this feeling. Your most prominent idea of God must be as Him "of whom all paternity is named in Heaven and on earth."[155] You must remember that the Spirit of Jesus is the one true Spirit, and that He is the Spirit of adoption, whereby we cry, "Abba, Father!"[156] You will never be right until your view of God as your Father swallows up all your other views of Him, or at least until they are brought into harmonious subordination to that view, which is the sweet soul of the Gospel and the life of our blessed Savior's teaching. A man could not do better than devote his whole life to be the apostle of this one idea: the compassionate paternity of God.

In matters of spiritual progress, our interests are identical with God's glory. This is another of His loving contrivances. Hence, we may still further persuade ourselves to the practice of thanksgiving by reflecting on its benefits to us from a spiritual point of view. Growth in holiness is nothing but the continual descent upon us of those fresh graces which crown every act of correspondence on our part to graces already received; and there is nothing, as we know, that so multiplies graces upon us, or causes God to throw the doors of His treasury so wide open, as the devotion of thanksgiving. But it is not only in this way that it helps us on in holiness. Its effects upon our mind must also be taken into account.

∞

Let thanksgiving call you back to God daily

Many persons try to advance in spirituality and are held back, as it were, by some invisible hand. The fact is — and they do not realize it — they have never been thoroughly converted to God.

[155] Eph. 3:15.

[156] Rom. 8:15.

They have stayed too short a time in the purgative way of the spiritual life, or they have bargained with God and kept back some attachment, or wished to loosen themselves from unworthy habits gently and gradually, so as to be spared the pain of conversion.

Now, thanksgiving swiftly but imperceptibly turns our religion into a service of love; it draws us to take God's view of things, to range ourselves on His side even against ourselves, and to identify ourselves with His interests even when they seem to be in opposition to our own. Hence, we are led to break more effectually with the world, and not to trail its clouds and mists along with us on our road to Heaven. Hence, also, we come to root and ground ourselves more effectually in the sense of our own vileness and worse than nothingness before God. And what is all this but to make our conversion more thorough and complete?

And the effect of thanksgiving is no less upon our growth than it is upon our conversion. All growth comes of love; and love is at once both the cause and the effect of thanksgiving. What light and air are to plants, the sense of God's presence is to the virtues; and thanksgiving makes this sensible presence of God almost a habit in our souls. For it leads us continually to see mercies that we would not otherwise have perceived, and it enables us far more worthily to appreciate their value, and in some degree to sound the abyss of divine condescension out of which they come.

Moreover, the practice of thanksgiving in ourselves leads us to be distressed at the absence of it in others; and this keeps our love of God delicate and sensitive, and breeds in us a spirit of reparation, which is especially congenial to the growth of holiness. Our hearts are enlarged while we are magnifying God, and when our hearts are enlarged, we run the way of His commandments, where we have only walked or crept before. We feel a secret force in overcoming obstacles and in despising fears, and altogether a liberty in well-doing, which we did not feel before; and all because thanksgiving has made us measure the height of God's goodness and the depth of our vileness: and so nothing looks too much or too hard where the glory of God is concerned. Like Areuna in the time of the pestilence,[157] we give to the King as kings ourselves, and in the spirit of kings. Our hearts are crowned with thanksgiving.

It is a great mistake to think lightly of happiness in religion, of enjoyment in religious services, of sweetness in prayer, of gladness in mortification, and of sensible devotion. True it is that when God subtracts them, it is not necessarily in anger or as a chastisement; and whatever be the cause, our plain duty is to submit ourselves to His sweet although inscrutable will. But this does not hinder all these things from being mighty aids in the spiritual life, and therefore to be desired and coveted with earnestness, although in a submissive spirit.

Who does not know cases where everything seems to go wrong because a person has no happiness in religion? Even at Mass, a veil is over their hearts, which neither music, nor brightness, nor the Divine Presence can go through. God's blessings are as dull to such people as His chastisements are to the generality of men. Prayer is a penance, confession a torture, Communion a very rack. What God blesses for them irritates like a sore. What He fills with peace, troubles them with disquietude. They have no light but the gloom of their own perverse moodiness; and they have no song but peevishness.

Inquire if such persons have ever had a spirit of thanksgiving, and you will find you have hit exactly on the characteristic omission of their lives, for happiness in religion comes from the spirit of thanksgiving.

[157] Cf. 2 Kings 24:18-25 (RSV = 2 Sam. 24:18-25).

Now for a few words to show how, by this devotion of thanksgiving, we can do our three things: promote the glory of God, advance the interests of Jesus, and help in the saving of souls.

∞

Glorify God through thanksgiving

First, as to the promotion of the glory of God: He has chosen to rest His glory in great measure on the praise and thanksgiving of His creatures. Thanksgiving was one of the ends for which He created us. And there is no matter in which He is so defrauded of His glory as in this, and none consequently in which He looks more for reparation from His faithful servants. No one ever thanks Him with devout intention who does not at once and thereby give Him glory. I said that joy comes of thanksgiving; and the spirit of thanksgiving seems not only to accompany that joy which is a special fruit of the Holy Spirit, but to be manifested in all the special devotions that have to do with joy.

Those who have had a special devotion to St. Raphael, the angel of joy, have generally had a more-than-usual gift of thanksgiving. We see this even in the book of Tobias, without coming to the examples of the saints most devoted to that dear spirit, such as St. John of God, Bl. Benvenuta,[158] St. Giacinta Mariscotti, and others. "Father, he gave joy":[159] this is the character the young Tobias gives St. Raphael. And when Raphael is about to make himself known, he says to them, "Bless ye the God of Heaven; give glory to Him in the sight of all that live, because He hath shown

[158] St. John of God (1495-1550), founder of the Order of Charity for the Service of the Sick; Bl. Benvenuta of Cividale (1254-1292), Dominican tertiary.

[159] Cf. Tob. 12:2-3.

His mercy to you. For it is good to hide the secret of a king, but honorable to reveal and confess the works of God." And again, "When I was with you, I was there by the will of God: bless ye Him and sing praises to Him." And again, "It is time that I return to Him that sent me; but bless ye God, and publish all His wonderful works."[160]

Probably as he parted from them, he let them see a glimpse of his angelic beauty, as they immediately went into an ecstasy of three hours, and what is left behind was a spirit of thanksgiving. "Then they, lying prostrate for three hours upon their face, blessed God; and rising up, they told all His wonderful works."[161] Then Tobias the elder, opening his mouth, said, "Give glory to the Lord, ye children of Israel. See what He hath done for us, and with fear and trembling give glory to Him, and extol the eternal King of worlds. Bless ye the Lord, all his elect, keep days of joy, and give glory to Him. Jerusalem, city of God . . . give glory to the Lord for thy good things."[162] And how beautiful was his life after the angel had left a mantle of joy and thanksgiving on the holy old man! "The rest of his life was in joy; and with great increase of the fear of God, he departed in peace."[163] And with the young Tobias, the joy lived after him, and there was joy instead of mourning for him; for it is said, "And after he had lived ninety-nine years in the fear of the Lord, with joy they buried him."[164]

Second, this devotion gives us great means of furthering the interests of Jesus. What was there upon earth that He sought more

[160] Tob. 12:6-7, 18, 20.
[161] Tob. 12:22.
[162] Tob. 13:3, 6, 10-12.
[163] Tob. 14:4.
[164] Tob. 14:16.

vehemently than His Father's glory? Although it is said of Him that He knew what was in men and would not trust Himself to them, yet He vouchsafed to appear surprised that only one of the ten lepers returned to give thanks to God.[165] And how full of mystery is that outburst of thanksgiving on His own part, when He thanked His Father and confessed before Him, because He had hidden His mysteries from the wise and prudent, and had revealed them to babes.[166]

∞

Spread the practice of thanksgiving

But there is one way especially that I would venture to suggest as a means of promoting the interests of Jesus, and in a most loving manner and with little trouble to ourselves. It is by assuming to ourselves a little apostolate to spread the practice of thanksgiving.

There are few of us who do not influence some others — children or servants or friends. Let us teach them to make more frequent, more systematic, more fervent thanksgiving. Let us say a seasonable word for this practice whenever we can.

If each person persuaded five people, in honor of our dear Lord's five wounds, to make daily thanksgiving, these five would, in turn, spread it to others, as the ripples spread on the surface of a pond; and anyhow, how much would Jesus rejoice at this harvest of God's glory from souls, making daily one act of thanksgiving more than they otherwise would have done. Think of all that is involved of grace, merit, glory, worship, praise, and acceptableness in one "Thanks be to God" said with devout intention; and yet, with but a little exertion, we could send up to the blessed but

[165] John 2:24-25; Luke 17:17-18.

[166] Matt. 11:25.

outraged majesty of God in each year millions of these supernatural acts!

Oh, why do we let so much that we could do for God slip by? What a homage of love to Jesus would this easy apostolate of thanksgiving be! Let us begin at once — this very day; for time is flowing from under us, and we have kept God's glory waiting long enough!

Thus also in schools and seminaries, and in domestic families, especially where there are many young children, out of whose pure mouths God has ordained praise, little associations might be formed to say some brief prayer of thanksgiving daily by themselves and, where it seems feasible, to make some little act of thanksgiving in common, as well as to endeavor to put more of a thoughtful intention into grace before and after meals.

The object of these little associations might be to thank God generally for all His goodness to His creatures, and especially for the Incarnation, and again for His mercifully giving us Mary to be our mother as well as His. We might thus unite morning and afternoon in a little act of thanksgiving for the gift of the most holy Roman Faith, and children could at once bless God for the national grace of their country, make reparation for apostasies, and also gain a habit that would be an effectual protection to them in the temptations of later life. These associations might be connected, if it was thought well, with devotion to the holy angels, whose life is one incessant song of grateful praise, and thus the virtue of purity, the attendant gift of this devotion, might at the same time be fostered in the souls of the youthful members.

If we think aright of the glory of God — in a word, if we love Him — these things will not seem small, nor their blessing insignificant. We have much lost time to make up in this matter of thanksgiving.

Oh, what glory cannot one man get for our dearest Lord if he only lays himself out to do it! St. Jerome, while he lived in the East, often heard the oriental monks intoning their doxology: "Glory be to the Father, and to the Son, and to the Holy Spirit." It appealed to him, and he asked Pope Damasus[167] to establish it in the Western Church, where, humanly speaking, were it not for him, it would never have been used. Who can count the million millions of times that doxology has been used in the West with loving and devout intention? Look how often it comes in the Divine Office.

Now, every time St. Mary Magdalene de' Pazzi said it, she accompanied it by a mental offering of herself to the Most Holy Trinity. Whenever St. Alphonsus, in his old age, heard of some good news for the glory of God or the welfare of Holy Church, he cried out with heartfelt emotion, "Glory to the Father, and to the Son, and to the Holy Spirit."

Great things are told us of the devotion of St. Paul of the Cross to this doxology, and he taught the same spiritual devotion to his religious. The lives of the saints would doubtless furnish us many other devotions of heroic love that have been connected with this doxology. Yet if St. Jerome had not one day asked Pope Damasus to introduce it in the Western Church, all this glory would have been lost to God.

When men do anything for God, even the very least thing, they never know where it will end, nor what amount of work it will do for Him. Love's secret, therefore, is to be always doing things for God, and not to mind because they are such very little ones. "Cast thy bread upon the running waters; for after a long time thou shalt find it again. In the morning, sow thy seed, and in

[167] St. Damasus (c. 304-384), Pope from 366.

the evening let thy hand cease; for thou knowest not which may rather spring up, this or that; and if both together, it shall be the better."[168]

∞

Practice thanksgiving to help save souls

Further, this devotion would be of great help in saving many souls. We ourselves, by the practice of it, would gain such favor with God as would enable us to impetrate graces that are far above the feebleness of our present prayers. Oh, we would see such things happen! Such a throwing open of the treasures of God's mercy, such inundations of grace, such obstinate hearts overcome, such new benedictions poured out over the whole Church! Then again, by making daily reparation to God for the ingratitude and unmindfulness of sinners, we would appease His anger against them, and thus avert from them many judgments and chastisements, both spiritual and temporal.

It is astonishing in how many indirect ways God lovingly allows us to cooperate in the salvation of souls. I wish we were more ingenious in finding them out, and more unwearying in the practice of them!

Oh, may I never forget that there may be souls on earth whose glory God has tied to my zeal and prayer! There may be a dear soul whom God has loved from all eternity, and decreed to call it out of nothing in preference to millions of souls He might have created instead; a dear soul whom Jesus thought of by name upon the Cross, and offered for it with distinct oblation all His sufferings; a dear soul for whose company Mary yearns in Heaven; and whether or not it shall see God, and be His king and priest forever, clothed

[168] Eccles. 11:1, 6.

with incomparable beauty, and crowned with inexpressible gifts, and plunged in an everlasting sea of joy, has been hung by an adorable venture of Divine Love upon my unconscious prayer!

Ah, Lord, when did I see Thee hungry and feed Thee not, thirsty, and give Thee not to drink? Oh may His answer never cease to sound in my love-frightened ear: "Inasmuch as thou hast not done it unto the least of these my brethren, thou hast not done it unto me!"[169]

[169] Cf. Matt. 25:45.

Chapter Eight

Praise God for His goodness

Men of science lead us into every nook and corner of the world to show us, even in the case of the vilest insects and the adaptation of their habits and instincts to their wants and weaknesses, how full creation is not only of the wisdom and the power, but also of the minute considerateness and tender compassion of the Almighty. We have seen precisely the same thing in the spiritual world and its supernatural arrangements. All is for love — and to an extent that almost tries our faith. God loves us with a surpassing love, and He longs to be loved by us, and He lavishes upon us with an incredible profusion the most unthought-of means of loving Him and increasing His glory.

Theology is the counterpart of physical science. It can tell us quite as wonderful things of the angels, whom we have never seen, as astronomy can of the stars we can never reach. The science of the laws of grace is a parallel to the science of the laws of life. The history and constitution of the Church is as startling in its wonders as are the records of geology. With the help of revelation, the Church, reason, and the light of the Holy Spirit, Catholic theologians have explored spirit with at least as much certainty and success as modern science has explored matter.

Those who smile when we speak so intimately of the different choirs of angels are like those who smile when they are told the bulk of a planet, or that it is made of some material as light as cork. The unbelief of ignorance causes the smile in both.

The immense intellect of man was once directed upon the life of God, His perfections, His Incarnation, and His communications of Himself. Revelation gave it countless infallible axioms, and that greatest glory of the human mind, Catholic theology, was the result. The same immense power is now brought to bear upon the currents of the ocean and the circles of the winds, upon electrical phenomena and the chemistry of the stars, and the result is wonderful enough in the system of modern science; yet hardly so wonderful, even as an exhibition of mental power, as are the summas of scholastic theology.

It is our ignorance of our religion that more than anything else prevents our discerning the extreme lovingness of God. To the savage, on whose unobservant mind no phenomena are forced but those of power, such as the storm, the flash, the sun, the sea, the wind, the Creator is simply a spirit of might. Could he see the affections and instincts of animals, as science would put them before him, he would come to change his notion of the Creator. So, when men are absorbed in worldly pursuits and do not occupy themselves in the things of God, it is only the phenomena of power in religion, such as death, mortal sin, judgment, Hell, and predestination that engage their intention. They must descend into the minute laws of grace, the secrets of prayer, the arrangements of merit and glory, the affectionateness of indulgences, and the sweet mysteries of Jesus and Mary, to get anything like a true idea of the length and breadth of God's amazing love. The thunderclap can strike the inattentive, but it is only the listener who catches the sealike whispers of the summer air in the pine treetops.

We have seen how God enables us to love Him by giving us all His own perfections, and the mysteries of His dear Son, to offer as our very own to His blessed majesty, and further, by teaching us how to unite our little services to the intentions and actions of our Lord. We have seen how all these things can be used alike for intercession, for thanksgiving, or for praise.

Praise God through holy desires

But we may now go a step farther, and say that in His anxiety to be loved, and to give us the means of loving Him, God raises even our ineffectual desires to the dignity of effectual acts, and enables us to worship Him with a most heavenly and delightful worship, with the passing wishes of our loving hearts. He does not call only for blood, pain, and sacrifice. He does not refuse to feed His glory on anything short of heroic self-immolation. The faintest heart in creation may love Him, and love Him with an abundant love.

Perhaps when we were young, we could sit at ease in our sunny nursery, on a rocking-chair, with the scattered toys and the dilapidated houses of wooden blocks around us — tokens of a play which had interested and tired us an hour ago — and amid all these comforts, we could, through books, cross the sandy plains of Africa, or thread the flowering forests of Brazil, or amuse ourselves with the mud volcanoes of Iceland; and if when night came on, we looked into our little beds to see if a cobra was lurking there, or we were perhaps shipwrecked in a dream, they were but the vainest of alarms, and even they could give a zest to the morrow.

Now, God's love has realized in our devotions something very like this. We can go from country to country on the earth, wishing God more glory and worshiping Jesus in neglected tabernacles. We can brood over the dim realms of Purgatory, and sigh and wish for God's glory and the interests of Jesus. We can range the courts of Heaven with undazzled eye, and worship there by inward wishes and by mental praises. We can pass from attribute to attribute of the Divine Majesty with praises, joys, and desires. And all the while, this is no mere amusement, no merely lawful occupation of our minds with the dear and deep things of God. But it is substantial worship, something with which the eternal Majesty is positively pleased, adoration impetrating actual graces and securing corresponding degrees of glory.

In truth there is nothing in the world so substantial as all these things. The rocky mountain is less real than true worship. Even suffering is but an unreality compared with that which has power to please the incomprehensible God. Grace, being a participation of the divine nature, is a thousand times more solid than the natures of men and animals: and the law of gravity is less certain than the unimaginable glory of the blessed.

Truly the ways of God are above our ways, and we soon get out of our depth in His loving counsels! If we, with the little dim discernment we can have of spiritual things, can touch and handle the amazing reality of everything that has to do with God, no wonder the saints have spoken so lightly and contemptuously of the things of earth, as if pain and pleasure, life and death, were so indistinguishably small that it mattered not whether one or the other befell a man. Verily there is no science like that of loving God.

The subject, then, that I want to bring before you now is that of praise and desire.

∞

Praise God with a childlike spirit

Praise is something more than thanksgiving. It is blessing God for His goodness, His power, His purity, and His beauty. It is congratulating Him that He is what He is, and that there is none like Him. It is calling on all His angels and saints to praise and glorify Him with all their might; and rising from them to Mary, we implore her to praise the majesty of God for us more worthily than we ourselves can do; and exhausting all the treasures of her almost divine prerogatives, we rise to the Sacred Heart of Jesus, which is like a boundless sea, every one of whose waves gleams and lightens with unutterable praise of God. But even that has limits. And by love, from excess of love becoming unabashed, we dare to throw ourselves into the bosom of the Most High, and listen ecstatically to His many-voiced praise and benediction of Himself.

This is a different spirit from that which measures the necessities of obedience, investigates its claim on God, ascertains the extent to which He has bound Himself by covenant, and follows the probable opinion that is in favor of the laxest practice. I am not saying this latter spirit is wrong. I am neither criticizing nor finding fault with anything. I am only saying what is clearly undeniable: that it is a very different spirit from the spirit of praise. Moreover, the spirit of praise is easier and sweeter. It brings no suffering along with it; it involves no austerity; it implies no arduous heights of prayer. There is not in devotion a more childlike spirit than it is. But it is not only a different spirit; it produces a different character, a different kind of spirituality. It entices us to serve God out of love. Hence, it finds its proper place in this treatise, which would not be complete without it.

∞

Desire that God be loved better and by all

By *desire*, I mean the devotion that results in the heart from the two loves of complacency and benevolence, to be afterward explained. It is wishing God more love, more obedience, and more glory from men. It is desiring for Him, out of love, the augmentation of everything in Heaven, earth, Hell, and Purgatory, on which His accidental glory can feed and be increased. It is wishing we could be martyred for the Faith, or clean Hell, or empty Purgatory. It is wishing, even until sorrow and condolence spring up in our hearts, that sins might cease, and scandals disappear, and lukewarmness evaporate from the face of the earth, and most of all, that we ourselves could serve such a Majesty otherwise than we do, and could have other hearts than those miserable icy stones which, so far as God is concerned, we carry about in our bosom all our lives long. It is wishing that every grain of sand and every leaf of the forests had a seraph's intellect and voice to swell the choirs of God's praise.

This, again, is a different spirit from wishing to escape hellfire, from desiring a short Purgatory — or to skip it altogether — from praying for a quiet life and an easy death, from asking temporal blessings and seeking cures from the relics of the saints, from desiring the peace, joy, and stability of Heaven, merely or mainly, because of the irksomeness of earth's contraries.

Once more, let me not be misunderstood. I am not saying that this last spirit is wrong. Not at all. I wish all the children of men were infected with it. But it is cognizably a different spirit from the spirit of desire. And the spirit of desire is easier and sweeter, and gives God greater glory. Besides this, it also, like the spirit of praise, produces a different spirituality and leads to the service of love.

Henceforth, I shall not speak of praise and desire separately; for they run in and out of each other so perpetually, that for convenience, we may very well regard them as one thing.

You see, to go back to my old story, what I want of you is confidence in God. There is no worship worthy of the name of worship, that is not the voice of confidence. There is no love that is not confidence. But there can be no confidence without the filial feeling. We always get back again to the same point: God is our Father!

Look at the perfections of God — His power as well as His love, His justice as well as His mercy. Consider one as much as the other; be as fair to one as to the other. So far as in our blindness we can at all estimate the character of God, or appreciate Him, we must acknowledge that there can be no acceptable worship of Him that is not based on confidence. This is the proper homage of the creature to its Creator. From the dreadful fear that worships the spirit of power with human sacrifice and fanatical suicide, to the mixed impertinence and superstition of fetishism, the absence of this filial feeling of confidence is the characteristic of every modification of false worship.

The beautiful worship of God as our Father is distinguished by this very thing: that its chief exercise of love is in putting trust in the very perfections of God, which, to an unloving mind, would produce fear. It is a great act of love to trust, like a son, God's tremendous power. It is greater still to remember what we are and, in spite of it, to put all our confidence in His justice; to repose, as in a mother's lap, upon that very attribute which haunts the unloving like an unconquerable specter as long as they believe and live.

All for love, and love for us all. All for Jesus, and Jesus for all. These are the two sides of religion. Everything is here — all theology, earth, Purgatory, Heaven. Jesus has come, softening and subduing all things to Himself, veiling His eternal glory in the sweet regards of human eyes, like unto His Mother's, pleasing not Himself, pouring love over the whole earth, to change the face of things. And yet alas for the interests of divine love! Alas for the Sacred Heart! How many Catholics contrive to make of this blessed Faith and service, a dry, cold, formal, stingy, ungraceful worship!

∞

Practice interior acts of worship

Perhaps nothing strikes converts in the devotional system of the Church so much as the value and importance assigned to interior acts. They are surprised at the duty, under pain of sin, of acts of faith, hope, charity, and contrition, at recurring periods or under given circumstances. They are startled at the commentaries on our Lord's doctrine about committing sin in our hearts. They have to reconcile themselves to the influence attributed to intention.

Now all this, just like the rest of the Catholic system, brings out God. God is a simple act. Whatsoever is done stands in a certain relation to God. All its meaning and reality is from this. Words, therefore, are but accidents. Overt acts add but little, comparatively, to the malice of the interior will. The thought has been assented to; the intention has been formed; the temptation has been deliberately admitted. The thing is irrevocable. It has touched God and is stereotyped. He needs no index of the voice, nor consummation of the hands. It is an act, and ranks as such with Him, for good or evil, for reward or punishment. Sins of thought, says the Council of Trent, have these frightful characteristics: first, that they sometimes make a greater wound in the soul than sins of deed, and second, that they are sometimes more dangerous. They are also more numerous, more easily committed, and their approaches frighten us less.

Now, the reality of the merit of devout desires, of mental praise, and of all interior as well as spoken acts of devotion is the loving side of this question. They need be nothing more than interior acts. Nothing more is necessary. They have touched God as such, and so have received their value and their merit. Thus, turning the tables on sins of thought, we may say that these interior acts of piety sometimes make a greater impression on the soul than exterior ones do, while they have the further advantages of being more numerous and more easily performed. But is it not enough to vex our love, to go and stand by the countless seas of men's hearts, and to watch the innumerable waves that stir and brighten in every one of them every minute, and to think there is not one wave or ripple that might not rival an angel's song for worth before the dear majesty of God, and yet, that this treasure is so little used, that men take so little pains about it, and that God is so defrauded of His glory? He so loves us, and He so longs for our love, that He has made it almost as easy, by the merits of Jesus, for our hearts to praise Him, as for the thurible to let the spires of sweet smoke issue through its perforated cover; and yet we will not do it!

It is hard to appreciate these interior acts at their true value. There was a nun in the convent of St. Mary Magdalene de' Pazzi, by name Sr. Maria Benedetta Vettori, whom the saint saw five hours after her death in a glory exceeding the beatitude of many other virgins of the monastery, and fearlessly gazing on the humanity and divinity of the Word. Wherefore, after a long time in admiring rapture, through joy at such a delightful sight, the saint began to exclaim, "Oh, happy thou, who knewest how to bear the hidden treasure! Oh, what a great thing to be singular among the singular, and yet regarded as an ordinary one! The Word, had He merely regarded the works, would have had little to reward, for short has been the time for working. But oh, the goodness of God, who rewards every thought, and word, and wish! Great and continual were thy works, and practiced by few, for they were interior! Oh, the greatness of interior works, so little understood! One interior work is worth a thousand years of exterior exercises!"

Remember, then, this is what we start with. There is nothing in the world so real and substantial as the love of God. One act of divine love is a more finished thing than a statue of Phidias or Praxiteles. It is more firm than the foundations of the Alps. It is more enduring than the round world that God has made so strong. All things are bubbles to it. They have nothing in them. They mean little. They soon pass away. An act of love is a complete work, and has greater power and greater consequences than any other act. The mere act of dying is not equal to it. And yet this act of love can be made by a mental glance, quick as lightning, and piercing Heaven.

Such acts can be multiplied at will beyond our power of reckoning, and in the midst of apparently the most distracting occupations. So far from being weakened by repetition, they only grow more intense and more powerful. Yet they require no effort. To elicit them is even a pleasure to us.

But when we put these facts alongside of our practice, it looks as if there must be a fallacy somewhere. All this can hardly be true, and yet we remain as we are.

How incredible is the hardness of our own hearts! It is a fair match for the excess of God's love.

Oh, welcome, then, that beautiful spirit of reparation to the majesty of God, which so many of the saints have had! It is like making sweet honey out of bitter flowers. The little love we have for God, thus, by this dear right of reparation, furnishes us with another means of loving Him still more. Who will say that all things are not contrived for love?

In order to get a clear idea of praise and desire, it will be necessary for us to enter somewhat into the question of divine love, its different kinds and manifestations. This, however, will be so far from leading us away from our subject that it will throw great light upon many of the preceding chapters. Indeed, if "All for Jesus" is the same thing as "All for love," then divine love is the very subject of the treatise. A holy longing for God as our last end, our sovereign good, our exceedingly great reward — as when St. Paul exclaimed, "I desire to be dissolved, and to be with Christ"[170] — this love we ought to have all our lives long, although God may not always give us the gift to feel it sensibly.

There is a remarkable passage in the revelations of St. Gertrude that shows how acceptable to God is this longing to see Him, while it illustrates also the drawing that devout people mostly have to gaze intensely on the Blessed Sacrament. She was divinely instructed that as often as a man gazes with desire and devotion on the Host, where the Body of Christ lies hidden sacramentally, so often does he increase his merit in Heaven; and that in the future Vision of God to all eternity there shall be to him so many special and congruous joys as the times that on earth he gazed with desire and devotion on the Body of our Lord, or, which is greatly to our present purpose, when he so much as desired to do so, and was reasonably hindered from doing it.[171]

Observe well that God is pleased to attach the same promise to the desire to see Him as to the actually doing so; so the remarkable words of St. Lawrence Justinian were no devotional exaggeration, when he said, "Let us persist in our prayers so that better gifts may be daily given to us. For it very often happens that what merits cannot do, the intercession of desires effects. Truly God rejoices so much in the prayers of supplicants, that He grants their wishes if only they come from a simple heart, a humble mind, and a faithful devotion. Only let these three conditions be united in a prayer,

[170] Phil. 1:23.

[171] *Revelations*, Bk. 4, ch. 25.

and whatever a man shall ask, according to God, he shall receive from the Father of lights and His Son, Jesus Christ."[172]

∞

Love God more by
striving to know Him better

"What is unknown," says St. Augustine, "cannot be loved; for, except as known it is not loved." It is this knowledge of God that leads us to those further kinds of love which we need to illustrate our subject of praise and desire; so I must try to do what seems very foolish: to describe God.

God is simple, without body or distinction of parts. He is simple, because He has nothing borrowed. He is good without qualities, great without quantity. He is Creator, yet needing nothing; everywhere, yet without place; eternal, without term; and changing all things, without change Himself. He is good with an infinite goodness, and good to all, but especially good to men. He is infinite in the multitude of His perfections, in their intensity, and in their magnificence. He is present everywhere, in different manners, yet nowhere contracting soil or stain. He is immutable; His eternity defends Him from time, His immensity from change of place, and His wisdom from change of purpose. He is eternal without beginning as well as without end, and eternal with a life that exists all at once and altogether, and with a perfect possession of it. He subsists by the incomparable unity of His blessed nature, and it is the crowning interest of every man in the world that God should be but one. He is sovereign purity, unspeakable sanctity, and most resplendent beauty. He is always in adorable tranquillity; no trouble can come near His Being.

[172] *De Exalt. Crucis.*

He is known to nature, to faith, to glory, yet He is incomprehensible by all. His name is the ineffable God. His science is beyond our thought and is the source of His ravishing joy. His being is truth itself, and His life is the inexhaustible fountain of life. His will is worshipful, unblamable, and supreme, and His liberty is without parallel and beyond words. His love of His creatures is eternal, constant, gratuitous, and singular; and His mercy is an unfathomable abyss of the most beautiful compassions and condescensions, and no less also of the most delicate judgments and the most tender retributions. His justice is as irreproachable as His sanctity and as benevolent as His mercy. His power is illimitable, and full of love; and His blessedness is inaccessible.

Yet all these are not separate perfections: but He is Himself all these excellencies, and He is one: Three co-equal, co-eternal, and consubstantial Persons, only one God. Such, in the dry language of the schools, is the description of Him who is our loving and indulgent Father, God over all, blessed forevermore. Amen.

Can we read it, and not see that no half-allegiance will do for Him? He cannot reign over a divided heart, for who is he that can share the throne with Him? What but love can be our religion, for with what else can we worship Him? When we have dared to trust Him, then we have worshiped Him.

And are not these attributes like the circles of the whirlpool, drawing us into themselves with the strong fascination of His beauty? What can we do more than cry out with St. Francis de Sales, "O goodness so infinite, O infinity so good!" Yet it is only in proportion as these dry definitions breathe and burn with the heat and light of the Holy Spirit that they touch our hearts with genuine love of God. But when they are so touched, as yours have long since been, they lead us not only to long for God as our own sovereign good, but to long for something more. But let us first see what comes of this sweet knowledge of God, where the will tastes what the mind perceives.

Now, if God cannot be loved unless He is first known, and if also He has arranged all creatures for the express purpose of communicating Himself to them and being loved by them, then it must follow that it is for the glory of God that His perfections should be known, and His goodness acknowledged. As our Lord said that when He was lifted up, He would draw all men unto Him, so when the Divine Majesty is raised up before the eyes of men, the hearts of multitudes will be drawn toward it in adoration and trembling love. Hence, as the glory of God is one of the three objects we are putting before ourselves at present, we see how much we can promote it, no matter what our rank and condition may be, by making God better known by those who come our way.

It is remarkable how few persons meditate on the attributes of God. They seem to imagine that little can be known, said, or thought about them; or at best that they are a subject for lofty contemplation rather than the humble meditation of beginners. If the mysteries of Jesus, the actions of the sacred humanity, were to be neglected for the divine attributes, there can be no question it would be a delusion and, as St. Teresa teaches us, a very dangerous delusion. But it really seems almost necessary to fruitful meditation on the sacred humanity of our dear Lord, that meditation of the attributes of God should go along with it.

It is sadly true, however, that with all classes of men, the perfections of God are infrequent subjects of thought. People will often start at being told things about God, as they would at some vision about the unrevealed actions of our blessed Lord and our dear Lady, or at some tremendous announcement of modern science that upsets half our previous knowledge and, for the time, throws it all into confusion. Surely this is the reason God is so little loved and why we are all so dry and unamiable in our way of serving Him, and especially why there is such a universal complaint that of all devotional practices, that of the presence of God is the hardest and most tedious.

∞

Reveal God's perfections to others

Now, we all have continual opportunities to say a word for God; to make others recognize His wisdom, or acknowledge His goodness; to take His side; and to contrast what He would like with what men at large are actually doing. We see pious and worthy people with their instincts in the wrong direction; we are pained by the inconsistencies of those whose fervent self-denial we joyfully admire; and it is all because God is not known, and His true glory not discerned.

But even if opportunities of thus glorifying God by teaching others about Him were wanting to us, we can always glorify Him by learning about Him ourselves, by reading about Him and meditating upon Him, and by perpetually offering to His majesty reverential and affectionate acts of praise and desire. We are dependent on nobody for this. We do not so much as need to speak. Yet we continue to glorify Him while we make acts of loving admiration of Him, or congratulate Him that His perfections are unspeakable, or offer to Him with humble reparation the praise due to Him from all those creatures that are this hour forgetting Him. Oh, how much could we do by patient love, by thoughtful love, by assiduous love!

And it is no less for the interests of Jesus that the knowledge of God should be spread upon the earth. He came to save sinners, not only by dying for them, but by making His Father known to them. This is eternal life: that we should know God and Jesus Christ, whom He hath sent.[173] Our Lord is Himself the brightness of His Father's glory and the figure of His substance. As the Second Person of the Holy Trinity, He is the Eternal Word, the Father's knowledge of Himself, whom He hath appointed heir of all things, and by whom also He made the world.[174]

Thus, to publish the perfections of God to others, or to acknowledge them ourselves, is of all works the most acceptable to our dearest Lord, for it is the likeness of His own work — rather, it is His own work with which He allows us to cooperate. It is His own grandeur, they are His own perfections, which we are thus publishing and acknowledging. There is no fitter devotion to the Person of the Eternal Word than to laud and magnify the splendors of the Most Holy Trinity.

The salvation of souls is equally concerned in the matter. What has been the experience of converts to the Catholic Church? It is not so much knowledge and love of Mary that they have acquired, as those they have left behind so often fancy. It is not so much the efficacy of grace, and the reality of the sacraments that they have come to learn by their new religion, although what they have learned of these things, and especially of the doctrine of grace, is indeed most wonderful. But the great, pre-eminent change in them since they became Catholics has been their knowledge of God.

The thought of God has been growing and expanding in them ever since, until their whole minds have become overshadowed with it. The chief fruit of an intense and enthusiastic devotion to our dear Lady has been to teach them more and more of God, and to magnify Him in their souls. When they look back on the old days of error, it does not look so much as if their ignorance had

[173] John 17:3.

[174] Heb. 1:2.

consisted in a disesteem of Mary or of the Blessed Eucharist, of penance or of Purgatory, as in having a low idea of God; so, in retrospect, a man is led involuntarily to exclaim, "Why, I did not believe in God!" and the cry is hardly an exaggeration. Then, for the first time, they know what a solid thing religion is.

And oh, how sweet has the knowledge of God been, as well as a solid gain! It has put another face on life, on trial, pain, vicissitude, and suffering. It has been within them a fountain of refreshment springing up continually, or, as the prophet says, "The shadow of a great rock in a barren land." And it is not only sweetness that has been in it, but power also — power to do and power to endure.

Men little know how great and good a work it is they are doing when they increase by ever so little another's knowledge of the Most High. They have stopped not one sin, but hundreds. They have been the channels not of one grace, but of thousands. They have taught not one devotion, but all devotions in that one which comes of knowing one thing more of God than we knew before. The knowledge of God is the establishment of Christ's kingdom in the soul. How many more would be converted if they would only read and meditate on God! How many would advance in the spiritual life who now stand still, because the divine perfections are not preached to them or are not made part of their spiritual reading! How many more Catholics would serve God out of pure love if they would make His character and attributes their study!

Let knowledge of God lead you to rejoice in His goodness

Let us now see what comes of this knowledge of God, which we receive by faith. We perceive Him to be the unspeakable fullness of all possible and incomprehensible perfections. As He is, then, an object immensely beautiful, He must therefore be immensely desirable, and is discerned as such by the understanding using the light of faith. Now, whenever the understanding beholds anything desirable, there is an immediate feeling in the will, which is not a free act, but the necessary result of the law of our nature. This feeling is called complacency. But although this is not itself a free act, it at once begins to act unless the reason forbids it. It begins at once to exercise itself freely in expressions or sentiments of joy, pleasure, praise, and desire.

It is thus that we come to this second kind of divine love — the love of complacency: rejoicing in God because He is so good, because He is Himself, because He is God. We praise Him for all this. We desire also that, as we can do nothing to increase His glory in Himself, we could at least increase His accidental glory, which comes from the obedience and love of His creatures, whom He has created for this end.

This complacency comes from the very knowledge of God that faith imparts to us; and it is continually growing in us, unless sin and lukewarmness hinder and kill it. The case between God and the soul, then, stands thus, if we may venture to use Scripture language for these mutual acts of love. The soul, looking in delighted wonder over all this sea of beautiful attributes and perfections, seems to hear a voice rising up from the surface of the many waters, and borne to its inmost ear: "I have loved thee with an everlasting love; therefore have I drawn thee, taking pity on thee; and I will build thee again, and thou shall be built, O virgin of Israel."[175] And the soul murmurs, half in thought, half in reply, "Know ye that the Lord, He is God. I have said to the Lord, 'Thou art my

[175] Jer. 31:3-4.

God. Thou art the God of my heart and the God that is my portion forever.' "[176] The voice of the many waters comes again, "If any man shall hear my voice, and open to me the gate, I will come in to him, and sup with him, and he with me."[177]

How delightful is this complacency in God! There need be no bounds to it; it may be, if it could be, as wide as God Himself. There can be no talk here of limit or of moderation. Moderation is baseness, fraud, and infidelity, where God is concerned. All God is before us, infinitely perfect, infinitely desirable, for us to rejoice in.

What is earth? What are the things of earth? Shall we not be lifted up far above ourselves, our own petty wretchedness and misery, our own groveling interests and low-born desires? God grows like a dawning splendor before us. We become like that good man mentioned in St. Philip's life who was seen retreating from the altar, step by step, with wonder and rapture depicted on his face, and who said that he was meditating on the greatness of God, and it was growing upon him like something in pursuit, and thrusting him backward.

The more we know of God, the more our complacency increases, because, to fill our minds and engross us, the simple thought of God must be multiplied and repeated from a thousand objects. It is like the sun lighting up a mountain chain. He is not multiplied Himself, but as His golden magnificence lights up peak after peak, we become more and more surrounded by his effulgence. It is thus with God: each attribute to which we give a name — although His attributes are in truth His simple Self — is to us as a separate height crowned and glowing with His glory, and so

[176] Ps. 99:3; 15:2; 72:26 (RSV = Ps. 100:3; 16:2; 73:26).

[177] Apoc. 3:20 (RSV = Rev. 3:20).

reflecting Him upon our souls, while the multitude of nameless perfections for which we have neither ideas, nor words, nor standards are to us like the consciousness of the glorious sea of mountain tops that are beyond our ken, but which we know to be resting in that furnace of golden light, and adding to the burning splendor that is circumfused over earth and sea and sky.

Who can think of self when he is thus with God? And who can have hard thoughts of His absolute empire and uncontrolled sovereignty, when he is lost, sweetly lost, in this complacency, joying over God that He is God, that He is just what He is, and that nothing is wanting to Him? He is the Lord; let Him do what seemeth Him good.

Ah, dear Jesus, how is it we do not cultivate this blessed complacency? It is so full of gladness and of peace, and of self-forgetting, childlike love! Oh, teach us to be ever looking over the sea of Thine interminable magnificence, and rejoicing that Thou art what Thou art, that Thou hast been thus from unbeginning eternity, and shall be thus, adorably immutable, for never-ending ages!

"The soul," says St. Francis de Sales, "that exercises the love of complacency cries perpetually in its sacred silence, 'It is enough for me that God is God, that His goodness is infinite, that His perfection is immense. Whether I die or live matters little to me, for my Well-Beloved lives eternally with a life all triumphant.' Death cannot sadden a heart that knows that its sovereign Love is living. It is enough for the soul that loves, that He whom it loves more than itself is heaped with eternal blessings; for such a soul lives more in Him whom it loves than in the body that it animates; for in truth it does not live itself, but its Well-Beloved lives in it."[178]

[178] *Treatise on the Love of God*, Bk. 5, ch. 3.

Praise God for His goodness

∞

Let complacent love blossom into benevolent love

The love of complacency, strictly speaking, is the joy we feel in the infinite perfections of God, that He is what He is. But just as the knowledge of God, by faith, cannot stop at knowledge, but passes into a necessary complacency — and that necessary complacency into free acts of praise and of desire — so, also, this free love of complacency cannot terminate in itself. It passes on to another and a further love, which is called the love of benevolence.

Our love of God is just the opposite of God's love of us. He loves us first with a love of benevolence, working in us all the good we have, and then when it is worked, loving us with a love of complacency in His own work within us. But our benevolence toward God is, as St. Francis de Sales points out, merely the natural consequence of our complacency in Him. We first rejoice that He is so good and perfect, and then wish Him, if it were possible, more goodness and perfection; and this last act is the love of benevolence.

To explain this, I will use the words of St. Francis himself.

"As it is not easy to understand how man can wish any increase of happiness or perfection to God, let us examine how far the love of benevolence we bear Him is a real and solid love. As God is the center of all good, as His perfections are infinite, and consequently beyond the reach of our desires and thoughts, it is evident that we cannot wish Him, at least with an efficacious desire, any perfection that could add to what He is in Himself. Besides, the object of desire is some future blessing, whereas in God all perfection is present, and so present that it forms one and the same thing with the Divine Essence, which exists from all eternity, and acquires no increase.

"As we cannot form any real or absolute desire, with regard to God, we form imaginary and conditional wishes: 'Thou art my God; Thou art so rich in Thyself that Thou needest not my possessions. But if it were possible that there was anything Thou didst not already possess, I should wish it to Thee, O my God! I should long to procure it for Thee, at the expense of my life. If, being what Thou art, and what Thou canst not cease to be, it were possible that some new perfection could be added to those Thou hast already, with what ardor would I desire it were Thine! I would wish that my heart were transformed into desires and that my life were consumed in sighs. Yes, O Lord! I am far from desiring that we could have room to wish Thee any increase of perfection. My greatest happiness is to think that we cannot add to Thy sovereign goodness even in desire. But if Thou couldst acquire any new advantage, if the desire of seeing Thee more perfect or more happy, chimerical as it is, could be realized, I would wish that my soul were totally transformed into this desire, that my ardor in wishing Thee any perfection which Thou didst not already possess, were as lively as the pleasure I now feel in not being able to desire for Thee anything Thou hast not. How sweet this impotence becomes to me, O my God, when I reflect that it is founded on Thy sovereign, immense, incomprehensible riches, which would be capable of satiating an infinite desire, could it exist, so as to be transformed from desire to infinite enjoyment.'

"These desires, although founded on imaginary and impossible suppositions, are very pleasing to God, and are usually formed amid the transports and holy ecstasies of charity. . . . We also testify love of benevolence for the Almighty, when, reflecting that we cannot add any degree to His perfections, which are His infinite and essential immensity, we endeavor to increase in ourselves His accidental greatness, which consists in the complacency we derive from knowing that He is infinitely perfect, and which increases in proportion as this complacency becomes more ardent. We do not then exercise the love of complacency on account of any pleasure we derive from it, but because it is a source of delight to God. We do not seek our happiness therein as our own happiness, but as conformable to that of God, and thereby calculated to unite us to Him, and procure us the enjoyment of His infinite perfections.

"To render this union and enjoyment more excellent, we desire to communicate, if it were possible, an infinite strength and boundless extent to complacency. The ever-blessed Queen and Mother of holy love gives us an example of this, when she says, 'My soul doth magnify the Lord!' To leave no doubt that the ardor of her gratitude derives its increase from complacency, she immediately adds, 'My spirit hath rejoiced in God my Savior.' "[179]

These explanations are sufficient for my purpose. What I want to bring you to is this: just as I have urged you to promote the glory of God, the interests of Jesus, and the saving of souls, by what is called the love of condolence, or sorrowing for other men's sins, and also by the use of intercessory prayers and thanksgivings, by offering up your own actions to God in union with those of our dear Lord, and also by offering up to Him His own perfections, and the mysteries of Jesus and Mary, the angels and the saints; so now I want you to glorify Him in like manner by those acts of praise and desire which come of these two loves of complacency and benevolence.

Such are acts of joy that God is what He is; acts of praise of Him on His perfections, His works, and the mysteries of His sacred humanity; acts of desire, wishing for Him impossible things, which

[179] *Treatise on the Love of God*, Bk. 5, ch. 6.

St. Francis de Sales has just told us are acts of real love, and very acceptable to Him; acts of desire, wishing for Him that He might have had more glory from the world in years gone by, from the lost souls, and the like; acts of desire, which intercession may make efficacious, that He may be more glorified than He is now, through the perfection of the saints and the conversion of sinners, and the more rapid liberation of souls from Purgatory; acts of praise, wishing that every sand of the sea and leaf of the woods had an angel's intelligence to praise Him, and offering to Him again and again with loving ardor the actual angelic praise of Heaven; and sighs of loving sorrow, condolence, and reparation, over His slighted love, His outraged majesty, His forgotten goodness, and His defrauded glory. It is true that all these things sound like the breathings of very saints. Yet they need not the austerities that repel us, nor the supernatural powers from which we shrink as much in dismay as in humility. And, as with all the other things recommended in the previous chapters, so with these, how much might we do at such a little cost!

If you look at any of the saints, you will see that they are made up of these things: obedience to the commandments of God and the precepts of the Church; strong and loving instincts for the glory of God, the interests of Jesus, and the salvation of souls; an intense love of suffering and voluntary austerities, accompanied by terrific interior trials and what mystics call passive purgations of spirit; and supernatural states of prayer, unusual gifts, and miraculous powers.

Now, the first of these things we may put aside, because we must all have it, or else we shall not be saved. The love of suffering, most likely, we honestly confess we do not feel, and we shrink from it, as well out of humility as out of cowardice; and, as a consequence of this shrinking, we are not quite so blinded by self-love as not to see that the last point is far above us and unsuited to our present attainment.

∞

Strive for love of God, not heroism

Thus the strong and loving instincts for the glory of God, the interests of Jesus, and the salvation of souls remains, as something beyond the common necessary practice of the faithful, and below the pinnacles of the saints. These three instincts seem open to us, inasmuch as the austerities that frighten us and the supernatural heights of prayer that are out of our sight are not requisite for them. Moreover — and this is a singular consolation — the beauty of the saints lies rather in the three instincts that are open to us than in the two heights to which we dare not aspire.

Now, devout people formed upon the three instincts for the glory of God, the interests of Jesus, and the welfare of souls abound in Catholic countries in good times and seem to be to the Church what the middle classes are to the prosperity of the state — not its heroes, but its life, strength, muscle, and independence. They are the growth of quiet times. Martyrs can be, and will be, made out of them by scores, when troubles come. But saints, the spiritual creations of an interior life, belong to another order of things. It is plain, then, that in uneventful times, it is our chief work to increase this middle class of the faithful; otherwise we shall be such dry and uninteresting Christians that we shall never convert those outside the fold, and, what is even of more importance, we shall have nobody to love our multitudinous poor, or to take any generous, persevering pains about them.

It is equally obvious that it is the Devil's game to lessen the number of this class; and this he does in two ways especially: first, by giving devotion a bad name, inspiring men to call it romantic, enthusiastic, pretty, youthful, the fervor of converts, fanciful, novel, unpractical, and the like; and second, by leading people to aim too high, to attempt too much, to read mystical books, to run after miracles and portents, to make rash vows, and to tempt God by burdening themselves with a multiplicity of prayers; and then, when their wax wings are melted off, in weariness and disgust, they sink down to the merest observance of precepts and, not seldom, even lower still.

The aim of this treatise is to draw a picture of this middle class, to give a view of their life, to exhibit samples of their devotion, and to make out a case for them. It was mainly this sort of people St. Philip set himself to multiply in Rome, and it is substantially the chief work he left his sons to do. I do not say the exclusive work, or else we should lose our right to the crowds of dear sinners that are ever gathering themselves to the odor of the saint's name, and to the lures of his little apostolate. If, then, you want to be a saint, like to one of the canonized, this is not the book for you. He that has climbed the rocks can alone tell you the secrets of the rough ascent. This is a map of the easy ways of divine love, higher than the plains and above their dust, yet not so high as to be beyond the region of sweet flowers and shady trees, and the coolness of bubbling springs.

If you have ever read the life of St. Philip, you may remember how someone who wanted to be a saint dreamed that the holy Father was dragging him through rude and prickly briers. I wish we all had the heart to face the briers; but it is not so, and it is of no use trying to be good by theories. Still, to love God is a great thing, to love Him more and more is a greater thing, and to make others love Him is so great that it is a joyous surprise, ever fresh, and new every day, that God should let such as we are do so great a thing.

You must not suppose that I hold cheap the practices of mortification, whether outward or inward, or that I think affective love renders effective love unnecessary, or even that I believe interior mortification can dispense from the obligation of bodily penances and discomforts, in the case of those who are aiming at perfection. My little book is not a summa of ascetical theology. But because we cannot rise so high, there is no need surely to sink so low. Some severe spiritualists speak as if affective love were little better than a delusion, or at best a mere service of fervent feelings. Oh, surely this is hasty, peremptory, unkind, and not like the Church or God. I grant we must not stop there, that we must go on to mortify our inordinate passions, and work and suffer. Yet surely merely affective love is good as far as it goes; and it cannot be with Catholics nothing more than a worship of feelings, for I have shown all along — and theology most amply bears me out — that the practices of it may be made most solid — nay, almost inevitably are so. And then affective love is the way to effective.

Besides this, by aiming exclusively at one only, we most commonly lose both. I know there are many people who have made up their minds not to be saints. Well, if God were angry with them, and counted their pusillanimity as sin, if Jesus turned away from them and left them out of His reckoning, we need take no pains for them. But He does not do so; and therefore we may well affectionately ask them to think, if they will not be saints, whether they will not love our dearest Lord as far as Calvary, without committing themselves to the crucifixion. This will come home to us most feelingly, when our poor ashamed hearts tell us that we ourselves are at least among the well-intentioned faint-hearted cowards of the army of our generous and unselfish Lord.

It is not unfair, although I pretend to be pleading for God's glory and a service of love, to assail you with arguments drawn from your own interests. I am sure many of you are not contented with yourselves. You want to love God more and to make more of Jesus. You want to get out of your cold, dry, unhandsome way with Him. You would fain have more liberty of spirit, and feel your affections more at large in religion, and be unaffectedly more familiar with the instincts and interests of Heaven. You see that the service of love has common sense on its side, that these half-and-half measures with God make you neither happy nor holy, and, besides, something in your heart is drawing you closer to God and winning you to better things.

∞

Let acts of praise and desire transform your perspective

Now, look what these acts of praise and desire will do for you. They will take the world out of your hearts and make its pleasures look small and dull to you. They will draw you into quite a different set of ideas and associations, of affections and sympathies. They will make the practice of God's presence as easy to you as it will be delightful. They will settle a host of cases of conscience for you, by raising you at once into a clearer atmosphere where the doubts and difficulties in question do not exist. They will make idleness, frivolity, and dissipation intolerable to you, because of the change they will bring about in your tastes.

Beautiful angels were dull to St. Mary Magdalene, for she was seeking Jesus that Easter morning. What were their celestial faces and their dazzling raiment to her? They had taken away her Lord, and she knew not where they had laid Him. The gardener, too, as St. Francis sweetly says, reminded her only of flowers, while her head was full of nails and thorns and crosses; yet as he has come in her way, she will out with her one thought, "Sir, if thou hast taken

Him hence, tell me where thou hast laid Him, and I will take Him away."[180]

The three kings hurried through Jerusalem; the court only made them fret; they could rest nowhere but with their star at the crib of Jesus in the cave of Bethlehem. The spouse met the watchmen of the city, and her heart also was on her lips: "Have you seen Him whom my soul loveth?"[181]

So these acts of praise and desire make new men of us. We are all for Heaven. Death even changes its aspect. All things seem easy that are for Jesus, all things welcome that are steps to Him. How differently people feel! When someone told Fr. Dominic[182] the Passionist, whose memory is dear to so many of us, that she feared the particular judgment, the tears started in his eyes, and he cried out in his natural way, "Oh, but how sweet to see for the first time the sacred humanity of Jesus." This is what praise and desire bring us to. We cannot be all we wish on this side of the grave, but we can get on toward it by means of love. We can bring matters to this comfortable simplicity of the Spouse: "My beloved to me, and I to Him, who feedeth among the lilies till the day break, and the shadows retire."[183]

Desire to love God more

My first example of practices of praise and desire shall be taken from no less authoritative a book than the *Raccolta of Indulgences*. There is in it a chaplet of acts of divine love, indulgenced by Pius

[180] John 20:15.

[181] Cant. 3:3 (RSV = Song of Sol. 3:3).

[182] Dominic of the Mother of God (1792-1849), theologian.

[183] Cant. 2:16-17 (RSV = Song of Sol. 2:16-17).

VII in 1818. I will extract some of those that illustrate the present subject.

I desire, O my God, to see Thee loved by all. Oh, happy me, if I could give my blood to make all men love Thee. Come, all creatures, and love my God. O my God, would that I had a thousand hearts to love Thee with, or that I had the hearts of all men, so that I might love Thee with them. Oh, would that there were more worlds than there are, so that all might love Thee! What a joy it would be! Happy he who could love Thee with the hearts of all possible creatures. I rejoice that the angels and the blessed love Thee in Heaven; and I desire to love Thee with all the love wherewith the saints most enamored of Thee loved Thee, and St. Joseph, and our Blessed Lady in each one of her mysteries, and our dearest Lord in each one of His mysteries, and in all the tabernacles where He is now lying hid in the Blessed Sacrament. I would fain love Thee with that very love with which He loves Thee in Heaven at this hour, and will love Thee to all eternity. And, last of all, I desire and intend to love Thee with all that love wherewith, O my God, Thou lovest Thyself.

∞

Praise Jesus for His love and merits

The following praises are recommended by Lancisius in his devotions to Jesus risen:

- Praise Jesus risen for the gifts of His glorified body and for all that He merited by his death, such as His triumphant Ascension, royal dignity, and dominion over the whole world, and plentitude of power in Heaven and on earth, the supreme headship of the Church, and His judicial office, and other things that we do not know and that are not enumerated by theologians.

• Praise Him for the manifold fruit of His life, Passion, and death, among both angels and men, and especially all the graces whereby the good angels were confirmed in grace, and all the graces of all kinds, innumerable and indescribable, by which men have had, to hinder sin, or to raise them out of sin, or to lift them to perfection. Praise Him for all sacraments and indulgences and for the resurrection of our bodies.

It will not be out of place here to mention a particular devotion of Sr. Maria Denise of the Visitation to her guardian angel. It was to praise him for the only fact of his history of which she had sure knowledge: the grace he received to stand in grace when the angels were falling all around him.

• Praise Jesus for the innumerable choirs of angels and holy souls in Heaven, who adore Him as their supreme Head, the Giver and Cause of all their graces and honors, and for the divine worship that is paid to Him in Heaven and out of Heaven, on earth, in Purgatory, by Masses, churches, images, vows, and all the good works that will ever be done up to the last day.

• Praise Him for that immense charity by which, as St. Dionysius tells us, He revealed to St. Carpus that He was ready to suffer death over again for the salvation of the human race; and by which also He revealed the same to St. Bridget. "Oh, my friends," said He, "so tenderly do I love my sheep that, rather than be without them, I would, if it were possible, die over again by a special death, equal to the one upon the Cross, for each separate one of them!" Another time He said, "Oh, if it were possible, I would, with most eager love, die over again as many times as there are souls in

Hell!" These things, alas for our stony hearts, help us, by our dearest Lord's — may I say it? — extravagant love of us, to measure our miserable pretense of loving Him!

∞

Renew your good purposes and holy desires

Thomas à Kempis tells us in the *Imitation* to renew our good purposes every day and excite ourselves to fervor as if we had been converted only today;[184] and Lancisius recommends certain classes of heroic acts and desires that it would be well for us thus to renew:

- *Acts of humiliation and our own nothingness:* Our blessed Lord said to St. Mary Magdalene de' Pazzi, "Whenever you make an act of your own nothingness, remember that as a creature cannot live without a heart, so you cannot live without me. As long as this knowledge remains in you, you may be sure that you will remain united with me; and my peace shall be with you even while you seem to be waging perpetual war against temptations, which, by my permission, shall assail you, but shall not overcome you; the more sharply they attack you, the more shall my favorable assistance superabound in you, although you shall not feel its presence or its sweetness."

  Another time He said to her, "They who serve me should do so with such humility as plunges their souls to the center of the earth; for just as a falling arrow does not rest until it touches the ground, so my Spirit rests only in the soul it finds in the center of its own nothingness."

[184] *Imitation of Christ*, Bk. 1, ch. 19.

Elsewhere God the Father said to her, "The ladder of the words of my Word is loftier than Jacob's ladder, for its foot is in the soul, which, by humility and self-knowledge, is lower even than the abyss in which, by lowly opinion of itself, it plunges, and by the true knowledge of itself it comes even unto my inmost being. And this is the difference between the two ladders: that Jacob's ladder did not reach beyond Heaven, nor descend lower than the face of the earth; but this ladder goes beyond the stars, in proportion as the soul humbles itself; nay, it is exalted even to my inmost being, for the soul's humility is its exaltation."

• *Desires and purposes to avoid all deliberate sin and even imperfection*, so that with St. Augustine we would rather die than sin; with St. Chrysostom, we would rather see the face of Hell than offend God; and with the heroic paradox of St. Alphonsus Rodriguez,[185] we would rather be thrust into Hell for no fault at all than offend God by the very least conceivable venial sin.

• *Desires and purposes to endure all sorts of things for the sake of our dear Lord*, such as St. Ignatius puts in the contemplation of the kingdom of Christ in the second week of his *Exercises*: "Behold, O supreme King and Lord of all, I, although most unworthy, yet relying on Thy grace and help, offer myself entirely to Thee and submit all I have to Thy will, declaring before Thine infinite goodness, and in the sight of the glorious Virgin, Thy Mother, and all the heavenly court, that this is my mind, my desire, and my decree, to follow Thee as nearly as I can, and to imitate Thee in

[185] St. Alphonsus Rodriguez (1532-1617), Jesuit lay brother.

bearing insults and adversities with true patience, both interior and exterior."

- *Desires and purposes about the love of our enemies.*

- *Desires and purposes to give up all our will and liberty to God,* without ever retracting them, and without excepting anything from the sacrifice. That these mere desires are, as sacrifices of love, most acceptable to Almighty God may be seen also from the fact of His so often inspiring His servants with pious designs, which He never intends them to accomplish, as in the case of Abraham's sacrifice of Isaac, and St. Philip's desire to go to the Indies to preach the Gospel and to shed his blood.

The lives of the saints furnish us with repeated instances of this. Thus it comes to pass that what St. Francis de Sales says is true: that even to wish impossible wishes about God Himself and His perfections is real worship and substantial love, and acceptable to Him. This opens out to us many trains of thought, and if our hearts were what they ought to be, it would open out to us many fountains of loving tears.

Develop liberty of spirit

While, for the good of our own souls as well as for the glory of God, we take pains to cultivate the spirit of praise in ourselves, we must not forget that in reality it is not so much a virtue of our own as a gift of God, and so to be sought from Him by special prayer. We should not omit to claim for this purpose the patronage of St. Gertrude, who was eminent even among the saints for her wonderful spirit of incessant praise. If we could imitate her in this, we might come at length to a participation in her equally wonderful liberty of spirit. How much depends upon this liberty, and how intimately it is connected with a spirit of praise! I wish men could be persuaded to study St. Gertrude more than they do, for most certainly our great defect is the want of liberty of spirit.

This is the chief reason the service of love is comparatively so rare among Christians. Surely, if persons living in the world, and in society, wish to lead a devout life, they should not suppose that a conventual life, diluted and lowered, can be the proper fashion of spirituality for them. From their position and their duties, they cannot command their own time, or break up their day into halves and quarters of hours, as if they were in a quiet cloister and had nothing to do but to follow the chimes of an abbey clock. Hence, in nine cases out of ten, to tell such people that they must draw up a written rule and keep to it, and that the captivity of set times for spiritual drill is their only hope, is as good as telling them that persons living in modern society must not attempt to lead what is called a devout life.

How many have given devotion up altogether, because they have tried a rule and found they could not keep it! How many have leaned their whole weight upon fixed hours and appointed ways of doing things, upon clockwork and over-division, and have broken down, because weak health, or a change of duties, or the interference of a London season have made their fixed hours and stereotyped ways impossible!

If spirituality is made dry, it will never wear. People living in the world are sure to put it disdainfully aside very shortly and to make themselves at home in a state of low attainments. They have tried spirituality, and it did not answer. It did not last. And so, because their own kind of spirituality was a failure, they have no faith in any other kind. It is incredible how soon people can make themselves comfortable in low things. It is as frightening, too, as it is incredible. If it were not for this fatal facility of settling down, common sense, honest shame, and reasonable discretion might win the day at last. But this settling down is like the hedgehog policy: roughness does not hurt it; sweetness cannot win it; and persuasion leaves it as it found it — prickly and imperturbable. Now, the failure of this regimental kind of holiness, as well as the idea that no other kind is safe or solid, comes entirely from the want of liberty of spirit.

It is difficult to speak well of liberty of spirit without seeming to recommend negligence, or to countenance unpunctuality, slovenliness, and caprice. But we may safely illustrate the manner from St. Gertrude herself. The following may be taken as specimens of her delightful liberty of spirit. We are told that she never stayed away from Holy Communion through fear of the dangers that her spiritual books told her were incurred by those who communicated unworthily. On the contrary, the more keenly she felt her imperfections, the more eagerly she ran to our blessed Lord, sustained by a lively hope and a zealous love of God.

On one occasion, when she was traveling, she fell by some accident from a dangerous height. Full of joy, she cried out, "Oh, my sweet Savior, what a blessing it would have been for me, if this fall had shortened my road to Thee!" Some of her companions were a little scandalized at this and asked her if she was not afraid of dying without the sacraments. "I should wish from the bottom of my heart," she answered, "to be fortified by the sacraments before I die; but I have the hardihood to prefer the Providence of my Lord and my God to all sacraments, and I think this the worthiest preparation for death. It is a matter of indifference to me whether my death be slow or sudden, provided it be agreeable in the sight of Him to whom I trust it will conduct me. For I hope, however I die, to find the mercy of God, without which I shall be lost eternally, no matter how long a preparation I may have made for death."

A pious person had prayed for a long time for some particular grace, and God had never answered her prayers, at which she fell into a state of dangerous discouragement. At last God said to her, "I have delayed answering you, because you have not sufficient confidence in the effects that my mercy produces in you. You should imitate my chosen virgin Gertrude, who takes her stand so firmly upon my Providence that there is nothing she does not hope for from the plenitude of my grace; and hence it is that I can never refuse her anything she asks."

Here is a picture of Gertrude's life. One day, when St. Matilda was singing in choir, she saw Jesus sitting upon a lofty throne, and Gertrude walking up and down before Him, without ever taking her eyes off His face, whichever way she walked, and at the same time she seemed busily occupied with a host of exterior duties. While Matilda was gazing in astonishment on the vision, she heard our Lord say, "This is the image of the life that my dear Gertrude leads before my eyes. She walks always in my presence. She allows no rest to her desires, no truce to her anxieties, to find out what is nearest and dearest to my heart; and as soon as she has discovered it, she executes it with care and fidelity. But the great thing is that she does not rest upon it, but is off again, always seeking some new thing in my will, in order to redouble her zeal by new actions and fresh practices of virtue, and thus her whole life is nothing but a linked chain of praises consecrated to my honor and glory."

St. Matilda thought at once of the besetting infirmity of active and zealous piety, for she had seen it — so she believed — in her dear Gertrude; and she ventured to say, "But, Lord, if Gertrude's life is so perfect, how is it she cannot bear the defects of others, and exaggerates them so much?" Our Lord, with admirable sweetness, replied, "It is because she cannot bear the least stain on her own heart that she feels so keenly the failings of her neighbors!" Nearly a volume of spiritual commentary might be written upon this.

Once more: let us listen to the testimony of God Himself. A holy man pressed God in prayer to reveal to him what it was in which His divine majesty took so much pleasure in His beloved Gertrude. God vouchsafed to reply that it was her liberty of heart. The holy man having esteemed the excellence of this gift much less than it deserved, answered in surprise, "And I, Lord, thought that what pleased Thee most in her soul was her perfect knowledge of herself, and the great love to which, by Thy grace, she has attained." "It is true," replied our Lord, "that those are two great perfections; but this liberty of heart implies both of them, and it is a precious gift, and a good so perfect that it is enough to raise a soul to the summit of perfection. It is this which disposes the heart of Gertrude to receive every moment of her life some new favors; and it is this which hinders her heart from attaching itself to anything that can displease me, or dispute with me the empire of her love."

∞

Let your love manifest itself in action

Having said so much of the failure of persons who live in the world and aim at devotion, I cannot refrain, although it is not necessarily connected with my subject, from adding a few words more. In the world, men must try to lead angelic lives, but with all the distractions of noisy life around them. To make a cloister about us in the world is to enclose the world along with us in our cells, and not to see the suspicious companion we have. Thus, trying to lead the lives of religious in the world, by a sort of spurious adaptation of monasticism to the world's circumstances, is one reason so many good people fail in trying to be better.

But there is another reason, too. The contemplative life is one thing, and the active life another, and each has its own retinue and appurtenances; and consistency is the secret of success. Now, except a few, a very few, singular vocations, devout people living in the world are called, as living in the world, to an active life. Yet here is a mistake into which they constantly fall. They make their spirituality to be all interior, while the whole of their active life is for the world, and essentially worldly. These good people have no Christian active life, and so the prayers and the church-going will not keep the peace with the parks and the parties, and at last devotion gets the worst of it, and signs away its rights in a base concordat.

In other words, dear reader, I suspect — I only say *suspect*, for I have no right to anything beyond a suspicion in spiritual science — that we can have no devout lives in the world without some active tending of the poor! Visiting the sick, looking after schools, attending hospitals, having to do with penitents and foundlings, immigrants and soup kitchens — I suspect the secret of perfection in the world, and of perseverance in devotion in the world, lies in these things. To live interior contemplative lives in the world for three hours a day is a glorious thing. But you see, unluckily, it hardly ever lasts. What now, if it really be that I am right, and that the reason for the failure is that to give all your interior life to God and all your exterior life to the world is an unlawful division; and that, if the rich are to be holy, they must either strip themselves of their riches, and hide themselves behind a convent grille, or they must labor with their own hands for those below them, and make themselves companions of the poor?

You see, your Christian life is made up of Mass, Communion, meditation, examination of conscience, some little austerities, and the like. But all this is more or less contemplative, so long as it stands by itself. It is all most excellent, but you are called to something additional — to an active Christian life, to the apostolate of the rich, which consists in assiduous and affectionate works of mercy for the poor.

Look abroad where the middle class of holy Catholic people so abounds and is so fruitful of good works, and so graceful in its spiritual beauty. It looks as if the secret there was in this glorious activity for the poor. When you come from prayer, or from church, you cannot without singularity carry your outward recollection into company, and somehow, prayer is like a delicate bloom upon the soul; the hot air of the world's rooms dissipates it speedily. But if you come from the garret or the hospital, the workhouse or the cellar, you have a charmed atmosphere around you, which is a sort of panoply of Paradise, from which the venomous arrows of the world glance off blunted and innocuous. It wears well. It cannot be smiled away, or talked of, or gossiped to pieces, like the exotic bloom of prayer.

Everywhere, where the world is, there is danger to the soul; but the gaiety, the pleasure, or the fashion can hardly be named that active mercy to the poor cannot disarm of all its perils, and even sanctify. Depend upon it: with you who live in the world, *mercy* is but another word for perseverance, and the touch of the poor is the real presence of your Lord.

What a wonder it is that God should love men! Intrinsically, what is there in them to love? If we compare our own natural gifts with those of an angel, how miserable we appear! If we consider how much more faithfully the beasts answer the end of their creation than we do, of what shall we be proud?

∞

Grieve that God is not loved more

Moreover, God has tried men over and over again, and they have always failed Him, and failed Him with every circumstance of unamiable selfishness that can be conceived. There was, first of all, Paradise and the Fall. Everyone knows what came of it. God was matched against an apple, and the apple carried it. The Flood was an awful judgment, but mercy went along with it. Yet we soon find the knowledge of God almost confined to one family and one line of Patriarchs. Then came the Israelites. Job's patience is hardly a picture of God's long-suffering with His people. He rewarded, and they despised Him. He punished, and they hardened their hearts. He sent them His Son, and their leaders crucified Him; and the Romans took away their place and nation, and burned up their city and temple.

Then here is the world since the Crucifixion. To look at it, you would say that our dearest Lord's Passion had been a simple failure. So little has the face of the world, or the tone of the world, or the way of the world changed. The results of the gospel on the world seem to be, first, a tinge of unusual romance in its history and, second, a great number of new words brought into its various languages to express the phenomena and genius of the Incarnation. Can anybody say that much else has come of it, looking at the world at large?

Then there are we Christians, a most unsatisfactory sight indeed! How do we treat our sacraments? How many of us are serving our Crucified Lord generously and out of love? Verily, God's love of men is a simple wonder. Yet how He must love them, seeing that He became not an angel for angels, but He became a man for men! There is no other account of the matter than the Scripture account of it. It is simply one of the mysteries of the character of God, as the Eternal Wisdom says of Himself: "I was set up from eternity, and of old before the earth was made. The depths were not yet, and I was conceived; neither had the fountains of water as yet sprung out. The mountains with their huge bulk had not as yet been established. Before the hills I was brought forth. He had not yet made the earth, nor the rivers, nor the poles of the world. When He prepared the heavens, I was present; when with a certain law and compass He enclosed the depths, when He established the sky above and poised the fountains of the waters, when He balanced the foundations of the earth. I was with Him forming all things and was delighted every day, playing before Him at all times, playing in the world, and my delights were to be with the children of men!"[186]

But it is a greater wonder still that He lets men love Him. Where are the words to tell the privilege it is to love the incomprehensibly beautiful, infinitely good, and immensely holy God? One would have thought such love as ours would be but an insolent profanation; and that were we allowed to be before God with such instinctive love as that of the patient cattle or the drinking birds, it would have been honor enough for us. Yet if, by permission of His inexhaustible compassions, we might love Him, surely it must be by blood, pain, suffering, shame, penance, and the costly offerings of a terrific austerity, and an appalling self-sacrifice.

Ah, dearest Lord God, and so, in truth, it is; but the blood and the pain, the suffering and the shame, are not ours, but His own! He weeps so that we may smile. He bleeds so that we may be whole. He is put to shame so that we may be glad and joyful. He is afraid, and anxious, and heavy, and sweating blood so that we may be at ease about our past sins, drinking in the sunshine of the

[186] Prov. 8:23-31.

earth, familiar with God, and sweetly confident about eternity. So far does He go that not only may we love Him most earnestly, but He has arranged all things to entice us into love. He coins our very desires into worship; and He lets us love Him, and glorify Him, and earn glory for ourselves by what would almost provoke a smile from an unbeliever, it looks so like mere make-believe, the artifice of a good-natured father, a very child's play of love.

If all this on earth, what will He be, what will He do, in Heaven? Isaiah and St. Paul have both told us how useless the inquiry is.[187] We must have other eyes to see it with, other ears to hear it with, and a far other range of thought to compass it and take it in. And will all this one day be ours? By the Blood of our sweet Jesus, we trust undoubtingly it will.

And what have we ever done for it? Where is the proportion between it and our deserts? There is none. It is all because of Jesus. Jesus is the secret of everything. Jesus is the interpretation of all the secrets of God. What a religion is this, and what a God! Oh, let it be told to every inhabitant of the earth that it is not as he thought it must be. We may all love God as much as ever we please, and in as many ways as we can think of. Would that angels might proclaim it every hour of the day and night, with the sound of the trumpet, to all the dwellings in the four quarters of the world. If, when they hear it, they neglect their worldly interests, and become like the men of Galilee, gazers into heaven,[188] it is only what we might expect: infinite permission to love! There is the creature's charter. The blood of a God bought it.

Do wonders end here? No! There is a greater still. It was passing wonder that God should love men. It was more marvelous that

[187] Cf. Isa. 64:4; 1 Cor. 2:9.

[188] Cf. Acts 1:11.

He should let men love Him. But man can outdo God, for his is the greatest wonder of all: it is that he does not love God when he may. This is hardly to be believed, although we see it. Oh, if we were not hardened by custom to this fact, it would breed in us some such horror as a cruel and savage parricide would do. It would take our breath away. We would not know what to make of it. Belief in it would only grow slowly into us, and would stupefy us as it grew.

Determine to make God better loved

But to forget God is the order of things, and we hardly notice the phenomenon at all. Alas, if we could see it altogether as faith would have us see it, we would long for tears of blood to wash away our infamy! And what can be said to make men love God, which is half as strong as what God has actually done for them? His mercy is so eloquent, His bounty so touching, His indulgence so persuasive, that if He has failed to win, why need men trouble themselves to proclaim His love?

This is what St. Paul must have meant when he talked about the foolishness of preaching.[189] Christ crucified was Himself the sermon and the preacher — what need of more? It was foolishness. Only in His love again God let us do this; we are always meeting love and running against it at every turn; He allowed us to take the words of His covenant into our mouths, and show our little love of Him by telling others His great love of us. And He showed His love again by letting the conquest of the world depend upon this foolishness of preaching.

But you and I love Him! Well, this is another wonder, for why do we do so, when so many more around us do not? It is simply His

[189] Cf. 1 Cor. 1:17-18.

own gift, simply grace. Here is Jesus again. He taught us how to love, and seeing what unapt pupils we were, He took some of His own love out of His Sacred Heart and put it into ours, so that we might love God with it. And all our share in the matter is that we have left the lamp untrimmed and caused the fire to burn far duller than it did before. It almost seems as if He purposely chose those who were least capable of loving Him. You and I must surely feel this. We could point to scores who do not love Him and yet are a thousand times nobler and more generous of heart than we are, and would have made far finer characters.

How miserable we are! Why did not God call other souls out of nothing who would have loved Him gloriously, and not been the mean things that we are? He loved us, our souls, ourselves. He chose us with an eternal choice, gave us an eternal preference, and loved us with an everlasting love. Why? There is no answering the question. Simply, He loved us, and so He chose us.

Then what are we to do with this world, which will not love God? Ah, there is the question. We may well have our heads and hearts full of all manner of wild heroic schemes for His love and honor. But it chafes us. What can we do? What is the nearest thing to infinite that we can attempt? How can we be in all quarters of the world at once? Here is an answer — not equal to the necessity, I admit; still it is an answer: by love and the spirit of reparation.

Oh, for the love of Jesus, do something! Can you see Divine Love begging from heart to heart, and not be touched by the piteousness of His poverty! There is no mendicant on earth so spurned as He who made it of old, and supports it now. Make one heart give Him an alms, in honor of the Father; make reparation for another heart's denial, in honor of the Son; and grow in love yourself, in honor of the Holy Spirit. Do we not see that a man hardly ever makes up his mind to a thing without doing it? Few men miss their end when they are obstinately bent on gaining it. I wonder what would take place if a few of us would do this — if we were to say resolutely, "I am determined to have God better loved in the world. I will not come into the world for nothing. Somebody shall love God the more for my having been created. If it be ever so little, divine love shall have been increased in the world by me."

Have we ever made such a determination? Let us make it now. I have huge faith in it. When do we begin? Today. Very well. Now we have a definite work before us, a work that shall be done.

Dear majesty of God, by the Heart Jesus, we will do something great and generous for Thee!

It would be a waste of words to show how the practice of praise and desire would assist us here, both in increasing our own love of God and making reparation to Him for others' want of love. But when we have done all, it seems so little that we may well fall back upon our doctrine and practice of oblation in order to supply for our deficiency. Where do we naturally turn? To Mary, the Immaculate Mother of God, to her who was not only conceived without sin, but was never so much as included in the decree that concerned sin.

Offer God praise for Mary

We would never know God as well as we do, if it were not for Mary. She reflects upon us the magnificence of God. Her dignity is the highest that can be and, St. Thomas tells us, even within the compass of omnipotence. She is a trophy of Divine Love, whereon the Three Blessed Persons have hung all their gifts and prerogatives that a mere creature is capable of receiving. She is clad from head to foot in the surpassing beauty of God. He has communicated Himself to her in a manner that we dare not put into words.

The Church calls her by names that startle us, as if she had borrowed the titles of the Most High and claimed common property in His attributes. We are bidden to speak of her in words that seem to belong to the eternal uncreated Wisdom of the Father. The Son has transferred to the Mother what is His.

She is more than all creation beside, more worthy, more beautiful, more mighty, and more loved of God. Thus, she is before God the unspeakable "hymn which befits Him in Sion."[190] She is all praise, all thanksgiving. She is the repose of the Creator's merciful complacency, the plenitude of His delighted benediction. With her He is well pleased.

Thus is Mary's praise an almost boundless worship we can offer to Him. In old times the servants of God called upon seas and mountains, fields and fishes, heat and cold, wells and green things, cattle and men to praise, exalt, and superexalt the glory of the good Creator.[191] But the Church teaches us to thank in strains of ardent love the Most Holy and Undivided Trinity for the gifts and graces of Mary, and has indulgenced several devotions to this effect. See what this implies. Enter into the Spirit of the Church.

Sweet praise of Mary! Can anything go beyond it?

Dear Mother, what a joy to us to know thou art such praise to God! Sweet praise, beautiful praise, the praise of the sinless! Can anything go beyond it? Yes, Mother, and none knoweth this so well as thou dost!

There was a cedar in Libanus, with fair branches, and full of leaves, of a high stature, and His top was elevated among the thick boughs. The waters nourished Him; the deep set Him up on high; the streams thereof ran round about His roots, and He sent forth His rivulets to all the trees of the country. Therefore was His

[190] Ps. 64:1 (RSV = Ps. 65:1).

[191] Cf. Ps. 148 (RSV = Ps. 149).

height exalted above all the trees of the country, and His branches were multiplied, and His boughs were elevated because of many waters. And when He had spread forth His shadow, all the fowls of the air made their nests in His boughs, and all the beasts of the forest brought forth their young under His branches, and the assembly of many nations dwelt under His shadow. And He was most beautiful for His greatness, and for the spreading of His branches; for His root was near great waters. The cedars in the paradise of God were not higher than He; the fir trees did not equal His top, nor were the plane-trees to be compared with Him for branches. No trees in the paradise of God were like Him in His beauty.[192]

∞

Offer God the praise of Christ

See how sweetly the prophet speaks of the sacred humanity of Jesus. It is to Him incomparably more than to our dearest Mother that the Father saith, "Show me Thy face; let Thy voice sound in my ears; for Thy voice is sweet, and Thy face comely."[193] And, oh, the glory of Mary! His voice sounds like hers, and His face wears the lineaments of hers!

But who can tell the praise that the voice of Jesus utters to the majesty of God? When an angel sang but a moment to St. Francis, the saint felt that he would have died of sweetness, had the music been prolonged an instant more. What, then, must be the voice of our Lord's most dear humanity? Oh, what a joy it is to kneel in silent praise, hushed with the sweet thought of all that divine, unutterable praise which the voice of Jesus is uttering to God! Oh, the consolation that God is now at least receiving praise — the value

[192] Cf. Ezek. 31:3-8.

[193] Cant. 2:14 (RSV = Song of Sol. 2:14).

of which is infinite — because of the blessed union of the Word with that sacred humanity!

But saints alone can rightly speak of these things. Let it be St. Francis de Sales. "When we have listened to the united praises which all creatures render their Creator, and then hear the homage and benediction of the eternal Son, we discover therein an infinite value and worth. We wake as if from a profound sleep, and, enchanted by the magical sounds of this heavenly music, we exclaim, 'It is the voice of the sovereign object of my love which strikes my ears; in comparison of this one voice, the harmony of all others is but a melancholy silence! Behold, He cometh leaping upon the mountains, skipping over the hills' — that is, elevating far above the benedictions of all creatures the homage He renders His eternal Father. His all-seeing eye penetrates more deeply than any other the infinite, uncreated beauty of the divine object He desires to glorify.

"The features that mark His boundless love are thus described in the Canticles: Behold, He standeth behind our wall, and clothes Himself with His sacred humanity. He renders Himself visible through His wounds and bleeding side, looking through these apertures as through the windows and through the lattices. We may consider divine love residing in the heart of our Redeemer as a sovereign seated on his throne. Through His wounded side it beholds the hearts of the children of men, never losing sight of them. As those who look through a lattice see without being seen, so the love of this divine Heart, which may be called the Heart of divine love, being in reality its center, incessantly considers all that passes in ours. As for us, we do not see Jesus Christ distinctly; we merely catch a glimpse of Him, for could we behold Him as He is in Himself, mortal beings as we are, we would expire for love of that infinite goodness which prompted Him to die for love of us, and which would induce Him to sacrifice His life for us again, if He were still liable to mortality.

"Could we hear the canticle which this divine Heart sings in honor of the Father, we would endeavor to burst our ties and soar to Heaven, so that we might listen to it forever. This God of charity does not deprive us of this advantage. He invites us to unite ourselves to Him, saying, 'Arise, make haste to fly to me, my love, my dove, my beautiful one. Come to this heavenly abode, where everything breathes supereminent bliss, where nothing is heard but canticles of benediction and notes of joy. The melancholy turtledove here changes her lamentations to the sweet strains of happiness. Come then, my love, my beautiful one, behold me through my wounds; they are the lattices through which I see you. My dove in the clefts of the rock, come and contemplate my heart through the opening in my bleeding side, made when my house was so piteously ruined on the Cross. Come and show thy face. Let thy voice sound in my ears. Let it be united to mine, and then thy voice will be sweet, and thy face comely. What transports of delight shall we not experience, when our voices, mingling with and made one with our Savior's, shall share in the infinite sweetness of those praises which the well-beloved Son renders to His eternal Father."[194]

Can the majesty of God need more than this? Shall not the aspirations of our wildest flights of love repose delighted and contented here? No, not even here, not even with the praise of our dearest Lord's sacred humanity. Love can still draw a distinction. The human actions of Jesus, such as this sweet praise, have indeed all infinite value because of His divine person. But they are not infinite in themselves. Here, then, is something in the praise which

[194] *Treatise on the Love of God*, Bk. 5, ch. 11.

falls short of the majesty it praises. We must mount higher still, until we rest in that perfect, infinite, sovereign praise that the Divinity offers to Himself.

∞

Let the loves of complacency and benevolence wing your soul to Heaven

But we must again call in a saint to speak. He shall sum up all I have tried to say of praise and of desire, of complacency and of benevolence. St. Francis de Sales asks, "Who can comprehend the sentiments of joy and complacency that animate a soul when it sees that God is infinitely glorified by the praise He gives Himself? But this complacency gives birth to a new desire. We long to glorify God for the power He possesses of worthily honoring Himself. We wish to annihilate our whole being to return Him thanks for it. We call anew to our assistance all creatures to bless Him, because He gives Himself an infinite glory which He can receive only from Himself.

"Thus, pleasure at seeing God worthily praised and an incessantly increasing desire to glorify Him, keep the heart, as it were, suspended between complacency and benevolence. It is continually wavering between these two sentiments, and always penetrating more deeply into the exhaustless sweets of love. It then reunites all its powers to praise God, and to thank Him that He can be adequately glorified only by Himself. For although the devout soul, in the first ardent effusions of its love, aspired to nothing less than to offer its God a homage worthy of His greatness, the soul afterward acknowledges that it had deceived itself, and declares that it would regret possessing the power to praise Him worthily. It prefers to all its desires the humble feeling of complacency, which it derives from seeing that God whom alone it loves, being infinitely worthy of homage, must be extolled in an infinite manner, in order to be praised as He deserves, and that He can be thus glorified only by Himself. After this avowal, the heart, unable to proceed, can only admire, and say with the prophet, 'A hymn, O God, becometh Thee in Sion.'

"Isaiah represents the seraphim, singing over and over again the same canticle, with their face and feet veiled, to show that they can neither know God perfectly, nor serve Him worthily. Feet, which support man, mark actions and services. However, notwithstanding their impotence which they unhesitatingly acknowledge, they always fly by the help of two wings; that is, the sentiments of complacency and benevolence keep them in continual motion. But this motion is not accompanied with agitation or disquietude, and is perfectly consistent with the calm and peaceful love by which they repose in God.

"The human heart is always agitated, when the movement by which it is incessantly dilated and compressed happens to be restrained, and it is most tranquil when this movement meets with no obstacle or resistance. In other words, its peace and calm depend on its movement. So it is with the seraphim and all who love God. Their love finds repose in the double and incessant movement of complacency and benevolence. By the first, they attract and — if we may use the expression — restrain the Almighty within the limits of their heart. By the second, they dilate their hearts in God. In this state, a heart inflamed with love, although perfectly tranquil, still experiences two kinds of movement. It desires to see the wonderful effects of God's infinite goodness, and then it wishes to render Him a worthy homage.

"But these two desires are the two wings which the seraphim cannot use. One they fold on their face, as if to acknowledge that God is infinite and beyond the reach of their comprehension. The other they fold on their feet, as if to express that they can do nothing worthy of the greatness and majesty of God. Love, then, retains only two wings of complacency and benevolence, which it employs to soar to the bosom of God, to absorb and engulf itself more and more deeply in the fathomless abyss of His infinite perfections."[195]

Ah, dearest Lord, why is it that we think of anything but this? Why is it that the world does not always seem little to us, as at this hour, and life a weariness, and death a gain? Why do our hearts leap up at other things besides the thought of God? Why art not Thou our only sweetness, who art, as we have ever found Thee, so passing sweet? Why art Thou not our only rest, our choicest recreation, who art our Father, our Brother, and our God? Why wilt Thou not take pity on our helplessness, and touch us with Thy fire, and make us serve Thee out of love? Ah, Jesus, we shall have reason to complain of Thee for being so lovely, if Thou wilt not give us love!

[195] *Treatise on the Love of God*, Bk. 5, ch. 12.

Chapter Nine

Assist the souls in Purgatory

It is incredible how dear the glory of God becomes to those who are continually on the lookout for it. The very search gives them new senses whereby they can find it, while daily increasing love is perpetually sharpening their discernment. "The earth is full of Thy glory." What a joy to a loving heart!

If Heaven and earth are full of the glory of God, so also is that most melancholy, yet most interesting land, where the prisoners of hope are detained by their Savior's loving justice from the Beatific Vision. And if we can advance the interests of Jesus on earth and in Heaven, I may almost venture to say that we can do still more in Purgatory.

Gain indulgences for the souls in Purgatory

Grace is such a great thing that we ought to try to increase it in all possible ways; and there are few ways in which we can increase it more rapidly than by turning satisfaction into merit. This is done by gaining indulgences for the souls in Purgatory. By this devotion, we acquire great spiritual treasures, and it is acceptable to God while it is profitable to ourselves.

Let us run through some of the fruits of this devotion, so as to animate ourselves to be more liberal toward these children of God and spouses of the Holy Spirit, to assist them with prayers, and with the satisfaction of our good works, offering it all for them without fearing that we shall thereby lose any of it. In truth, he will gain immensely who shall not reserve to himself any part of his satisfaction, or any of his indulgences, but shall offer them all for the holy spouses of our dear Redeemer who are detained in those terrible pains.

- *Increase in merit:* The first fruit is the great increase of our merits by this; for, of the three things that the good works of the just include — merit, impetration, and satisfaction — the greatest of all is merit. By it we become more acceptable to God, and more His friends, receiving greater grace, and so acquiring a new title to greater glory. Doubtless, then, if a man could turn all the satisfaction of his good works into so much fresh merit, over and above the merit there was there before, he would be a gainer by it, because the glory of the blessed is without comparison a greater good than the pains of Purgatory are an evil; and so the right to greater glory is a better thing than the right to less pain.

  He, then, who offers the satisfaction of his good works and his indulgences for the soul in Purgatory, does just this: he converts his satisfaction into merit. In this charity is a heroic act of great virtue, by which he will acquire eternal life by means of that satisfaction turned into merits, which is no help at all as simple satisfaction toward eternal life. As satisfaction, it would not have helped him one iota to that, but he makes it do so by turning it into merit, and at the same time helping others.

Now, this deserves reflection; for, besides the fact that glory is a greater good than Purgatory is an evil, we must remember that the increase of glory is a thing that is eternal, whereas the lightening of Purgatory is only temporal, for Purgatory itself is merely temporal; so the distance between the increase of glory and the lightening of Purgatory is as good as infinite. And yet to enjoy eternal goods, even in the very lowest degree, would be cheaply purchased by the endurance of the greatest temporal evils.

We must add to this that we ought in all things to do that which is most pleasing in the sight of God, not seeking our own interest or convenience, but His greater good pleasure. To please God is a better thing than to avoid suffering. A man who keeps his satisfaction and indulgences to himself does so from a desire of avoiding suffering, whereas he who offers them all for the souls in Purgatory thereby makes himself dearer to God, by a refinement of love in this heroic exercise of mercy and charity, which he was not bound to, but does out of the sweet freedom of his own will.

• *Gratitude of released souls toward their benefactors:* The suffering of the holy souls is without any gain or profit to themselves, whereby they can increase their merits, and so long as they are detained in Purgatory, so long is the heavenly Jerusalem deprived of her citizens, and the Church upon earth of new protectors and advocates with God. Hence comes another fruit of this devotion. The soul that we help release from Purgatory is laid under a particular obligation to us, both because of the singular benefit it receives from entering all the sooner into glory, and also because of the tremendous sufferings from which it is delivered. Thus it is bound to obtain for its benefactors perpetual graces and blessings from God. The blessed know that the good they have received is infinite, and being most grateful, they strive to show gratitude proportionate to the greatness of their enjoyment. Thus he who gives his indulgences to the holy souls will have so many agents in the court of Heaven to look after his eternal interests; and it is a greater good for a man to secure his salvation in this life through the graces obtained for him by this multitude of heavenly protectors, than to avoid the risk of being somewhat longer in Purgatory, because he has given away his satisfaction and indulgences.

But we gain more than the friendship of the souls we deliver; we gain the love of their guardian angels and of the saints to whom those souls were especially devoted; and we became also more dear to the Sacred Heart of Jesus, because of His pleasure at the release of His dear spouse and its entry into His celestial joy.

• *Souls to worship God on our behalf:* But there is a third fruit of this devotion which is very much to our purpose. It is a great thing to have someone in Heaven who shall love, praise, and glorify God on our behalf. He who loves God fervently and tenderly can never rest without doing all he can so that the infinite majesty of God should be exalted and glorified. Yet with all the miseries and sins of this life, we cannot magnify and adore that most dear majesty as the blessed can in Heaven.

Oh, then, the joy and consolation to think that others, whom we have released from Purgatory, are doing this great work for us in Heaven, and that, while we are still here, they have begun their praise already! Surely there can be no soul that has been fortunate enough to reach Purgatory which is not holier than ours, and more fitted to glorify God. And if so, then we ourselves have already put one in Heaven who shall give God greater glory than we would do if we were there ourselves. While we are eating, drinking, sleeping, and toiling here on earth, there in Heaven — refreshing thought, most solid consolation! — is the unsleeping soul, or, please God, the many unsleeping souls, whom we have hastened thither, worshiping and exalting the beautiful majesty of the Most High, unspeakably and incessantly.

• *Joy in the Church:* This is not all: there is a fourth trait of this generous devotion. We gain invaluable treasures not only for ourselves, but for others also; for we cause great joy in the Church, both Militant and Triumphant. Great is the feast in Heaven as the number of its citizens is increased; for if there is joy there over one sinner who does penance,[196] and yet he can return to his sin again, what must the joy be over that new citizen who can sin no more? That person's guardian angel, too, rejoices and receives a thousand congratulations from the celestial spirits at the successful issue of his guardianship. There is joy also among the saints to whom the soul was especially devoted, and among his relatives and friends. Our Lady, too, rejoices at the success of her multiplied intercessions, while Jesus reaps the harvest of His Precious Blood with love and with rejoicing. The Holy Spirit vouchsafes to joy over the triumph of His gifts

[196] Cf. Luke 15:7.

and countless inspirations; and the eternal Father, in the perfection of His chosen creature, whom he has borne with so long and so compassionately. And the Church Militant is no less interested in this joy. She has gained a new advocate. The relatives, friends, family, community, and country of that soul have especial reason to rejoice. Nay, all the predestinated, and indeed all nature, have cause of joy that another creature has entered into the joy of its Creator.

• *Immediate use of indulgences:* But there is a fifth fruit of this devotion. Love brooks on delay. Shall a treasure that can do wonders for the glory of God and the interests of Jesus stand idle, it may be, for years? At present we may be in no want of our satisfactions and our indulgences. And if they go into the treasury of the Church, who knows how many years may elapse before they are used? Shall not this talent, then, be used for God at once, by at once releasing from Purgatory souls who may begin, perhaps this very night, their sweet sacrifice of everlasting praise?

• *Blessings for us:* Last of all, what we are giving away comes back to us most abundantly, and this is the sixth fruit of this devotion. First of all, in this very act of such great charity and generosity, there is satisfaction for our sins; for if alms given to relieve bodily wants satisfy above most other good works, what will not spiritual alms do?

Second, he who loses anything for the glory of God receives at last a hundredfold. And God will either give us such grace so that we shall need little Purgatory, or He will inspire others to pray for us when we are there, so that, if we had kept our indulgences to ourselves, we might have been long in those fires; whereas if God sets many to gain indulgences for us, we shall enter much sooner into glory. It is an axiom that no one loses who loses for God. And when we are in Purgatory, the blessed, who by our means went sooner into Heaven, will look upon us as their benefactors, and on our release as a debt of justice.

∞

See how devotion to the holy souls touches many aspects of your Faith

It is not saying too much to call devotion to the holy souls a kind of center in which all Catholic devotions meet, and which satisfies, more than any other single devotion, our duties in that way, because it is a devotion all of love, and of disinterested love. If we cast an eye over the chief Catholic devotions, we shall see the truth of this.

Now, Purgatory is simply a field white for the harvest of God's glory. Not a prayer can be said for the holy souls, without God at once being glorified, both by the faith and the charity of the mere prayer. Not an alleviation, however trifling, can befall any one of the souls, without His forthwith being glorified by the honor of His Son's Precious Blood and the approach of the soul to bliss. Not a soul is delivered from its trial, without God being immensely glorified. He crowns His own gifts in that dear soul. The Cross of Christ has triumphed. The decree of predestination is victoriously accomplished; and there is a new worshiper in the courts of Heaven.

Moreover, God's glory, His sweetest glory, the glory of His love, is sooner or later infallible in Purgatory, because there is no sin there, nor possibility of sin. It is only a question of time. All that is gained is real gain. All that is reaped is true wheat, without chaff or stubble, or any such thing.

Again, what devotion is justly more dear to Christians than the devotion to the sacred humanity of Jesus? It is rather a family of various and beautiful devotions, than a devotion by itself. Yet see how they are all, as it were, fulfilled, affectionately fulfilled, in devotion to the holy souls. The quicker the souls are liberated from Purgatory, the more is the beautiful harvest of His blessed Passion multiplied and accelerated. An early harvest is a blessing, as well as a plentiful one; for all delay of a soul's ingress into the praise of Heaven is an eternal and irremediable loss of honor and glory to the sacred humanity of Jesus.

How strangely things sound in the language of the sanctuary! Yet, so it is. Can the sacred humanity be honored more than by the adorable Sacrifice of the Mass? And here is our chief action upon Purgatory. Faith in His sacraments as used for the dead is a pleasing homage to Jesus; and the same may be said of faith in indulgences and privileged altars, and the like. The powers of the Church all flow from His sacred humanity and are a perpetual praise and thank-offering to it. So, again, this devotion honors Him by imitating His zeal for souls. For this zeal is a badge of His people and an inheritance from Him.

Devotion to our dearest Mother is equally comprehended in this devotion to the holy souls, whether we look at her as the Mother of Jesus, and so sharing the honors of His sacred humanity or as Mother of Mercy.

Next to this we may rank devotion to the holy angels, and this also is satisfied in devotion to the holy souls. For it keeps filling the vacant thrones in the angelic choirs, those unsightly gaps that the fall of Lucifer and one-third of the heavenly host occasioned. It multiplies the companions of the blessed spirits. They may be supposed also to look with an especial interest on that part of the Church that lies in Purgatory, because it is already crowned with their own dear gift and ornament of final perseverance, and yet it has not entered at once into its inheritance as they did. Many of them have a tender personal interest in Purgatory. Many are guardians to those souls, and their office is not over yet.

And devotion to the saints is not without its interests in this devotion for the dead. It fills them with the delights of charity as it swells their numbers and beautifies their ranks and orders. Numberless patron saints are personally interested in multitudes of souls. The affectionate relation between them and those devoted to them not only subsists, but a deeper tenderness has entered into it, because of the fearful suffering, and a livelier interest, because of the accomplished victory. They see in the holy souls their own handiwork, the fruit of their example, the answer to their prayers, the success of their patronage, and the beautiful and finished crown of their affectionate intercession.

Perform the works of mercy through your devotion to the holy souls

The royal devotion of the Church is the works of mercy, and see how they are all satisfied in this devotion for the dead! It feeds the hungry souls with Jesus, the Bread of Angels. It gives them His Precious Blood to drink in their incomparable thirst. It clothes the naked with the robe of glory. It visits the sick with mighty powers to heal, and at the least consoles them by the visit. It frees the captives, with a heavenly and eternal freedom, from a bondage dreader far than death. It takes in the strangers, and Heaven is the hospice into which it receives them. It buries the dead in the bosom of Jesus in everlasting rest.

When the last doom shall come, and our dearest Lord shall ask those seven questions of His judicial process, those interrogatories of the works of mercy, how happy will that man be — and it may be the poorest beggar among us, who never gave an alms because he has had to live on alms himself — who shall hear his own defense sweetly and eloquently taken up by crowds of blessed souls, to whom he has done all these things while they waited in their prison house of hope!

∞

Let this devotion strengthen your faith, hope, and love

Another point of view from which we may look at this devotion for the dead is as a specially complete and beautiful exercise of the three theological virtues of faith, hope, and charity, which are the supernatural fountains of our whole spiritual life.

It exercises faith, because it leads us not only to dwell in the unseen world, but to work for it with as much energy and conviction as if it were before our very eyes. For, what to us, either in interest or importance, is the world we see, to the world we do not see? This devotion exercises our faith also in the effects of the sacrifice and sacraments, which are things we do not see, but which we daily talk of in reference to the dead as undoubted and accomplished facts.

It exercises our faith in the Communion of Saints and acts with regard to indulgences as if they were the most inevitable material transactions of this world. It knows of the unseen treasure out of which they come, of the unseen keys which open the treasury, of the indefinite jurisdiction that places them infallibly at its disposal, of God's unrevealed acceptance of them, and of the invisible work they do, just as it knows of trees and clouds, of streets and churches — that is, just as certainly and undoubtingly; although it often can give others no proof of these things, nor account for them to itself.

And this devotion is not a less heroic exercise of the theological virtue of hope, the virtue so sadly wanting in the spiritual life of these times. For look what a mighty edifice this devotion raises: lofty, intricate, and of magnificent proportions, into which somehow or other all creation is drawn, from the little headache we suffer up to the sacred humanity of Jesus, and which has to do even with God Himself. And upon what does all this rest, except on a simple, childlike trust in God's fidelity, which is the supernatural motive of hope? We hope for the souls we help, and unbounded are the benedictions we hope for in their regard. We hope to find mercy ourselves, because of our mercy; and this hope quickens our efforts without detracting from the merit of our charity. If we give away our own satisfactions and the indulgences we gain to the souls in Purgatory, instead of keeping them for ourselves, what is this but an heroic exercise of hope? We throw ourselves upon God. We hardly face the thought that we ourselves are thus sentencing ourselves, it may be, to abide years and years longer in that unconquerable fire. We shut our eyes, we quell the rising thought, we give our alms, and throw ourselves on God. We shall not be defrauded of our hope.

Then, again, this devotion has to do altogether with things beyond the grave, and there is the region of hope. Its dwelling place is behind the veil. "For we are saved by hope. But hope that is seen is not hope. For, what a man seeth, why doth he hope for? But if we hope for that which we see not, we wait for it with patience."[197] For the state of the dead is no dream, nor our power to help them a dream, any more than the purity of God is a dream, or the Precious Blood a dream. Thus, although there may be many consolations, yet it is we who have "the strongest comfort, who have fled for

[197] Rom. 8:24-25.

refuge to hold fast the hope set before us, which we have as an anchor of the soul, sure and firm, and which entereth in even within the veil, where the forerunner Jesus is entered for us."[198]

As to the charity of this devotion, it dares to imitate even the charity of God Himself. What is there in Heaven or on earth that it does not embrace, and with so much facility, with so much gracefulness, as if there were scarcely an effort in it, or as if self was charmed away, and might not mingle to distract it? It is an exercise of the love of God, for it is loving those whom He loves, and loving them because He loves them, and to augment His glory and multiply His praise. There are a hundred loves of God in this one love, as we should see if we reflected on those holy souls, and realized all that was implied in the final entry of a soul into everlasting bliss.

It is love toward the sacred humanity, because it magnifies the copious Redemption of Jesus. It honors His merits, satisfactions, ordinances, and mysteries. It peoples His Heaven, and it glorifies His Blood. It is filled with Jesus, with His spirit, with His work, with His power, and with His victories.

How abundant is its charity to the souls themselves, who can exaggerate? It does not matter whether we give them the good measure of all the Church tells us to do, and some spontaneous alms besides; or the full measure of all our satisfactions during our lifetime, which are not by justice due elsewhere; or the measure shaken together, which adds all that shall be done for us when we are dead; or the measure running over, which heaps upon all the rest special works of love, such as promoting this devotion by conversations, sermons, and books, and by getting Masses, Communions, penances, and indulgences from others for them.

[198] Heb. 6:18-20.

All men living on the earth, even unconverted sinners, are included in it, because it swells the Church Triumphant, and so multiplies intercessors for us who are still warring upon earth.

To ourselves also it is an exercise of charity, for it gains us friends in Heaven; it earns mercy for us when we ourselves shall be in Purgatory, tranquil victims, yet, oh, in what distress! And it augments our merits in the sight of God and so, if only we persevere, our eternal recompense hereafter.

Now, if this tenderness for the dead is such an exercise of these three theological virtues, and if, again, even heroic sanctity consists principally in their exercise, what store ought we not to set upon this touching and beautiful devotion!

Let this devotion enrich your spiritual life

But a further excellence in this devotion is to be found in its effects upon the spiritual life. It would seem as if it were a devotion specially intended for interior souls. But the fact is that it is so full of doctrine, and embodies so much that is supernatural, that we need not be surprised at the influence it exercises over the spiritual life.

In the first place, it is a hidden work from first to last. We do not see the results, so that there is little food for vainglory; and it is not a devotion whose exercise appears in any way before the eyes of others. It implies, moreover, an utter ignoring of self, by making away with our own satisfactions and indulgences, and keeping up a tender interest in an object that does not directly concern us. It is not only for the glory of God, but it is for His greater glory, and for His sole glory.

It leads us to think purely of souls, which it is very difficult to do in this material world, and to think of them, too, simply as spouses of Jesus. We thus gain a habit of mind that is fatal to the spirit of the world and to the tyranny of human respect, while it goes far to counteract the poison of self-love. The incessant thought of the holy souls keeps before us a continual image of suffering; and not of merely passive suffering, but of a joyful conformity to the will of God under it.

Furthermore, it communicates to us, as it were, by sympathy the feelings of those holy souls, and so increases our trembling yet trustful devotion to the adorable purity of God; and as, except in the case of indulgences applied to the dead, it requires a state of grace to make satisfaction for the sins of others, it is a special act of the lay-priesthood of the members of Christ. The spirit of the devotion is one of pensiveness; and this is an antidote to frivolity and hardness, and tells wonderfully upon the affectionate character that belongs to high sanctity. And who can tell what will come, after patient years, of thus keeping constantly before our eyes a model of eagerness, unspeakable, patient eagerness, to be with our dearest Lord?

Oh, what a wonderful thing is the life of a fervent Catholic! It is almost omnipotent, almost omnipresent, because it is not so much he who lives as Christ who liveth in him![199] Oh what is it we are touching and handling every day of our lives, all so full of supernatural vigor, of secret unction, of divine force, and yet we consider not, but waste intentions and trifle time away in the midst of this stupendous supernatural system of grace.

It seems useless to enumerate the various ways in which we may practice this devotion. The adorable Sacrifice and indulgences will, of course, always be the principal means of extending our charity to the departed. It is wished that the beautiful devotion of

[199] Cf. Gal. 2:20.

setting apart the month of November for the holy souls, in the same way as we consecrate the month of May to our dearest Lady, could become naturalized among us, and of universal observance.

∞

Achieve your three goals through devotion to the holy souls

Giving opens a man's heart, and makes him love to give, and those who have more to give know best how little it is compared with the necessity. Yet, this yearning to give alms comes from the Sacred Heart of Jesus, and it must be satisfied; and how can we better satisfy it than by giving alms to those who need it most: the holy souls in Purgatory? And we can all do this. And how much might we do, even for our dear poor on earth, if we commended their cause to the souls whom God allows us to liberate, and made a sweet bargain with them that when once in the free air of Heaven, their first homage and salutation over, they should pray for an abundant outpouring of grace upon rich men, that their hearts might be opened like the hearts of the first Christians, to deny themselves, and to feast the poor of Christ?

This doctrine of Purgatory, and the marvelous powers put into the hands of devotion for the holy souls, prove more than anything else how God has contrived all things for love, all things to show love of us, all things to win for Himself His creatures' love. No less does the neglect of this devotion illustrate the ingratitude and waywardness with which we repay God's love, and which is as wonderful as that love itself. How touchingly beautiful was the description God vouchsafed to give of Himself, and His pursuit of souls, to St. Gertrude! "Just as a poor invalid," said He, "who cannot walk, having with difficulty got himself carried into the sunshine, to be a little cheered by the warmth, sees a storm come on suddenly, and has to wait, patient but disappointed, for bright skies again — so am I. My love for you conquers me, and compels me to choose to dwell with you amid the violent tempest of your sins, hoping for the calm of your amendment, and for the quiet harbor of your humility at last."

Well may we cry out with St. Catherine of Genoa, "O Lord, if I could but know the cause of Thy so great and pure love of rational creatures!" But our Lord answered her, "My love is infinite, and I cannot help loving what I have created. The cause of my love is nothing but love itself; and seeing you cannot understand it, be at peace; and do not seek what you will never find!" Whereupon the saint exclaimed, "O Love, he who feels You understands You not, and he who wishes to understand You cannot know You!"

I would only be repeating what I have said elsewhere, if I were to draw out in detail the various ways in which this devotion promotes our three ends: the glory of God, the interests of Jesus, and the salvation of souls. In fact, the peculiarity of this devotion is its fullness. It is all quickened with supernatural life and power. It teems with doctrine. It reaches everywhere and has to do with everything. We are always touching some hidden spring in it, which goes further than we intended, and effects more than we hoped. It is as if all the threads of God's glory were gathered up into it and fastened there, and that when one is touched, all vibrate, and make melody to God, part of that sweet song that the Sacred Human Heart of Jesus is singing ever, in the bosom of the most compassionate Trinity.

Biographical Note

∞

Frederick William Faber
(1814-1863)

Frederick William Faber was raised amid the cold fire and strictures of Calvinism, but in his university days, his childhood convictions were shaken by his encounter with the traditionally oriented Church theory of the then-Anglican John Henry Newman. Newman finally won him over, and Faber was ordained an Anglican priest in 1839. He worked as a tutor until 1843, when he was appointed Rector of Elton, Northamptonshire. During these years, Faber made two tours of Europe, which he described in poetic letters. These letters reveal his growing enthusiasm for the Catholic Faith.

That enthusiasm manifested itself in action. In 1844, he established the practice of confessions at Elton, began preaching Catholic doctrine, and wrote a biography of St. Wilfrid, who was himself a great defender of the supremacy of Rome. In 1845 he completed his spiritual journey by following Newman into the Roman Catholic Church, just a few weeks after his great mentor had been received. The following year, Faber founded a religious community called the Brothers of the Will of God, or the Wilfridians, for their patron, St. Wilfrid. In 1847, he was ordained a Catholic priest.

With his fervent community, then forty strong, he converted his entire Anglican parish to Catholicism — with the exception of "the parson, the pew-opener, and two drunken men."

The following year, Newman returned from Rome with his new congregation, the Oratory of St. Philip Neri. With striking humility, Faber and some of his community quickly joined Newman's Oratory as novices. In 1849, Newman sent him to London with orders to found and lead the Oratory there. The London Oratorians converted an old tavern into a chapel. There Faber introduced hitherto-unknown devotions, including processions of the Blessed Sacrament. For these he composed fine hymns that were noteworthy for combining theological soundness with fervor and poetic grace. His preaching was well loved; Faber had few peers in the quality of his delivery, the keenness of his expressive ability, and the compelling power of his exhortations. He was also a sympathetic confessor and a wise counselor of souls.

In 1847, Fr. Faber began writing his *Lives of Modern Saints*. These remarkable spiritual biographies went beyond merely providing biographical data; they demonstrated the growth of holiness in each saint, showing how each one attained supernatural perfection under the operation of grace. Faithful to the Holy See and deeply devoted to the Blessed Mother, Fr. Faber had a spirit of unworldliness and a profound spiritual insight that enabled him to sift through the lives of the saints and glean from their various practices and devotions the simple, joyful ways of serving Jesus. These he distilled into numerous other writings. He wrote with the same unflagging dedication that he brought to all his labors for God; in addition to two volumes of *Notes on Doctrinal Subjects*, a volume of poems, sundry essays and other brief works, he wrote eight books: *All for Jesus*, *Growth in Holiness*, *The Blessed Sacrament*, *The Creator and the Creature*, *The Foot of the Cross*, *Spiritual*

Conferences, *The Precious Blood*, and *Bethlehem*. His joyful spirit shines through his writing and continues to move the hearts of today's Christians to take up the service of love he preached with such devotion.

Sophia Institute Press®

Sophia Institute™ is a nonprofit institution that seeks to restore man's knowledge of eternal truth, including man's knowledge of his own nature, his relation to other persons, and his relation to God. Sophia Institute Press® serves this end in numerous ways: it publishes translations of foreign works to make them accessible for the first time to English-speaking readers; it brings out-of-print books back into print; and it publishes important new books that fulfill the ideals of Sophia Institute™. These books afford readers a rich source of the enduring wisdom of mankind. Sophia Institute Press® makes these high-quality books available to the general public by using advanced technology and by soliciting donations to subsidize its general publishing costs.

Your generosity can help Sophia Institute Press® to provide the public with editions of works containing the enduring wisdom of the ages. Please send your tax-deductible contribution to the address below. We also welcome your questions, comments, and suggestions.

For your free catalog, call:
Toll-free: 1-800-888-9344

Sophia Institute Press® • Box 5284 • Manchester, NH 03108
www.sophiainstitute.com

Sophia Institute is a tax-exempt institution as defined by the Internal Revenue Code, Section 501(c)(3). Tax I.D. 22-2548708.